JUST THE TICKET

My life, the entertainment business and beyond

Tommy Higgins

ORIGINAL WRITING

All profits from this book go to
The North West Hospice
www.northwesthospice.ie

North West
Hospice

ISBNS
Parent : 978-1-78237-962-1
epub: 978-1-78237-963-8
mobi: 978-1-78237-964-5
PDF: 978-1-78237-965-2

A cip catalogue for this book is available from the National Library.

Published by Original Writing Ltd., Dublin, 2015.
Printed by Clondalkin Group, Glasnevin, Dublin 11

*This book is dedicated to my wife Eileen,
children Clodagh & Melanie,
my sister Maura and my late parents.*

Cover illustration by Annie West

www.anniewest.com

Author portrait by Frances Muldoon Photography

I would like to acknowledge the excellent editing work
done by Tony O'Brien and Jackie Hayden of *Write*Right
Editorial Consultants.

They turned my first draft manuscript into this book.

CONTENTS

FOREWORD

I never intended writing a book. But some years ago, as I was sitting with my Aunt Chris during her final days, she related to me some old stories about the Higgins family. I then realised I hardly knew anything about my own family, and thought it would be an interesting and worthwhile project to document its history for future generations. So what started out as a 'few pages' on the family history ended up with this book!

The world can change so much in the span of one person's lifetime that a younger audience can be enthralled, and often bemused, at how life used to be only a few decades back. So I believe we need to hear and record the stories that people like my Aunt Chris have to tell, before they are lost in the mists of time.

But those who have lived through periods of change may also like to reminisce about how those changes relate to their own lives and the people they've met, known and loved (and one or two others!).

So this book is, in my humble way, intended for both younger and older readers. It shows how every life brings fresh challenges and new opportunities that enrich us as human beings. Those challenges can test us, and the opportunities can lead us who knows where. In my own case, I developed a love of music that took me into the upper echelons of the entertainment business where I dealt with many of the top names in both the Irish and International music industries. Yet I never lost touch with my Sligo roots and always looked forward to coming home no matter where I'd been or who I'd met.

But in a way, this book records the journeys of several people, including my own family, friends and neighbours, so I hope that you will feel rewarded if you accept my invitation to step a while along the road with me.

Tommy Higgins
Sligo, 2015

In Memory:

Eamonn O'Connor

1961-2013

MY SLIGO ROOTS

Early Years

I was born on May 2, 1947, at 5a Upper John Street, Sligo. My father William (Willie) Higgins, and mother Mary (nee McGuire), lived there from the time they got married in 1945. It was an extremely harsh winter, and has gone down in folklore as "the winter of the big snow". Indeed, there was still snow on the ground in May. My father told me later that the snowdrifts were over 6ft in our back yard and he had to dig a path to the outside toilet.

There was no running hot water in the house, and cold water came from an outside tap which frequently froze during that winter. Nurse Maloney, the District Nurse, lived next door in Number 4 and was a great help to my mother during her pregnancy, and was on hand when I was born. It seems I arrived before my time and my mother hadn't purchased a cot. Improvisation was the order of the day, and I was placed in blankets in a drawer until the cot arrived a few days later.

The house at 5a was originally a laneway. There was a field at the back, and the entrance was through a gate where the house now stands. Around the corner is Sligo Cathedral which had been advertised for tender by the Bishop of Elphin, Bishop Gilhooly in 1867.

A parish hall was built in the field directly behind our house. Its building started in 1904 and was completed in 1906 and named The Gilhooly Memorial Hall in memory of the Bishop, who died in 1895. A dividing wall was then built to separate the houses in Upper John Street from the Gilhooly Hall land. As there was no further need for the laneway into the field our house was built in the gap around 1900. At the time, all Churches owned property, and our house was then owned by the Catholic Church, with my parents as tenants.

The Higgins family lived in Rosses Point, County Sligo, for generations. My great-grandfather, William, was born in 1836 and married my great-grandmother Margaret Gillen circa 1863. She'd been born in 1846. My grandfather's name was Thomas. He was born in 1879 and married Catherine Gorman in 1912. She came from Mullaghmore, Co Sligo. She had four sisters, Ellen, Molly, Brigid, and Mary Ann, and one brother, James. After my grandparents Thomas and Catherine married, they lived in a rented house not far from the family holding in Rosses Point. My father Willie was born in Rosses Point on August 26, 1914. He had three sisters, Molly, Christina (Chris), Katherine (Kitty), and two brothers, Thomas and Frank. In 1916, while the family were at Mass, the house went on fire.

It had been understood that my grandfather, Thomas, would inherit the family holding, but a dispute arose and it went to another member of the Higgins family. My grandfather at the time earned a living ferrying people between Sligo and Rosses Point by horse and sidecar - a taxi driver! Following the dispute, my grandfather moved his family to Sligo where they lived in a tiny house in 3 New Street. After the move he earned a living as a fireman and then as an employee of the Sligo Gas Company in Wine Street, currently the site of Dunne's Stores.

As was common at the time, for space and financial circumstances, children were reared by other family members. In 1918, my father, Willie, was sent to Mullaghmore, Co. Sligo, to his mother's sister Molly, and husband Frank. Willie's sister Molly was sent to Downpatrick, Co. Down, to her Aunt Ellen, another sister of her mother. Willie stayed in Mullaghmore until 1925. His Aunt Molly and Uncle Frank were very good to him, but it was a strange upbringing in a way, as he hardly knew his brothers and sisters who lived only 18 miles away in Sligo. My Aunt Chris told me that she'd see him maybe three or four times a year, and although she knew he was her brother, it was confusing for the young family.

My father attended the National School in Mullaghmore. The Sisters of Mercy nuns had a holiday home there, but were also involved in the community. They suggested that my father should return to Sligo to enhance his education, and arranged for him to start in Quay Street School in September, 1925. The school entrance was directly opposite the New Street house, a short 30-yard walk.

My Aunt Molly stayed in Downpatrick, and after her education worked as a housekeeper for a Fr. Lennon for over 20 years. She later returned to Sligo and worked as a nanny for the Gilroy family until her retirement. Aunt Katherine (Kitty) worked in Lipton's, O'Connell Street (now Boots) in Sligo. In 1952, she moved to Dublin where she worked again for Lipton's, at that time one of the largest grocery store chains in the country. My Aunt Chris worked as a waitress in Lyon's Café, Quay Street, and then at Best's Cafe in Wine Street until her retirement. Uncle Frank worked as a counter clerk in Sligo Post Office before becoming a telephonist.

My Uncle Thomas studied for the priesthood in Maynooth and was ordained in 1945. I always knew him as Father Tom. He moved to Africa in late 1945 and became a missionary in Liberia. Finances were difficult then, and he earned money for the Order by starting a rubber tree plantation. After some years, and the trees had grown to the required height, he extracted the rubber from the trees and sold it to the Firestone Tire Corporation who had a factory in Monrovia, the capital of Liberia.

I never met my grandfather Thomas who died in a work accident in 1939. But I've very clear memories of my grandmother, Catherine. She was a very frail lady who always dressed in black. Crippled with rheumatism, for as long as I could remember she could only walk very slowly with a stick. When I was very young, I couldn't pronounce the word Granny, and could only manage Ga Ga. The nickname stuck until she died in 1964. I guess she was the first Lady Ga Ga!

New Street was a typical, tiny, two-up two-down house with a very small back yard. It had a parlour, a kitchen with a black range for cooking, and two bedrooms upstairs. Visitors were always entertained with the best china in the parlour. Of the six children in the family, only two married - Willie and Kitty.

Before my sister Maura was born, I was the only young child in the family and, needless to say, got endless attention.

My mother Mary Kate McGuire was born in Banagher, Fivemilebourne, Co. Leitrim. Her birth certificate states she was born on September 10, 1919, but she claimed she was born on July 4 (probably the correct date), but was registered on the later date. My grandfather Patrick McGuire married my grandmother Mary Ann McGoldrick in 1908. The McGuires lived in the townland of Upper Banagher, situated about a mile off the Sligo-Manorhamilton road. It was a picturesque site, perched on top of a steep hill overlooking Lough Gill in the valley below. It was a very small holding of a few acres, and the family lived off the land.

Like my father's family, there were six children. My mother had one sister, Margaret (Maggie), and four brothers, Patrick (Pa), Phillip (Phil), Michael and John. The custom at the time was to call the youngest boy Sonny and the youngest girl Baby (pronounced Babb-ie). So John was rarely referred to as John, but nearly always as Sonny. All the family attended Leckawn National School, to which in the summer they walked barefoot, a daily five-mile round trek.

In 1929, an opportunity arose in Newtown, Fivemilebourne, when my grandfather Patrick purchased a 25-acre farm. Life was too hard in Upper Banagher, and the new farm was on the main Sligo-Dromahair road, with better land and offering a better opportunity to provide for the family. It's still possible to see the location of the original home where the family were born. It's about two miles uphill from the new farm, but very difficult to reach due to a very steep uphill climb.

Regretfully, my grandfather did not have much time to enjoy his new purchase as he died in 1931. Uncle Pa took over the running of the farm at a very early age. He and Phil worked the farm and lived with my grandmother Mary Ann at Newtown. The family always called the new place Banagher, after the old home. My grandfather's only sister Kate spent most of her life in America, but came home in the 1940s and lived at the house in Banagher until she died in

1956. She was my mother's aunt and she was always referred to as just 'Aunt'.

My Uncle Michael moved to Dublin where he worked as a building labourer. Uncle Sonny worked as a shop assistant in Brady's grocery store in Dromahair. He married Winnie Walsh from Dromahair, and they moved to Kilburn, London, where Sonny worked at the food counter at Harrods. My Aunt Maggie married Patrick (Paddy) Cunningham in Dromahair Church on December 27, 1935. Paddy came from Killery, County Leitrim, about four miles from Dromahair, but as with my father, he was reared by his aunt at Magurk, a few fields away from Maggie's house at Banagher. Paddy's brother John was groomsman at the wedding and my mother was bridesmaid. The newly-weds moved to Dublin the day after the wedding and lived initially in South Circular Road before moving to Charlemont Street.

When in 1939 my mother Mary started work in Woolworths in O'Connell Street, Sligo, her work schedule was Monday to Saturday, with a half-day off on Wednesday. The family home at Banagher was only eight miles from Sligo, but public transport was non-existent in the area, so my mother had no option but to live in Sligo. She had room and meals as a tenant of two elderly sisters, the Miss Sweeneys, at 5a Upper John Street. This was not uncommon, and almost every house in Upper John Street had boarders, sometimes called lodgers.

In 1940s Ireland, young men and women mostly first met at dances, and the main dancehalls in Sligo were The Town Hall, The Ritz in O'Connell Street, The Plaza, Strandhill, The Elsinore in Rosses Point, and the Gilhooly Hall. My parents met at a dance in the Town Hall and were married at Dromahair Church in August, 1945, with Uncle Sonny as groomsman and Aunt Kitty bridesmaid. The wedding reception was at the Abbey Hotel in Dromahair. Because of World War Two there was a shortage of food and materials, but somehow they obtained enough material to make a suit for my father and a two-piece for my mother. The wedding photographs show both had outfits made from the same ream of cloth.

After one of the Miss Sweeneys died, my now-married parents moved into 5a Upper John Street. Shortly after, the other Miss Sweeney moved to a nursing home and my parents became the sole tenants of the house.

Of the twelve children from the McGuire and Higgins families, only five married. Sonny and Winnie had no children. Kitty married Tom Meaney and had one child, Gerrard. Maggie and Paddy had six children, Willie and Mary had two, my sister, Maura, and me, Thomas Higgins.

1947 – 1959

How far back can I remember? This is a difficult one. When I was quite young my mother asked me the same question. I told her that I remembered sitting in a pram at the junction of Pearse Road and Mail Coach Road watching a funeral pass by. There was a very big crowd, and I can still picture the people walking behind a hearse, and all the cars passing. My mother was standing beside my pram with her friend Rose O'Connor. She told me that the only such occasion she could remember was when the remains of W.B. Yeats were brought back from France to Sligo to be re-interred in Drumcliffe Cemetery in September, 1948. She remembered that she and Rose had stood at that spot watching the funeral. I was seventeen months old at the time, but I can still recollect that scene very clearly.

Other memories from back then include my aunts Chris and Kitty calling to the house every week and bringing me for walks. I would have been between two and three at the time.

One day, I was sitting outside our front door playing with toys when a gentleman crossed the road towards me. He was the local schoolteacher, Mr Shine who lived further down the street. He had the nickname 'Daddy' Shine, so I said *"hello, Daddy Shine"*. He approached me with a very cross face and pulled my cheeks. This hurt, and I ran into the house crying. In those days, schoolteachers, clergy and policemen were undisputed authorities, and not to be questioned. My mother just said *"don't call him daddy again, just Mr. Shine"*. This was before I went to school, so I was under four at the time.

It was around this time, perhaps 1950, when I began to notice I had cousins. My mother and her only sister Maggie were very close, and Maggie and her husband Paddy had five children older than me - Marie, Babs, Ena, Sean and Josie. At the time they lived in Charlemont Street, Dublin. They moved to Bluebell Road in 1953 and had another child, Bertie, now deceased. Paddy worked in the *Irish Independent,* and the family came to Sligo and Banagher for their summer holidays. I think for the first visit only Marie, Babs and Ena came.

Hardly anybody had phones then, so communication was by letter. My mother and Maggie wrote to each other every week, so Maggie would have written to tell us the day and time of arrival. I remember going to the railway station with my parents, and after waiting an age, the steam train came into sight. This was so exciting for both families. It being shortly after the war, the coal was of poor quality. The black smuts from the engine infiltrated the carriages, so some passengers had black spots on their faces. We lived only 10 minutes' walk from the station so we were home in no time. I've no idea where everybody slept, but that was not unusual in those days where everybody just piled into a bed if that was all there was. This was the start of a long and close relationship with my Dublin cousins that happily still exists today.

My father was a bus driver with CIE. But women often had to give up work after they got married. That was the rule in the Civil Service, although not in the private sector. So I remember my mother being around all the time.

Although I must have met them earlier, my first recollection of meeting my grandmother and uncles was during a night visit to Banagher. I was around three or four at the time. My father had bought a second-hand car, and I remember going up the lane in the dark, passing a house with scaffolding and entering a big room with lights on. I learned later that I'd passed the main house, and had entered the dairy attached to the house. The main house originally had a thatched roof, and it was being re-roofed with slates, and while this was being carried out, the family moved into the dairy.

Every farmhouse had a dairy where supplies were stored, milk churned for butter, and so on. It's hard to believe now how they were all able to live in the dairy, albeit for a short period. It was no more than 20 feet by 20 feet with a fireplace. But my grandmother, Pa, Phil and 'Aunt' Kate made it work. There were two beds, one for the women and one for Pa and Phil. Electricity didn't arrive in Banagher until 1957, so the room was lit with paraffin lamps, with a big table in the middle of the floor. The farm was completely self-sufficient, as I'll expand on later.

I can clearly remember 'Aunt' that night, sitting by the fireplace in her black wrap-around pinny and a hairnet. My grandmother used to have to a similar outfit. Pa and Pill were 'curing' a pig they had killed earlier, and were chopping up the various parts. Pa explained to me the process whereby they wrapped the meat in muslin cloth and placed the pieces in a barrel of salt which was left in the corner. It's over 60 years since that visit, and it's still clear as a bell to me .... my first car trip, the sounds and smell of the dairy, plus, of course, the fuss made of the little boy. But if that was an exciting occasion for me it was nothing compared to my first trip to Dublin. It was the summer of 1951, and I was due to start school in September. John Rooney lived over the road from the Banagher farm where he had his own small farm, but he was also a hackney (taxi) driver. He had a car and a van for his business, two of the few vehicles in the area, and on Sundays he'd drive local people to mass in Dromahair. But on that day back then he was going to Dublin to collect someone travelling home from America, and as he had an empty car travelling up he offered to bring my father who needed to go to Dublin.

My father had decided to take me along too. This was going to be my first long journey in a car, and I couldn't sleep for days. Even on the day, my excitement mounted by the hour until, at last, we were off! When we stopped at a garage outside Edgeworthstown, with petrol then costing only £1 for 4 gallons, John and my father 'argued' about who'd pay. The £1 note was thrown on the seat and thrown back again. I smile every time

I drive by the site of that garage, although it's closed now. But 'Peace' eventually broke out, one of them paid for the petrol and we eventually arrived in Dublin. It was a wonderful sight for me, bigger and noisier than any place I'd ever seen before. As we turned the corner into Charlemont Street my father spotted my cousin Marie waving on the pavement. I'm sure she'd been waiting on the street for hours, as nobody would have known what time we would arrive, and only the date would have been included in the letter. We were given a marvellous welcome by Aunt Maggie and the other cousins. I remember Uncle Paddy coming home from work on his bike later, but very little else remains with me from that momentous first trip to Dublin.

Back in Sligo, visits to Ga in New Street were naturally more frequent, as they were only about 10 minutes' walk from our house. But the cultures of the two sides of my family were quite different. The McGuires were country folk, while the Higgins's were 'townies'.

Ireland in the 1950s was a very grim place. Nearly everybody was what we would today call 'working class', with hardly any 'middle class'. The Higgins family had moved from Rosses Point in 1916 with nothing left after the afore-mentioned fire. Then my grandfather died suddenly in 1939. He'd worked for the Gas Company, so I can't see how any great wealth might have been created. Yet life seemed to be that little bit more posh in New Street, with good linen and china always available. Food, although simple, was a tad better than we had at home too.

Whenever the family travelled to Mullaghmore a taxi was hired, as they wouldn't travel by bus. It must also have been a huge sacrifice to fund Father Tom through Maynooth Seminary, yet the family always seemed 'comfortable'. It added hugely to one's social standing to have a priest in the family, and Father Tom's visits home from Africa were occasions of great rejoicing. Initially, he was allowed home for a three-month holiday every seven years. Later, it was reduced to five years.

What I remember most about those very early pre-school years is how I was loved and looked after so well by my parents, grandmothers, aunts, uncles and Dublin cousins.

Starting School

And did I follow the pattern of crèche, kindergarten, play-school like most kids to-day? Not at all. It was cold turkey for me, straight to school in September, 1951. My primary school history ran like this:

Year	Class	School	Teacher
1951	Low Babies	Scoil Fatima	Sister Vincent
1952	High Babies	Scoil Fatima	Sister Emyard
1953	1st Class	Scoil Fatima	Miss Currid
1954	2nd Class	Scoil Fatima	Sr. Mercedes
1955	3rd Class	St. Johns	Mr. Shine
1956	4th Class	St. Mary's	Brother Flannan
1957	5th Class	St. Mary's	Brother Flannan
1958	6th Class	St. Mary's	Brother Conan
1959	7th Class	St. Mary's	Brother Conan

My mother dropped me off to start my very first day at Scoil Fatima. I felt no apprehension myself, although I remember several children crying outside. My teacher Sister Vincent was a small, elderly, wiry nun. I had Sister Emyard in Second Class, a tall pleasant nun. There was a statue of a 'black baby' outside her classroom, and Sister Vincent encouraged us to put a penny in the box after which the 'black baby' nodded his head. That my uncle, Father Tom, worked with the 'black babies' in Africa was mentioned at various times during class.

It was mostly nuns who taught in Scoil Fatima, but I had a lay teacher in First Class. Katie Currid was an elderly, frosty lady with grey hair tied in a bun, a 1950s female teacher straight out of central casting. Sister Mercedes taught us in Second Class. A pleasant, smiling nun with glasses, *The Sligo Champion* reported in 2008 that she'd died in San Diego aged 104.

Upper John Street in the 1950s was a community in itself. Although only about 80 metres long, there were three shops and a post office. On our side of the street, Miss Burns had the shop on the corner, mostly selling vegetables and a small selection of groceries. She was a big heavy woman who always dressed in black. In 1953, after she died, the Kilduff family took over the shop and lived over it. Mrs Kilduff was the proprietor, and she had five children. She embarked on an extensive refurbishment and substantially increased the range of groceries stocked. Opposite Kilduff's, in No 3, Frank and Annie Cummins ran the local Post Office. I had an account there, and every time I got money from relatives I was encouraged to put something into it. Across from our house, Jim and Nell O'Neill had a small shop in their living room. They sold some groceries, as well as an enticing selection of sweets and lollipops. Jim and Nell were fanatical Fianna Fail supporters for whom de Valera was God. It was well known that Nell had been actively involved in gun-running with Countess Markievicz during the War of Independence (1919-1921). Jim died in the 1960's, but Nell continued with the shop into the 1970's. When she died in her 80s, the shop closed and the building converted back to a residence. Three sisters, the Miss Flynns, moved into it from Wolfe Tone Street.

At the other end of the street was Banks's, another grocery shop, run by brother and sister John and Annie Gilmartin. In the 1930's, next door to our house, the Foley family had a shop but it had closed by the time my parents moved to John St in the 1940's. In those days there were no supermarkets, but there were several grocery stores down town, including Blackwoods, Higgins and Keighron, O'Connor Brothers, Bellews and many other establishments. Although much larger than the local corner shops, the downtown stores were noticeably smaller than modern supermarkets.

Our main shop for food was Henry's at the top of Lower John Street. It was run by two Miss Henrys. Later their niece Mary came to town and married Tom Byrne, and Tom and Mary ran the shop into the mid-1980s. They provided a great service to the community and offered a credit facility. Customers could get their groceries on 'tick', with purchases listed in a book and paid for at the end of the week.

Further down from Henry's was Verdon's Dairy where Tom Verdon's daughters Molly and Nora served. They sold only milk, buttermilk, bread and butter. Tom also sold milk by the pint door-to-door from a cart with a churn. Of course it was a problem in the summer, as this was way before fridges became standard in households, and milk was put in a jug of water in the back yard to cool. Whenever ours went sour, my mother would use it to bake soda bread. Kevinsfort Dairy on Strandhill Road also had a door-to-door bottle milk service, but most people supported Verdons. Tom worked in his shop up to a late age. His great-grandson is Marc Feehily who became an international pop star with the pop group Westlife.

Next door to Kilduff's shop resided Larry and Molly Dowdall and their son Jim. Jim worked in *The Sligo Champion* and was a part-time drummer in Eamonn McCole's Dance Band. He was a generation older than me, and I had a chat with him before he died in 2009. Although I've been able to recall most of the people who lived in the neighbourhood at the time, Jim helped filled in any gaps. One of the memorable stories he told me was that in the 1930s a man called 'Jap' Foley lived in 3 Adelaide Street and he kept a few cows in a field at Maugheraboy. Jap would herd the cows from there to Adelaide Street, driving them right through the front door of the house to a shed in the backyard. He milked the cows there and sold the milk door-to-door around the locality. This spectacle happened every day, so the condition of the house must have been, er, somewhat charming!!

Our neighbourhood extended to College Road, Flynn's Terrace, Adelaide Street and Lower John Street to the back of the Cathedral steps. Thus, everybody knew each other on a very friendly, neighbourly basis. Wolfe Tone Street was very close too, but was deemed to be a posh street, as the houses were much nicer and the people had better jobs. Crime was almost unheard of in the locality in those days, and house keys were put on a string or chain and dangled inside letterboxes. The police enjoyed total control in the town and, apart from a handful of tearaways, there was widespread respect for authority.

A laneway called Ramsey's Row lay opposite our house and led to a big farmyard. Johnny and Annie Conlon were 'town' farmers. They lived in Temple Street but housed their animals in John Street. Johnny had 10 or 12 cows and they grazed at the Showgrounds, about half a mile from the yard. Every morning and evening he herded the cows from the Showgrounds to John Street for milking. Unlike 'Jap', Johnny had proper cowsheds. He also kept pigs, and Annie raised chickens. Tony Burrows from Jinks Avenue had a part-time job after school. Three days a week he'd call to houses, including ours, to collect 'brock' in a handcart for Johnny. 'Brock' was leftovers from meals - potato skins, bits of meat - anything that could be fed to pigs. The Conlons had no children and, as far as I can remember, operated this schedule for 51 weeks of the year. For week 52 they took a week's holiday and had their nephew Paddy Gilmartin look after their cows.

There were maybe twelve children in a street that was mostly populated by elderly people. My playmates included John Fowley and Sean Cullen from our street, Joseph Doherty from Flynn's Terrace, and Pat and Freddie Chrystal from Adelaide Street. Wherever we found a patch of ground we'd play football until parents started calling us home for tea and homework. We had cuts everywhere from playing on concrete. Knees, elbows there was blood everywhere. *"Look at your shoes"* my mother would say: *"just look at them"*. It didn't matter; we were back at it again the next day after school.

Occasionally we'd go to Treacy Avenue. It provided us with a 'natural' football pitch, a street with very little traffic and gateposts for goals. We were always outnumbered as there were large families in Treacy Avenue. The Treacy boys would put Josie Kelly in goals. He was handicapped, and wore braces on both legs up to his thighs, but was very brave. They'd prop him between the gateposts where he held on for dear life, but if the ball came his way he'd let go of the posts and dive in a heap on the ball. We all helped him back up again with a congratulatory *"good man, Josie, great save"*. The games usually continued until we were exhausted.

Mamie O'Shea lived in Charles Street just off Lower John Street. She had a heavy limp and carried a stick. Winter or summer she wore the same outfit - a brown coat and beret. She was a dressmaker and ran an under-age football team called John Street Rangers, and had a set of jerseys and togs, the only set in our neighbourhood. Her team played on grass, usually in the Fairgreen. For us, this was the big time. I was seven or eight when I first played for them. Putting on a real jersey and togs felt like magic. It didn't matter that they were three or four sizes too big, they were a REAL football kit, dark gold shirts and blue togs. But there was one problem. Mamie hardly ever washed the gear, so the jersey you put on was often wet or stinking with sweat. But a major attraction came at half-time; Mamie brought us into the centre circle and distributed pieces of orange - one piece each, and gave the team talk. I don't remember if we ever won a game.

The big local sporting attraction was Sligo Rovers. My father brought me to my first match in 1954, and we attended most matches for years after that. When he went to England, Uncle Frank would call for me every second Sunday and bring me to the games. Charlie Courtney, who lived in Wolfe Tone Street, was the local Postmaster, but he was also Chairman of Sligo Rovers. I used to hang about with his son, Damian, which sometimes gave me access to the Rovers' dressing room, a big perk for a football fan like me.

As with most boys in the neighbourhood, I served as an altar boy at the Cathedral until I was about 10. Of course the big gig was being picked for a wedding, as the Sacristan, Joe Whelan and the two altar boys usually received a few bob from the wedding couple. In the early days, I only once witnessed a very unusual occurrence after a wedding ceremony. When the Bride and Groom exited the church, the Groom flung a big batch of coins on the ground. Quite a number of people were waiting for this, and they scrambled on the ground trying to scoop up the money.

I asked my father about this later, and he said it used to be the custom for rich people to show their wealth by giving money to poor people on their wedding day. Of course there were hardly any wealthy people in Sligo at the time, so it rarely happened.

Looking back now it was a horrible age-old custom, and thankfully it was banned by the Church shortly after. Across the road from the Cathedral was The Manse, where the Rector of the Presbyterian Church, Mr. Davis, lived with his family. As Catholics, religion was 'bate' into us at school, and we plotted to do our bit for our church. One day after school myself, Pat Chrystal, Sean Cullen and Joseph Doherty spotted Mr. Davis's eldest son, Christian, walking home from school alone. He was about our age, and we frog-marched him into the Cathedral and proceeded to Baptise the poor fellow. Pat performed the blessing, while the rest of us dunked the kicking and screaming Christian into the holy water font. We were delighted with our day's work and took the vow of omerta. Despite the inevitable uproar, we all held the line and denied any involvement. I heard later that Christian had been immediately dispatched to a boarding school in Belfast. I remember Pat saying, in his Sligo drawl: *"Good riddance. At least he's baptised anyway"*.

In 1953, my cousins, the Cunningham family, moved to a new development in Inchicore on the outskirts of Dublin. My mother, Granny McGuire and I headed off to visit them on the afternoon train. The old steam trains had been replaced by new diesel trains which were luxurious by comparison. The big deal was afternoon tea in the dining car and it cost 2/6d. Mary Ann said it was her treat, so I was chuffed. Cousin Babs worked in Dame Street, so she and Uncle Paddy were waiting for us at Westland Row station. We then walked to College Green to pick up the No 21 bus which dropped us off at Inchicore Church. There was another long walk to their new house in Bluebell where, of course, the usual big welcome awaited. I remember the first visit particularly well because everything in the house was new.

After a week or so, my mother and granny went home; I stayed in Bluebell for another two weeks before going back to Sligo with Aunt Maggie and some of the children. This was the pattern for the next 5-6 years - a constant flow between Dublin, Sligo and Banagher. A few years later a new bus service was introduced from Westland Row direct to Bluebell and that was a blessing.

It was a magical time for me. My cousins were exceptionally kind, and I was taken to various places, including shopping in town. Babs and Brendan brought me to my first film in Walkinstown Cinema. Marie and Eddie took me to a Bingo session in the National Stadium on South Circular Road. Uncle Paddy loved football, and brought me to League of Ireland matches in Richmond Road and Glenmalure Park. I could go on forever. Nothing was too much trouble for them, and I will always remember their kindness.

From 1953 I also started spending some time in Mullaghmore and Banagher during the Summer school holidays. I'd stay three or four days with my father's Aunt Molly in Mullaghmore in the house he was reared in from 1918-1925, a small cottage at the top of the hill and with wonderful views. Every day I was brought down to McGloin's shop in the village for an ice cream. One day, as Aunt Chris and I were entering the shop, a tall man with a hat was exiting. He bent down, shook my hand, and started talking to me. I told him I'd come for ice cream. He immediately bought me a huge ice cream, and Chris said, "*Say thank you to Lord Mountbatten*".

Back then, Lord Mountbatten of Burma holidayed in Mullaghmore annually for the month of August in Classiebawn Castle which he owned. I didn't know at the time that he was a significant historical figure who had played a major part in World War II. After that war, he was Viceroy of India until that country gained Independence in 1947. He went fishing most days from the harbour across from McGloin's shop, and was very popular with the local villagers, many of whom worked in his castle. Tragically he was murdered by the IRA on his boat just outside the harbour in August, 1979.

Between the ages of six and eleven, I spent three or four weeks every summer on the farm in Banagher. At various times, different cousins would also arrive from Dublin. The farm was completely self-sufficient, with no car or tractor. There were four milking cows, a horse and a dog, as well as a donkey for a short while. It was considered one of the better farms in the area at the time.

Granny bought day-old chicks from Elmbank in Lower John Street and raised them in the chicken coop beside the cow byre. She was well into her 70s then, but was very energetic, a strong woman who ruled the roost. Both Uncle Pa and Phil were extremely hard-working, with Pa the leader. Phil was what today would be regarded as a little 'innocent', but he contributed substantially to the day-to-day workings of the farm.

The house was beautifully located at the bottom of a valley, and had three rooms, kitchen, bedroom and parlour. The parlour doubled as a bedroom for visitors. Life centred on the kitchen, with its open fireplace where Granny did the cooking on a turf fire. At the back was a settle-bed, a wooden bench-type piece of furniture that could be sat on during the day but folded out as a bed at night. Most farmhouses in those days had a similar settle-bed.

There was no bathroom, running water or electricity. The house was lit with paraffin oil lamps, and drinking water was drawn from a well in a bucket. This required a 150 yards uphill climb from the well to the house. Water for washing clothes and cleaning utensils came from rainwater collected in barrels at the side of the house. There was a unisex organic toilet, one of the early 'green' toilets ... Well, not quite! The 'toilet' was actually the field beside the byre, and one wiped one's bum with a dock leaf - none of your kitten-soft double-ply toilet rolls for us! We were possibly the first to understand the concept of carbon footprints; - we had to step carefully in the field to avoid the human turds! To my knowledge, every other house in rural farmlands operated the same system.

The day started around 7am when the men rose. Granny and Aunt would follow at around 7.30am. Pa lit the turf fire and Phil collected the four cows from the field and brought them to the cow byre beside the house. Pa and Phil usually milked two cows each by hand, before arriving in for breakfast at 7.55am. The timing was crucial, because a battery-operated radio sat by the window and it was very important to catch the weather forecast. Forecasts in those days were notoriously inaccurate, yet everybody swore by what came out of that crackling radio. We then got to hear the news headlines, but the radio was switched off immediately after "to save the battery".

But old habits die hard. Although electricity arrived in 1957, the radio was still switched on at 7.55am and off again after the weather forecast and headlines, even though there was no longer a battery to 'save'.

My cousins and I would be sent to the chicken coup to collect fresh eggs for breakfast. Maybe a couple of times a week, we had a few thick slices of bacon. It was all washed down with very strong tea and at least three or four spoons of sugar.

After breakfast, Granny would start baking white and brown soda bread in a big black skillet pot. Sometimes she'd throw some raisins into the white floor and wholemeal that was bought by the hundredweight sack. We had fresh bread every day, and there was that wonderful smell of fresh bread baking on the open hearth. While the bread was baking she'd go to the dairy to take the milk fat and pound it into butter. This was back-breaking stuff, as the pounding could last up to an hour. Sometimes my cousins and I were asked to help out, but I had a low boredom threshold even at that early stage. Somehow the process produced buttermilk and this was used for baking bread.

After the cows were milked, the milk was strained and divided into two churns. Con Healy collected the churns from the farmers to be brought to the Creamery in Calry. Every month a cheque arrived, one of the small income streams for the farm. Granny stopped churning butter when the Creamery started producing butter for shops, and Con would deliver a few pounds of butter when returning the empty milk churns.

The area in front of the house was called 'the street', a concrete path leading to a three-foot high wall. On the other side of it sat Granny's garden, with wonderful drills of vegetables, cabbage, turnips, parsnips, onions, scallions, lettuce, rhubarb etc. From time to time she would grow flowers and display them in a vase in the parlour.

Potatoes were plentiful too, and Pa and Phil would have a least one large field of potatoes. Pa sold them by the sack at the monthly market in the Market Yard, Sligo, and also sold cabbage plants which he tied with a hay-rope. I often helped prepare for the market, counting cabbage plants into a 'set' of 100 and tying them together after first weaving a rope from hay in the hayshed. In the early days, Pa brought his sacks of potatoes and plants to Sligo by horse and cart, and on the way he'd drop off a sack of potatoes to our house.

Dinner was the main meal and always took place around 12.30pm, except when hay had to be saved or turf cut. A chunk of pig would have been retrieved from the barrel in the dairy the previous night and steeped overnight. Bacon was boiled in the skillet. Cabbage was plucked from the garden, then washed and boiled. A large pot of potatoes was then placed on the crook in the fireplace. The cooked potatoes were put in a big tin basin, and we all tucked in to a tasty meal of bacon, cabbage and potatoes with heart-stopping chunks of butter and handfuls of salt. Pa and Phil usually drank buttermilk too, but it was not to my liking. After dinner the men went back to the fields.

I remember setting traps for rabbits, and we sometimes had roast rabbit, although a disease called 'myxomatosis' wiped out the rabbit population for a period. We nearly always had chicken on Sundays. I remember the ritual well. On Saturday afternoon, Granny would head out to the chicken coop with a breadknife, dive in and behead one or two chickens, depending on how many people were to be fed. The racket was awful, and she'd emerge with the unfortunate headless chicken or two, a cloud of feathers and a bloody breadknife. She then plucked the chicken on the 'street', and it was prepared for the following day's dinner.

The evening meal was very simple, just tea and bread, and maybe an egg. Then the moment my cousins and I dreaded - the ritual of the rosary, recited every night of the week except Sunday, because we went to Mass. Aunt was too frail to kneel, but the rest of the household knelt on the concrete floor, leaning on chairs. The five decades of the rosary was bad enough, but the 'trimmings' went on forever. De Valera was prayed for, the Bishop, the Pope, all the Saints in the Universe, the dog, the cat, Jim Fowley's tractor, all prayed for! I was generally fine when by myself, but it was impossible to keep a straight face with my cousins there.

The custom was for everybody to get a turn at the 'Hail Mary' and the rest would answer 'Holy Mary'. Pa had a loud voice, and as the prayers progressed the 'Hail Mary' would become a loud *'HAAAAAIIIIL MARY'*. Then the skitting would start, with Ena the worst culprit. I remember one evening when she and Sean were in the house. We started off with the good intention of getting through the prayers without skitting, so we knelt on the floor facing away from each other. But I glanced around when Pa turned up the volume, and noticed Ena's shoulders shaking. When it came to her turn, nothing came out ... she was wetting herself. Pa then roared *"Tommy!"*. I started but I was in trouble early on. *"HailMaryfullofgracethelordiswiththeeblessedarethou"* and then a dead stop! Pa was getting very agitated and called *"SEAN"*. Sean tried to get it going but he was done as well. After the end of the ritual, which lasted over 30 minutes, we got a severe bollockin'.

I dreaded Sunday Mass in Dromahair. 1950s Ireland was run by the clergy. It was not too bad in the towns and cities, but a more brutal regime reigned in rural areas, especially the Mullah of Dromahair, Father Traynor, who ruled the Parish with an iron fist. He controlled the entire congregation by terror. His sermons thundered on and on, roaring, mocking, scolding, whatever it took to keep the peasants in line. He also had numerous ways of extracting money from people who really didn't have much to begin with. His most notorious practice occurred at funerals. When a parishioner died, EVERYBODY in the parish was expected to attend the evening removal whether connected to the deceased or not. Fr. Traynor would say the usual prayers, and then came the announcement for the main event. *"We will now proceed with the offerings"*, where the parishioners placed money in a basket for the parish. Fr. Traynor then proceeded to read out from a list of parishioners the amount of money each

of his subjects had contributed. *"Pa McGuire five shillings .....
Michael McGoldrick ten shillings......Vincent Bird five shillings
..... Din O'Hara ....* (long pause) ...... *NOTHING".* After
the "NOTHING", came another long pause to let it sink in.
Then he'd resume his mantra. *"John Rooney ... five shillings"*
etc. boomed out all over the church, and on it went while his
congregation cowered reverently in their seats. Farmers had
cows waiting to be milked, but nothing interfered with Fr.
Traynor's evangelical Dyson, hoovering up the money.

John Rooney, as mentioned earlier, had a Ford van, and it
was equipped with two wooden planks on either side, and he
collected local people and brought them to Mass. Granny wore
her best black coat and hat with the mandatory hat-pin, Phil
and Pa were scrubbed up in their best Sunday suits. Fr. Traynor
patrolled the aisle before Mass, hands behind his back, shuffling
reluctant people up the front just for badness.

One particular summer it rained heavily for weeks. Farmers
were way behind with saving the hay, essential for feeding cattle
in the coming winter months. Then came a sunny day. The talk
in John's van on the way to Mass was whether Fr. Traynor
would allow the farmers to save hay on that sunny Sunday as
the window for saving hay could be very limited.
Despite the fact that I was very young, I could feel the tension
in the Church as the Great Enforcer gave his usual long sermon,
but still no announcement. Farmers shuffled in their seats, but
still nada. Then towards the end he started the tease, a lecture on
how to make hay, the size of the cocks, the height, the diameter,
the texture etc. It was excruciating, but having tortured his
subjects enough, he finally gave the green light and the tension
lifted. When I see the Mullahs from Iran and Afghanistan on
TV, I can't help wondering if they received tutoring from Fr.
Traynor?
Pa bought a few acres of meadowland at Moneyduff, a few
miles from the house. Many of us helped save the hay, as we
spread and forked until we produced big round cocks of hay.
On at least one occasion my mother and Maggie helped out too.

The hay was later transported by horse and cart to the hayshed beside the house.

One of the most important Summer tasks was bringing in the turf from a bog close to the meadow at Moneyduff. As was the practice, the bog was shared by a number of farmers. First the turf was cut with a slean, and left to dry on the ground. After a few weeks it was moved to the side of the road where it was stacked upright in groups of three sods. This was called "footing". Then, at the end of the summer when the turf was dry, it was brought back to the turf shed.

Pa and Phil, and maybe a neighbour or two, would go to the bog after the cows were milked, and it was my task to bring the mid-day meal to the men. After Granny baked the bread, she'd sometimes produce a beautiful rhubarb tart using rhubarb from the garden. Tea was made, including milk and fistfuls of sugar, and poured into tin cans. It was all packed into shopping bags for me to bring to the bog, where the men were usually famished and delighted to see me.

Once the hay was saved and the turf brought home, everybody was happy. The family had hay for their cows, and turf for cooking and heating. Although there was a wood on the farm, it was rarely used for firewood. At the end of the summer, Pa would chop up some wood and deliver a load plus turf to our house in Upper John Street, providing our heating needs for the winter.

While nearly all our needs were produced on the farm, supplies had occasionally to be purchased in Dromahair or Sligo. Phil was dispatched to buy red meat maybe every 10 days or so, arriving back with the meat in a brown parcel clipped to his bicycle carrier. But by the time he got home, the meat would be fossilised to the paper and a trail of blood behind him on the 'street'.

Joe Hennigan had a travelling shop and called every two weeks. He operated the family shop on The Mall, but headed out to the hinterland with his range of groceries, hardware, baking flour, towels, dishcloths, and so on, providing a fine service to the community. Paddy Verdon (Tom the milkman's son) worked with Macarthur's bakery in Sligo, and he called door-to-door with bakery products every Wednesday afternoon. Granny supplemented her home cooking with Macarthur's bread, and, whenever I was there, she'd buy me something sweet as a treat.

I was about eight when I went to my first cattle fair in Manorhamilton. Pa woke me from the settle-bed around 5am, and after breakfast we headed off on foot to Upper Banagher, a difficult uphill trek through the fields. We collected the cattle and headed out on the main Sligo-Manorhamilton road. My job was to stay in front of the cattle and stand at laneways to block them off, wait until Pa drove the cattle past, and then run again in front to repeat the procedure. It was an eight-mile trek, so I was fairly tired when we arrived around 11am.

The Fairgreen in the centre of the town was packed with farmers, cattle, sheep, donkeys, horses, drovers, vets, hucksters, three-card trick men and people just there to gawk. We took up a position near the edge of the green, and a handful of buyers threw a few shapes, looked under tails, examined teeth, all part of the posturing. At around 12.30pm, somebody agreed to mind the cattle, and we went to a house down the street where I had my first "mate tay", also known as a *musician's wedding cake*. The meat tea was an Irish institution, consisting of a few slices of ham decorated by a single limp tomato, with tea, bread and butter. Everybody in that room had 'mate tays'.

After replenishing our appetites, we went back to the Fairgreen, where the participants were getting down to serious business. Pa was selling his four cattle for, I think, £24. It was pure theatre. A man started bidding at £20, but was immediately rejected. The bidder would move away and somebody would drag him back again. There was a lot of spitting on hands, and after a long time there was only 10 shillings between them, the bidder at £22, Pa holding out for £22.10s. As I was dreading the walk back I urged him to take the money. No chance, he was holding out. The deal collapsed, and I couldn't understand how he walked away from £22. We headed back the eight miles to Banagher. But we were about two miles along when Pa waved down a cattle truck. A deal was done for 5 shillings to transport myself, Pa and the four cattle to Upper Banagher. So there was only a 5 shillings gap in it in the end. I slept in the settle-bed until 2pm the next day. (*Lesson: Don't be too greedy in a deal*) 'Aunt' Kate died in 1958. It was the first funeral I attended. I went in my father's car with Granny and my mother. The custom was for the men to walk behind the hearse for the three miles from Dromahair to Newtownmanor graveyard. We were about to climb a very steep hill, about 200 yards from the church, when the cortege stopped. Nobody knew what was going on until Pa came back and told us that the hearse had broken down. After what seemed like an age a large car arrived. The coffin was hoisted onto the roof and tied on with big thick ropes. There was consternation in the car, and rosary beads were produced. We debated if the coffin might slip off the roof, but 'Aunt' Kate held tight and all was well.

My Uncle Sonny came home from London every two years or so. He would stay with Aunt Maggie for a few days before hiring a car for the trip to Banagher. Some of my cousins might travel with him, although for one trip I returned from Dublin with him. It was usually torture, and not unusual for the trip to take six or seven hours as Sonny seemed to stop at every pub along the way. He was a big heavy man with a huge capacity for drink. For every drink he had, we got lemonade, but in truth, all we wanted was to get home. But we loved Sonny as he always dispensed large quantities of cash (three or four shillings was a fortune to a six-year-old). He had a large pocketful of coins, and would tease us by rattling them in his pocket before planting a handful in our sweaty palms. It was then straight across the road to Nell O'Neill's for a swag of lollypops, lucky bags, bull's eyes and other assorted goodies.

My sister Maura was born on April 15, 1955. I didn't know much about the pregnancy until Nurse Maloney told me my mother was going into hospital "*to buy a baby*". I stayed next door with her while my mother was in Sligo General Hospital. Mothers had to remain in hospital for a week in those days, and it was maybe five days after Maura was born that I was allowed visit. I headed off by myself on what was a very sunny day. I entered the hospital grounds and saw an open window. When I looked in I saw my mother with Maura at the end of a ward with maybe ten other women. My mother saw me and waved me in. I held Maura for a few minutes and then went home again. I can't remember much about her early days at home, but I must have taken it all in my stride.

My Aunt Chris said that the Higgins's always had itchy feet, meaning they travelled a lot. My grandfather's sister Kathleen, emigrated to England and South Africa. Another strand of the family moved to Liverpool, and one of them, Francis, became a sea captain. I met him in New Street only once, and he wore his captain's uniform which was very impressive.

Not long after Maura was born, my father went to England to work. All the family, including my Granny McGuire, went to Dublin on the train. My mother didn't tell Granny that my father was emigrating but pretended he was visiting Sonny in London. Aunt Maggie and Paddy had moved to a new development in Bluebell in 1953, and on the way there, Granny decked what was happening and was livid. I also suspected something was up. From Bluebell we went to Westland Row station. The trip to London was punishing, including a train to Dun Laoghaire, the mail boat or cattle boat to Holyhead, and a very slow twelve or fourteen-hour train journey to London.

Thankfully, my father was back with us in Sligo within a year. He went back to CIE, but had to take a job in Athlone. His bus left Athlone at 8am, arriving in Sligo at 11.30. On its return journeys it left Sligo at 4pm, arriving in Athlone at 7.30m. So he arrived home at noon, ate his dinner and was back to the bus at 3.45pm. On weekdays I'd only see him for half an hour during my school dinner break. He organised lifts back to Sligo on Saturday nights, and was home on Sunday but back to Athlone on Sunday night. It was a gruelling schedule he had to put up with for two or three years, and his health suffered eventually.

I'd moved to St John's School, only five minutes' walk from our house. It was run by Marist Brothers and a few lay teachers. My first teacher was – yes - Daddy Shine! He was a very good teacher and very humorous, despite his stern appearance, and he never mentioned our earlier incident. Some of my classmates in third class talked about moving to St. Mary's School on The Mall for fourth class. St. Marys was also run by the Marist Brothers but had a better reputation. It had an unusual arrangement, only two teachers with slightly smaller class sizes. Brother Flannan had fourth and fifth in one room, Brother Conan had sixth and seventh in the next room.

About twelve Brothers lived in a large house at the end of our street, and were part of the community. They attended 7.30 mass every morning. Flannan was very interested in music, and had a very good school band. Nearly all of us learned the tin whistle at some stage, starting in Scoil Fatima. In addition to the tin whistle band, Flannan had started an accordion band at St. Mary's. So in September, 1956, I moved to St Marys where I knew quite a few of my classmates as we'd nearly all started in Scoil Fatima in 1951.

I played the tin whistle during the music class during school hours. Accordion practice took place after school hours. Flannan was very encouraging, and although I didn't own an instrument, I hung around and would occasionally pick up an instrument during a break just to feel it in my hand. Eventually I told my parents I'd like to learn the accordion.

One day around November, 1956, I arrived home as usual for my dinner break. My father was at the table, and I noticed a cloth cover on the chair I would normally sit on. Both my father and mother were smiling, and asked me to lift the cloth. To my great surprise, sitting there was a gleaming red Paolo Soprani two-row accordion. I was ecstatic. I learned later that my father was paying up on the instrument in a music shop in Athlone. The accordion cost £19, over twice my father's weekly take home pay and a truly great sacrifice for my parents at the time. I headed back to school with the accordion under my arm looking forward to joining the after-school class. Little did I know then that my life and career would evolve around the entertainment business. That day was the start of a wonderful journey for me. I didn't take long to pick up a few tunes. Flannan had a very relaxed teaching style, and these were happy days. Classes seemed to fly, and I looked forward to strapping on my accordion for each lesson. After about a year I could play quite well and joined the school band. The pattern for 1956 and 1957 was much the same - school, music, football, and summer holidays in Mullaghmore, Banagher and Dublin. When in Dublin, Aunt Kitty would arrange to take me and one of my cousins out for an afternoon.

It was also around this time that we moved from New Street to a much more spacious house at 70 Doorly Park where Ga Ga, Frank and Chris lived. I'd heard of my Aunt Molly, but I can't remember when I met her first. After working in Downpatrick, County Down, she came home to Sligo to work as a nanny with the Gilroy family. I'm assuming she lived with the family, but I don't remember seeing her in Doorly Park very often.

The family moved again, in 1960, to 2 Temple Street, almost opposite St John's School. This was the first time I heard about 'aunty' Kathleen. She was not really my aunt, but my father's aunt. She was one of the itchy-feet Higgins clan, having left Rosses Point as a young girl and travelled the world. She spent over 20 years in South Africa where she was in charge of a large hospital. She was a very formidable woman with a very plummy English accent. But she had recently retired from work and wished to live in Sligo. Her arrival also dove-tailed with Aunt Molly's retirement from Gilroy's .

The house in Temple Street was quite large, so Ga Ga's family and Kathleen pooled their resources and had joint ownership. Kathleen converted two rooms into a self-contained apartment upstairs, and was independent from the rest of the family. It was obvious she was well-travelled. She had lots of exotic antiques too, including a beautiful hand-carved Chinese chest, decorated in ivory. I dropped by her apartment regularly because she was always interested in what I was doing.

I moved into Brother Conan's class in September, 1957. If Flannan's class was heaven, this was hell, as Conan was an alcoholic with a violent temper. He was ok sometimes, but when he was on the bottle he was a nightmare. The Marist Brothers House was within view of our house, and I often spotted Conan nipping across the road to Holland's Bar at the corner of Church Hill and John Street. He didn't drink in the bar, but the Holland family lived upstairs and he could gargle there unseen into the early hours. I was usually an altar boy for 7.30 mass, and I always knew when he was hung-over as he'd have his head buried in his hands. Before he arrived in school I had the grim onus of telling my classmates to prepare for the worst. It was not a good time.

One day for homework we were asked to write an essay. I didn't bother doing it, hoping it wouldn't be noticed. The next day Conan was in one of his moods and said *"I'm not correcting homework today, but I'll ask some of you to read your essays to the class"*. Great, I thought, with luck I'll escape. *"Higgins, will you read out your essay? What did you write about?"* says Conan. I was too terrified to say no, and said *"My New Bicycle"*, but with little conviction. *"Very good"* said Conan, *"let's hear it"*. Up I stood with the empty copybook and started to make up a story. *"Excellent...can you read the last paragraph out again?"* The game was up, and I had to confess.

He went for his cane, but it was badly splintered from his previous beating. So he gave me 6d and told me to go to Billy Peebles in Market Cross to buy a new one, and sent my classmate Davy Curran with me to make sure I came back. Billy had a newsagents, bookshop and general hucksters shop, and also operated a printing press at the back. Sheepishly I asked for a cane. Billy said *"ye are for the high jump today, ha ha"* and proceeded to test the cane by hitting the books with it. Back to the scene of the crime, Conan give me six or seven full-force welts on both hands, one of them right on the bone of my thumb.

That evening at tea, I had difficulty holding my cup. My father said, *"what's wrong?"* I denied it for a while but, expecting sympathy, I blurted out my tale of woe. I then got a clatter across the head from my father. *"That'll teach you to do your homework in future."* So, no sympathy from that quarter. *(Lesson: Take the knocks, and don't look for sympathy)* Those two years with Conan in sixth and seventh class were tough, but the music was an outlet. We practiced after school in the next room with Flannan, and I was in the school band, a mixture of accordions and tin whistles. We played at school concerts, football matches and any gathering that required music. The Marist Brothers were about to open a new school in Ballina and were having a fundraising concert in Ballina Town Hall. Flannan was asked to bring our band, but it was impractical to take twenty-four 10-year-olds for a night-time concert 35 miles away. Instead, he asked myself and four others to play at the concert. Needless to say, I was chuffed.

Sean Forde was the manager of the Provincial Bank (now AIB) in Stephen Street. Actively involved in the community, he agreed to drive us to Ballina. It was a big deal for me, as the five lads plus Flannan on his accordion played three or four tunes to a packed audience. It was a very frosty evening, and on the way home Sean lost control and crashed the car into a wall outside Dromore West. Nobody was hurt, but the car was too damaged to continue. There were very few cars in Ireland in 1958, especially in such a remote area, so we'd waited for over an hour before the driver of a cattle truck stopped to help. We all got in the back of his truck and travelled to Sligo standing up, holding onto the cattle bars. Welcome to show business!

John Fowley, who lived across the road in John Street, had started to learn Irish dancing. My mother pushed me to take it up too, and although I had very little enthusiasm, I went along with her wishes and attended weekly lessons at Madge Fallon's house in St. Bridget's Place. Madge's brother Bernie was a champion dancer, and the house was full of his trophies. It would be reasonable to say that I was not the most delicate of dancers, no budding Michael Flatley.

Dancing lessons would lead up to the Sligo Feis where competitors from all over the country vied for a variety of cups and medals.

I was entered in the under-10 reel competition. I was fitted out with a kilt, jacket, shawl - the full works. Competitors had to dance in various heats to eliminate the dross, so I did a reel with three others. The single reel was danced in a circle of twelve steps. Madge had coached me to be sure to get to the half-way point in six steps so I could coast after that.

Her brother, Danny Fallon, was the resident fiddle player for the Feis and had a seat on the floor at the front of the stage. My mother, Auntie Chris, Uncle Frank and some of the John Street neighbours were waiting in the audience. But I noticed a disapproving look from my 'supporters'. I had been playing football earlier, and appeared with a bloodied knee and blood on my socks. The shame of it!

Anyway, what could possibly go wrong? Danny fired up the 'Mason's Apron' reel and we took off. It was another kind of bloodbath. I scattered all around me, elbowing the others out of the way to make sure I had clear road in front of me. I can still see the look of terror on Danny's face as I rounded the corner. He thought I was going to fall on top of him, so he flinched backwards, still playing the fiddle. Oh shit, I was in trouble. With my long strides, I was at the half-way point in three steps. I had the stage ahead to myself, and negotiated nine short steps to finish the circle with a great sense of achievement. The others stayed well away from me for the rest of the dance.

Needless to say I didn't qualify. Madge said, diplomatically, *"You did well Tommy. You'll be better the next time"*. That was the end of my dancing career. Madge probably told my mother it'd be easier to teach an octopus to dance Irish reels, and I don't remember seeing the dancing outfit again, so it must have been sold.

After about two years, my father got a new route, much closer to home. He was now based in Blacklion, only 30 miles away. A 90-minute bus trip, it was less arduous. As with the arrangement re Athlone, he stayed overnight in Blacklion and had much more time at home, including a full day off on Wednesday and Sunday.

I slept in the back room of our house in Upper John Street. It faced towards the Gilhooly Hall where every Sunday night a dance was held, featuring a variety of professional bands. I loved to hear the music, which sounded very clear, but especially in the summer nights when all the windows were open. My usual manoeuvre was to slip into the hall while the band was setting up and hide behind the stage for the first hour of the dance, unless I was caught and asked to leave. I'd be home by 10pm and would listen to the music in bed before drifting off to sleep. As I started my last year in national school, the talk among my classmates was about what we would do next. Most would go to the Technical school to learn a trade, while others would go to College. I was just an average student, having passed all my end-of-term exams, but I was nothing special. I knew during that last year that I was entering a different cycle.

My mother was remarkable, as it must have been very difficult for her bringing up two children with such little resources. She had very high standards, and passed on all her values to me. She dressed immaculately every time she left our house. I recall the fireside chats during which she reminded me to be respectful to women, and I clearly recall her saying to me *"Treat others as you'd like to be treated yourself"*.

It was terrific advice that I've always tried my best to follow, and it stood me well in the decades to come.

1960 – 1969 Summerhill College

After we returned from the Christmas holidays in January, 1960, most of my classmates started to focus on either College or Technical School. My father had gone to England again, and my mother was keen for me to attend Summerhill College, only a 10-minute walk away, but there was no pressure. I was aware that it was financially tight at home. I was entering my teenage years and becoming aware of the ways of the world.

My father sent money home weekly by telegram. Every Saturday, between 11am and 12.30, the telegram boy Aidan Sexton arrived on his bike with the magic envelope. I would usually go to Henry's, pay the grocery bill and bring back the change. My mother would then go down town. Hard to believe now, but our weekly grocery bill then was in the region of £3-£4, about 30% of the weekly take-home pay at the time. We trudged off to sit the entrance exam for Summerhill College at the Mercy school during the Easter holidays. I was secretly hoping I'd fail, but somehow scraped through. I hardly spent any time in Banagher that summer. My cousin Sean, although reared all his life in Dublin, loved the country life and increasingly spent his holidays there. The music was still going strong and I'd accumulated quite a number of tunes, but since I hadn't learned to read music, I picked them up by ear.

I started first year in Summerhill College in September, 1960. The fees for the year were £100 plus the cost of books, a substantial amount for us, considering the average income was about £12 a week. I've no idea where the money came from, but I suspect the grannies pitched in. I knew several of my classmates, as most of us had started out in Scoil Fatima, while about half the class was made up of boarders from County Sligo and Roscommon. The teaching roster was mostly made up of priests with a small number of lay professors. We'd no idea what to expect. It was to be a new experience, because, unlike the previous one-teacher system, we'd have a different teacher for each subject.

When our first teacher breezed into the class we were not expecting what was to follow. "*Hello. I'm Fr. Devine, your Latin teacher*" was spoken in a fabulous American drawl. He was a young priest in his 20's, looking not much older than us. He was subsequently called 'Ricky'. After he was ordained, Ricky spent two years in Florida and then 'subbed' for other priests during their holidays. He was our first college teacher, and we were his first students. Meeting him was the start of a fabulous relationship that has continued to the present day. He seemed so exotic, with his accent and his deep tan. He had a positive effect on us, with his wonderful method of teaching, introducing drama, soccer, basketball, debating and a host of other activities to the college.

In 1960, soccer was banned in a Gaelic sports school like Summerhill, but Ricky organised a soccer game between two classes. On the day of the match he arrived on the pitch in white shirt, shorts, socks and to cap it all, white boots, and all set against his super tan. We mere mortals wore a ragbag of assorted colours against bony snow-white skin. We played the soccer match on the Summerhill Gaelic pitch which was sacrilege, but as soon as somebody spotted the school President, Fr. Kelleher, we'd get a signal from Ricky and instantly start to play Gaelic football. He also introduced us to various strands of American music which had previously been totally unknown to us. (A remarkable feat was achieved in 1970 when Summerhill won the All-Ireland schools soccer championship for the first time. They were coached by Ricky.)

The first year passed very quickly, and despite my initial indifference I thoroughly enjoyed the experience. The talk turned to what to do during the three month summer break, as you were considered a failure if you didn't have a summer job. I was fourteen at the time, and scoured *The Sligo Champion* jobs section. I spotted an ad for 'Help Wanted' in Rowlette's, Wine Street, only five minutes from our house. It was a guest house with six bedrooms, and run by two elderly ladies, Florence and Olivia Rowlette. It seemed like a handy gig, so I headed off for the interview.

I was hired immediately and started the next day at 30 shillings a week. My duties consisted of waiting on tables, cleaning, dusting, washing dishes, and making beds. I worked from 7.30am to 1pm, and 5pm to 7.30. The house was always busy, but I picked up the routine very quickly. Jimmy Rowlette, a brother of Florence and Olivia, was visiting from Dublin for the week. He gave me a tip of 10 shillings, an enormous sum then. I received an envelope with my wages of £1.10 shillings, and as I had the tip from Jimmy I gave the envelope to my mother. I felt really good about contributing to my upkeep for the first time.

Killavil Hall

I started back in second year at Summerhill in September, 1961. Flannan was still involved in music, and he'd call to our house some evenings to play music with me and a few others. One night in mid-December he called with news that, although I didn't know it at the time, would set me out on the path to where I am today. He said that Fr. O'Hara from Killavil wanted us to play at a dance just after Christmas. This was a big deal, as we'd never played at an adult function before, so we picked five guys from the school band and practiced every night over the Christmas holidays.

We called ourselves St Mary's Ceili Band. We'd no amplification so we hired a 15 watt amplifier and two x 12" speakers from Bernie Morahan's shop in Teeling Street (a U2 concert would have 100,000 watts of amplification and at least 250 speakers!) Killavil, a few miles outside Ballymote, consisted mainly of a church, pub and shop. When we arrived, the gubby was lighting the paraffin oil lamps (*every hall had a gubby= caretaker/odd job man*). He then spread resin on the floor to make it easy for the dancers to glide around. The hall had no electricity, so we took the battery from Fr. O'Hara's car to power up the amplifier. A huge turf fire beside the stage provided heating .... no health or safety issues back then! A door each side of the stage lead to the toilets.

We set up our meagre collection of instruments and Fr. O'Hara took up his position at the door to collect the money. As soon as we started playing at 9pm, people started coming in, and by 10pm the hall was packed with maybe 150-200 people. It being Christmas time, many were home from England. The Killavil hall was typical of thousands of parish halls around Ireland at that time. It was used for a variety of functions, but mostly dances, and helped to supplement the income of the local priest. Nearly all social events in rural areas took place in the local hall.

Our programme was mostly Irish ceili music and waltzes, plus a few ballads, and it didn't matter that we had to repeat some a few times. The place was jumping, aided by the men coming from the local pub fuelled with copious amounts of whiskey and poteen. For me it was just wonderful playing at a grown-ups dance. The entire occasion was intoxicating - the smell of turf, paraffin oil, resin, cheap perfume, sweat, pee from the toilets behind the stage, all mixed into a magic concoction. We had a 15-minute break around 11pm. Around midnight the battery gave up, but nobody cared. We just played louder, and I was disappointed when the dance ended at 1am. Fr. O'Hara was delighted, and I was knocked out when Flannan gave us 15 shillings each. We put the battery back into Fr. O'Hara's car and pushed him down the road. He waved out the window when the engine fired up, and we headed back to Sligo deliriously happy. The fact that I got paid nearly eight week's pocket money made the occasion all the sweeter, and I was hooked on the music business forever.

Fr. O'Hara must have spread the word, because enquiries started to come in from other parish halls around the county. That Flannan, 'a man of the cloth', was involved with us did us no harm. However, there were no further gigs for a while, as parents quite rightly wouldn't entertain such activities during school term. Our next outings came during the Easter holidays when we played for Fr. Fleming in Carney Hall and Fr. Ward in Maugherow, both very successful performances. This was heady stuff, if short lived, as we had to finish our final term at Summerhill.

The highlight of the year was the launch of Telefis Eireann on New Year's Eve, 1961. There were few televisions in Ireland up to the launch of the national TV channel which was only going to be available in black and white. Up to then, our only form of home entertainment had been the radio with its one channel. Now, nearly everybody had to have a TV set installed, mostly rented. RTE started transmitting from just before 6pm to 11pm. I'd just turned fifteen when Florence Rowlette called to the house one evening and asked if I'd be interested in working at the guest house again during the summer as she had very heavy bookings. She also asked if I knew of another person looking for summer work as I'd need help. So I contacted Pat Chrystal who lived in the next street, and he was delighted with the opportunity. We were a lethal combination. The guest house being very busy, there was a lot more washing up, but we broke more than we washed, and when we broke a cup or plate, we kicked the broken pieces under the cupboard. This was fine until we were rumbled.

One day Florence said *"Boys, it's time for Spring cleaning"*, and started pulling out tables and chairs at the other end of the kitchen. Pat turned to me. *"Tommy, we are fucked"*, and indeed we were. In due course, Florence got around to our dumping cupboard and swept out the broken crockery. Pat dead-panned: *"I've no idea where that came from"*. It didn't work. Florence read the riot act .... *"I am very disappointed"*, and we had to take it on the chin. In fairness, they were lovely ladies and our misdemeanour was quickly forgotten.

Summer 1962 flew by. In addition to my job at Rowlettes, the band had increased its profile and we played at least once or twice a week. But there was a new urgency when we went back to college, as the Inter Certificate was coming up the following June. I was finding it increasingly difficult to summon much enthusiasm for college, having been irreparably "damaged" by the Killavil experience.

The year ended on a sad note when my Uncle Michael died in December, 1962. I'd met him maybe no more than three or four times.

Teenage kicks

My parents assumed I was studying at night, but I'd smuggle our new transistor radio up to my room. As I mentioned earlier, there was only one Irish station at the time and the music was awful. On the other hand, Radio Luxembourg was a commercial station, although as we were at the outer edge of Europe, the signal was unreliable. Whenever possible, I'd tune in to the 208 band and listen to fabulous pop music with the radio under the blankets to deaden the sound. The DJ's were wonderful compared to the Radio Eireann presenters, Barry Aldis, David Jacobs, Brian Mathews, Alan Freeman .... I knew them all.

Then one night in October, 1962, everything changed for me. A band called The Beatles had released their first single, 'Love Me Do'. The DJ played it and then interviewed the band. They were so different, Lennon making quirky jokes, Ringo saying stupid things, Paul and George chipping in. I was hooked, as the whole world was soon to be hooked.

Being a teenager in the 1960s was fabulous. In the 1950s, Ireland had been a dark, foreboding and oppressive country ruled by Church and State. If the decade was to be described as a colour, it would be dark brown or black. But the 1960's were a kaleidoscope of colours. We were assaulted with sights and sounds never experienced before, JFK, The Beatles, Elvis, Cassius Clay (Muhammad Ali), Pele, The Rolling Stones, Carnaby Street fashion, George Best, Tamla Motown, endless new wonders.

While Elvis and rock 'n roll had started in the 1950's, the music scene exploded in the 1960's, and it was impossible to keep up with it all. The Beatles released several singles a year and they were all huge hits, and their initial success paved the way for the Mersey Sound. Hundreds of artists created brilliant new music and it came in waves, and Radio Luxemburg introduced us to trans-Atlantic music too.

It was magic stuff. We threw away the shackles of the fifties, the dark clothes, the oppression and the baggage of the past. It seemed as if an enormous weight had been lifted from our shoulders. Instead of depression and darkness, we had coloured shirts to match the colourful music. The Beach Boys introduced us to surfing and California Girls. Simon and Garfunkel sang about Scarborough Fair. Bob Dylan was Bob Dylan, and that was more than enough, and in the mix we also had a brand new sound from Motown with the Jackson 5, The Supremes, Smokey Robinson and The Four Tops.

Of course TV became an important factor too, and even if it was in black and white, we didn't care. We now had access to sports, music, drama and politics on a scale never experienced before. We'd heard of Pele from the 1958 World Cup, but didn't see him on TV until after the 1962 World Cup in Chile, which might as well have been on the moon. It could take 24 hours or more before results trickled through.

Meanwhile, college became more serious as the exams loomed. But my head was filled with music and I found it difficult to concentrate on my studies. The band continued playing gigs, but with a few personnel changes due to parents insisting on studies being a priority. When exam time came in June 1963, I was not optimistic, and dreaded the day of the results. I wasn't too concerned for myself, but I didn't want to disappoint my parents. I was heading up to the college expecting the worst when one of my classmates on his way back told me, "*I think you're ok. There were only two failures*". I had scraped through, with two honours, English and Geography, plus passes in five other subjects. This would be considered poor by today's standards, but I was a happy bunny and family honour was saved.

The Sligo Champion

It was getting to crunch time. I couldn't face going back to Summerhill, and broached this with my parents. I was 16, and they seemed to trust my judgement. Apart from haring around with the band, I caused very little trouble at home. They said that I'd have to think of the future and suggested training for a trade. So I enrolled in Sligo Technical School in September, 1963 with no particular subjects in mind. It was quite undemanding, no more than three or four hours per day.

For reasons I can't remember, I embarked on a course of shorthand and typing. There were more females than males in the class, and the girls expected jobs as secretaries at the end of the course. Shorthand and typing schools were useful for males going into journalism. But I merely drifted into the class, with no endgame in mind. Although I was there for only a short time, I liked typing, and picked it up very quickly.

After about a month my mother mentioned an advertisement in *The Sligo Champion* looking for apprentices to the printing trade. This was one of the plum jobs in town, described by my mother as "*a good pensionable job*". Flannan dropped by that night. He was friendly with the Townsend family who owned the newspaper, and said he'd put in a word for me. As good as his word, he was back the following night with the news. *"You're in. You start next Monday"*. My parents were happy with this development, and I was thinking it'd allow more time for the band. The hours were great too, Monday to Friday only, so no Saturday, Sunday or Bank Holiday work. And the office was only five minutes' walk from home. Happy days.

I started in *The Sligo Champion* in October, 1963. My job title was apprentice compositor, and the apprenticeship period was for five years. I started a three-month probation, with a salary of £1.10 shillings a week, to rise to £2.50 a week after the three months, in all about £150 a year. My neighbour Jimmy Dowdall worked there as a machine-man (printer) and he introduced me to my colleagues.

The process of producing a newspaper then was entirely different from today where it's mostly computerised. For instance, a modern reporter covering a sports event can type his/her report on a laptop as the event is taking place. The report is then e-mailed to the editors who can insert it on a page via computer. It's the same for photographers. Photographs taken from pitch-side are e-mailed back to the office. The editor can choose the most suitable photo, attach the reporter's match report, and electronically transfer the finished page directly to the printing press, a doddle compared to my day.

Take the 2014 World Cup in Brazil. England v Italy was played deep in the Amazon jungle in Manaus. The match ended at 1am on Sunday morning. 7 hours later, I was able to walk into my newsagent in Sligo and read a *Sunday Times* 4-page account of the game in full colour photographs and graphics. Considering the papers had to be printed, sorted by region/shop, distributed and transported to the West of Ireland (at least a three-hour journey) it was still a remarkable achievement only possible with modern technology.

When I started in 1963, the reporter wrote up the event in short-hand. If the location was close to the office, he/she would then transcribe his notes onto a typewriter. Sometimes (if lucky) the reporter could phone in his report to another reporter at the office who'd type it out on A4 sheets. The reports were then sent to the linotype operators.

On my first day, I was directed to the poster department and shown the basics of designing posters that contained probably no more than six or seven lines in large letters. I had to learn where each letter was in the box, as they were not arranged in alphabetical order. Joe Carter had started a few months before me, and he helped me get started. This is how every apprentice started in the trade. As the last man in was also the designated gopher, I was at the beck and call of all the senior staff, running for errands here and there. I then looked at the orders in the tray. They were mostly for dances in the locality, including one featuring my own band!

With the huge change in the worldwide music business, primarily driven by The Beatles and Elvis Presley, the genie was out of the bottle. But there was a revolution of a different kind in Ireland, the showband scene. Dancing has been around for thousands of years, evolving in various forms, but in order to dance you have to have music, and the composition of musical groups evolved down through the centuries.

Bands as we know them probably came out of the jazz scene which originated in the latter half of the 19th Century. The American Civil War played a key role too, as nearly every military and navy unit had a marching band. As the Confederate army was forced back South and defeated, tens of thousands of musical instruments were abandoned in New Orleans. It was a bonanza for the locals, and a New Orleans style developed, generally recognised as a form of jazz. Various groupings evolved into bands, and a typical jazz band would consist of trumpet, trombone, saxophone, drums, banjo, double bass or tuba, and vocalist. Eventually this line-up expanded, and in the 1920s big band and swing music became very popular. Most popular bands in the 1940s and the 1950s consisted of 10-15 musicians, all sitting down, reading from sheet music.

There are various claims to the title and origins of rock'n'roll, but one theory is that it probably developed from a mixture of blues, jazz, gospel and country music in the 1940s. Hank

Williams had some early rock 'n roll hits in the early '50s, and Jerry Lee Lewis, Johnny Cash, Carl Perkins and other seminal figures emerged around then too. But one record that exploded around the world was Bill Haley's 'Rock Around the Clock', released in 1954. The following year it spent over 30 weeks in the UK charts and was equally popular in Ireland. It revolutionised the music scene, and Elvis and others enjoyed dozens of massive hits around the globe.

The mass reaction against the 1950's meant that, while the parish halls were still there, new commercial ballrooms started to spring up. Parish halls were usually small affairs, the largest holding no more than 500, but some ballrooms could hold over 2,000. They were a considerable improvement on parish halls, with larger stages, maple floors, cloakrooms, and better facilities. The better ballrooms also had a balcony, or a raised area where revellers could enjoy refreshments, although no alcohol was sold. The centre-piece was the mirror ball, revolving slowly, throwing sparkling lights on the dancers below.

But best of all, people could escape the beady eyes of the parish priests and indulge in a little mischief. Although the clergy held out for a while, it was the beginning of the end of their stranglehold on us young people. Bands promptly moved from parish halls to ballrooms where the rewards were far greater. They played covers of pop hits, and the whole experience was fresh and exciting. With the explosion of new music, they had plenty of material to play.

From 1960 to around 1975, over 500 professional bands played in hundreds of ballrooms in every nook and cranny around the country. It was a phenomenal time, and it was not unusual for people to attend dances four or five nights a week, even travelling great distances. The Reynolds brothers Albert and Jim from Longford had the largest chain, over 30 at one point. Even the names had an exotic theme, Cloudland, Danceland, Jetland, and so on. Albert eventually went into politics and became Taoiseach (Prime Minister). Jim owned the Longford Arms Hotel too. Although the ballrooms are closed now, his son

John founded the very popular annual Electric Picnic festival, now owned by Festival Republic.

The ballroom owners were smart entrepreneurs. Most of them were 'colourful' characters who required careful watching, but it was all part of the game. Our two local ballrooms were the Silver Slipper in Strandhill, owned by the Byrne family, and the Las Vegas in Finisklin, Sligo, part of the Associated Ballroom chain. The *Sligo Champion* produced the posters for "the Slipper", and other venues in the surrounding counties, The Rainbow, Glenfarne (the original Ballroom of Romance); The Central, Charlestown; Tooreen Co Mayo; The Astoria, Bundoran; and The Pavesi, Donegal.

On my very first day at work, 'Boss' Byrne swept into the poster department with orders for the 'Slipper. His sons, Sean and Patsy ran the business, but Boss was in charge of the posters. I never knew his first name, and he was a larger-than–life man with a big booming Yorkshire accent. *"Son, I want them posters tamarra or you'll be paid nowt'*. When he'd got his posters he'd head out around midnight putting them up around the county. I soon realised that the poster department was a useful source of information, and that it gave me access to the venues and, most important, to the owners. This was more like it!

2
MUSIC TAKES OVER

With no school distractions, I concentrated on the band, and over the summer a new line-up really gelled: Andy Healy, accordion; Padraic McManus, saxophone; John Bray, drums; Ray Wickham, guitar and vocals, and myself on accordion. We were all aged between 15 and 17. Flannan also joined in from time to time, and the bookings flowed in, mostly in parish halls, but that was fine by us. We got a booking in the Irish Club in Dublin, an important gig that went so well the promoter gave us one Saturday night booking every month for the next year, 12 dates in all. This was massive. We invested nearly all our money in equipment, and I traded in my first accordion for a bigger, better model. Around the same time I bought a record player. There were two record shops in Sligo at the time, Broderick's in O'Connell Street and Morahan's in Teeling Street. My father was from the old school, and sang old parlour songs from time to time. "*Never mind those bloody Beatles, they'll never last. You should be listening to proper music, Joe Loss, Victor Silvester, and not that rubbish*". Forty-five years later I was selling tickets for Paul McCartney shows. They'll never last? The old man sure got that wrong!

Sadly, my grandmothers died within four weeks of each other in 1964. Fr. Tom had moved to Ghana where he was involved in setting up a new missionary house. Communications were very patchy, and it took four days for word to reach him that his mother had died. He was unable to attend the funeral, but I attended the evening removal and the funeral the next day, and we paused for a few moments at her house on the way to the cemetery. I didn't attend grannie McGuire's funeral. My mother was very upset, and thought it best I looked after my sister.

On the personal front, 1964 continued the upward trend for me. The band was doing excellent business, and I was enjoying working in *The Sligo Champion*. But some of the older, seasoned workmates were fond of the drink, and Monday mornings were the worst. Some colleagues could go on serious benders.

I soon learned that on Mondays I basically had three hugely important jobs to do:

1. Collect the Irish Press from Jimmy McGoldrick's newsagents

2. Get buns from the Cafe Cairo for the teabreak

3. Most importantly, collect my colleagues' 'cure' from Alec McGarrigle's pub in O'Connell St.

Yes, I was working in the media!

The summer was very busy with band bookings all over the West. Every Friday and Sunday we played in Mayo or Galway, and some week-nights closer to home. In the summertime, there was an increase in musical activities in the seaside towns, especially Salthill, Ballybunion, Bundoran, Courtown, and Youghal. Salthill, outside Galway, was the best, always throbbing with people. It had two big ballrooms, The Seapoint and The Hanger, as well as a few smaller ones and dozens of singing pubs. That summer, we played in The Hanger every month to huge crowds for a flat fee of £18 per night. We seemed to be in County Galway every week, Carraroe, Spiddal, Ballyconneely, Tuam.

Then Flannan was transferred to Athlone. I've no doubt the Marist Order frowned on his activities. It was fine when we were playing at school concerts and local events, but as the band became popular and played at dances all over the place, his superiors understandably decided to take a stand. He was very unhappy about the move, and eventually left the Order and married. Left in charge, I became musician, band manager, paymaster, transport manager, general dogsbody.

For our instruments we bought a trailer which we parked outside our door. I doubt if the neighbours were impressed. We'd arrive home around 5am, and bring the instruments into our front room, probably waking up the whole street. It was very unfair on my mother, but she never said a word. The pattern was the same after every Sunday gig: arrive home at 5 am or even later, grab a few hours' sleep and get to work at 9am. Yet I never missed a day's work. I've been blessed with a fine fund of energy all my life, and can operate on a few hours' sleep. I suspect the groundwork was laid in those days.

Although the normal age for entrance to dances was 18, I never had much difficulty, as I was tall and could pass for 18. There was no dancing in Ireland on Saturdays, apart from Dublin and Cork, so we had Saturdays off. Nor were dances held during Lent, creating serious problems for professional musicians relying on the income. Taking six weeks out of a schedule was a major challenge for managers too, so bands headed off to England and Scotland's thriving Irish ballroom scene. Following the mass emigration to England in the 1940s and 1950s there was a ready-made market for Irish bands. Some of the ballrooms were fabulous, far superior to Irish venues, but some of them were awful too.

I made my first visit to the Slipper in 1966 for a guest appearance by the Everly Brothers. They were hugely popular, having had million-selling hits like 'Cathy's Clown', 'Bye Bye Love', and 'Wake Up Little Suzie'. They played for about 45 minutes before heading off for another spot at The Silver Sandal in Enniskillen, a sister venue of the Slipper also owned by the Byrnes.

New Line-up

We had to make major changes in the band in 1965 after Andy Healy and Ray Wickham emigrated to Boston and New York respectively. John Bray also left to pursue his studies.

We were merely one of a number of bands in Sligo at the time. The Clefs, the envy of the semi-pros, had emerged as a full-time professional showband from the Clefonaires. They'd been operating from Tubbercurry under various names since the early 1950s, but turned professional, and were based in Sligo Town from 1961. They broke up in 1964.

The semi-professional groups playing in Sligo in the early to mid-1960s included: The Renowns, The Offbeats, The Apaches, Stanley Tymon and Robert Burnside, The Sapphires/New Sapphires/Sensations/The Tokens (1961-1965); The Heartbeats, who became The Heartbeats Showband and later the La Bamba Showband (1964-1969) and the mostly professional Stylos Showband (1965-1968).

Although we were not the best band in town, we had the best bookings by far, so when the word went out that Ray, Andy and John were leaving, I'd no difficulty recruiting new members. Bernie Fallon (drums) and Sam Devins (electric bass) came from The Tokens, and Padraic Fox (guitar/vocals) from The Heartbeats. Despite being somewhat cobbled together, this was a far more commercial line-up. Bernie was a terrific dancer and an exceptional drummer - rhythm flowed through his veins. He could also sing, and was a comedian. I'd never played with a bass before, and Sam added great depth to the sound. Padraic Fox played electric guitar and had an impressive range of songs. With this new sound we could switch between Irish ceili music, country music and pop. Andy Healy had left his organ with us, so I taught myself to play the basic organ chords (badly) to fill in the gaps in the background. But, more important, it looked well! We tweaked the name from St Mary's Ceili Band to St. Mary's Bandshow to reflect our expanded repertoire.

We had a successful two years full of fun, as Bernie had us in stitches and our enjoyment rubbed off on the dancers. The band 'office' was *The Sligo Champion* or Hunts, a guest house in Upper John Street run by Annie and Leo Hunt. We had no phone, but they had a pay phone in the hallway. If a call came for me, one of the Hunt children would run across to our house to tell me. It was nearly always somebody, like a hall manager, wanting to book the band.

Booking was a simple procedure. I'd a diary, we'd check dates, agree a price, and the transaction would be confirmed in writing. During work hours, the same procedure applied in *The Sligo Champion*. One of the reporters would shout down "*Higgins, phone call. Hurry up!*" The biggest challenge then was actually seeing the phone through the cigarette smoke. The old-style reporter's room was a nightmare. Four reporters on typewriters, chain-smoked in a small room swamped with sheets of paper: Tom Palmer the Editor, Dermot McHale, Deputy Editor, and the two reporters Pat Chatten and Paddy Clancy.

Rainbow

It was around this time that we first played in the Rainbow Ballroom, Glenfarne, about 25 miles from Sligo. It was owned by John McGivern who had returned home from the US to operate the dance hall. Like many other venues in Ireland at the time, it was in the middle of nowhere, but people came from miles around. The border with Northern Ireland was only about five miles away, so going to dances could be a great cover for a spot of late night smuggling.

One of the features in John's dances was his famous *Romantic Interlude*. Around midnight, he and his sidekick Mickey Dolan would arrive on stage in tuxedos. We knew that what was coming would be excruciating. Mickey would dim the lights, and John would take the microphone and proclaim "*Now we will proceed with our romantic interlude*". He would then give a short speech about romance and love while we all fiddled with our instruments. "*Turn to your partner and look into their eyes*". After some more talk he'd turn to me and say "*please continue with a slow waltz*". I'd never be so unkind as to say that the farmers' sons and daughters gazing into each other's eyes were the most handsome in the world, but they were unlikely to appear on the cover of *Vogue* or *Vanity Fair*.

But we 'slow waltzed' for about 15 minutes until Mickey turned the lights up again. What a relief! People today will find this too mushy for their tastes, but John ran a very successful operation and claimed that over 200 marriages resulted from his *Romantic Interludes*. He was a gentleman to deal with too. In the 1970's, as the ballroom scene declined and the Rainbow closed, John moved to Sligo where he became manager of the Savoy Cinema in High Street.

Texas King

Mickey Feeney was our driver/roadie. He had a taxi business, and the best car in town, a top of the range Opel Admiral. We were too young to have driver's licenses and too poor to own our own transport. So his car was perfect for the band, a bench seat in front and a roomy rear seat. All six of us plus Mickey crammed into it, with our equipment behind in the trailer. What better way to grow up than as part of a bunch of teenagers travelling and playing music around the country?

Mickey was a fabulous character, full of life and mischief. He teased us about how useless we were, constantly saying he'd be a big star himself and appear in some of Ireland's largest venues. *"Just wait, and you'll see my name up in lights"*.

Then one day at work in *The Sligo Champion*, an advertisement arrived via the 'in' tray. It was for The Mayflower Ballroom, Drumshanbo, one of the best known venues and 25 miles from Sligo. I was setting it up for printing when I was struck by the content. *"Saturday next, Special Guest from the USA, Texas King"*. But I was staring at a photograph of Mickey dressed up in a cowboy outfit.

I had to see this, and went to Drumshanbo as a punter. The place was always packed on a Saturday night, and at midnight came the big announcement. *"All the way from Nashville Tennessee ....TEXAS KING!"* And out jumped Mickey in a fabulous suede jacket with frills, shirt, boots, hat, the lot. I stood open-mouthed with all the other punters. Nashville Tennessee??.... Texas King?? But this is Mickey Feeney from Treacy Avenue, our driver! Then in a great Southern drawl mixed with a Sligo accent..."*Ladies and gentlemen, for my first number, I would like to sing....I Won't Go Huntin' With You, Jake, But I'll Go Chasin' Women"*.

I don't know where he'd got the band, but they kicked off anyway. Mickey (*sorry*, Texas) kicked off in a different direction, and was either behind or in front of the beat for the entire song. It was obvious they were under-rehearsed, and the whole thing was a train wreck. Then he started to

yodel. "*She Taught Me How To Yodel.....yo do leh he dee...
yo do leh he dee*"...... It was painful. He sang about six or
seven numbers, and that was the end of the special guest
from Nashville.

A couple of nights later we were travelling to The Hanger in
Galway with Mickey behind the wheel and had three hours of "*I
told ye, but ye'd never believe me*". Later, halfway through our
gig and completely without warning, Mickey jumped out of the
dressing room in full cowboy regalia, grabbed the microphone
and announced himself as a special guest and of course we
were "treated" to "*I Won't Go Huntin' With You, Jake*". Taken
complete unawares, we'd no choice but to go along with the
charade. We couldn't risk causing a scene or a row, as he was
driving us home.

A few weeks later, we were on a photo shoot in Doorly Park,
and Mickey was due to pick us up for a gig after the session.
I saw his car arriving and out stepped Mickey in his cowboy
outfit. He asked to sit in for a few photographs. I didn't
have the heart to refuse, but the photo shows Mickey to one
side away from the band. Thankfully, Texas King's career
petered out, and Mickey emigrated to New York.

At the time I didn't know how Mickey got the gig at The
Mayflower, but years later the full story unfolded. Mickey was
friendly with Sean Doherty, a cop in Sligo at the time. Sean was
a colourful character, and persuaded the owner to hire 'Texas
King', whom he claimed was an up and coming star from the
US. More likely, Sean made him an offer he couldn't refuse, like
"*Hire Texas or I will raid the place*". I'm joking, of course. After
Sean resigned from the police he entered the political arena and
later became Minister for Justice in the Government......not
joking this time!

Thirteen years later, my friend Pat Ely was doing a few gigs in New
York when, you guessed it, out pranced Mickey unannounced,
and "*started yodelling like a lunatic*". He obviously hadn't
given up, but this irrepressible character passed away in New
York some time afterwards.

Taxman

I was coming back from my usual Cafe Cairo bun run one morning when Brendan Larkin approached me on the street. He was a tax inspector, and I met him frequently around the area. He and another tax inspector Mr. Colleary ran the Sligo-Leitrim tax collection service from two rooms over Quirke's butchers in Wine Street. He said he'd noticed that the band was doing well, judging by the advertisements in the paper, and wondered if I was paying tax on my earnings. I innocently said I didn't think I had to pay such tax, so he asked me to call into his office the following week.

Before that meeting, I consulted Don Molloy, a solicitor and part-time musician. I remember Don's words well, as he waved the obligatory cigarette. *"Of course I cannot advise you to avoid, or not pay tax, so my advice is to give him something to keep him quiet"*.

I then went to Dessie Monaghan, a bookkeeper with an office in Teeling Street. He gave me a few hints in advance of the taxman's meeting, including *"Don't forget to get an allowance for clothes and instruments"*. He then extracted 10 shillings from me for that advice. It was steep, but I paid up, and it worked out fine. In fairness, Mr. Larkin wasn't too pushy. We agreed that I played two nights a week and earned £3. (It was more than that, but I said nothing). I brought up the issue of allowances for clothes and instruments, to which he smiled and nodded. In the end, we agreed that I'd pay 5 shillings a week. As I was leaving, he said he'd arrange for the 5 shillings to be deducted from my wages in *The Sligo Champion*... a bit sneaky, I thought. I was not expecting that, but was happy to leave with what was a very good deal. Today, there must be two hundred people working in the tax office in Sligo. *(Lesson: The taxman is always watching, so pay up, as there's no escape)*

The Swing Seven

I got a call one day from John Healy who owned a very well-known band in Leitrim called The Savoy Swing Seven who'd been around for quite a while. He asked to meet me as he had a proposal that might interest me. His band was breaking up, and he suggested that if we joined forces we would make a great combination. This was an attractive proposal, with the possibility of playing in a band with a wider reputation. The S.S.S. were a professional band, with a good PA system, transport and a lot of bookings, including a weekend in Manchester.

I knew John was a very good trumpet player, and he said he had a saxophonist also available. I felt that St Mary's had run its course and was not good enough for the new showband world. So we hitched our wagon to John's SSS, but it was not a good move. John's diary had a few decent bookings in good venues, but they were few and far between. It was ok at the start, as I had some bookings from the old band, and we were booked to play two nights in the Carousel in Manchester, a venue with a high reputation. It was owned by Bill Fuller, a big heavy Kerryman who'd made his fortune re-building Manchester after the World War II bombings.

We were booked to travel over on the Dun Laoghaire-Liverpool ferry, but John's van broke down in Kinnegad. Sam was a mechanic and got us going again, but we arrived at the terminal as the ferry was departing. It was agreed that we had to fulfil the date, so it was arranged that John would stay behind to repair the van, and the rest of us would fly to Manchester. John would miss the first night, but re-join us for the Saturday dance.

The entertainment industry was notorious for heavy drinking, although, strange as it might seem today, most young men didn't start drinking seriously until they were well over 18. They may have dabbled earlier, but 21 was the norm for when you got "the keys to the house". Padraic Fox was the only guy in our band who took any alcohol, maybe as much as a glass of beer each night. But John was a serious drinker, never went on stage without a skinful, and always had a cargo backstage.

After a few nights I asked about the saxophonist. *"He'll be joining next week"*, said John. But when the saxophonist arrived our faces dropped. He must have been 50, with a big bush of red hair. His name was John Armstrong but was known only as "Red Cloud". This new arrangement was turning sour. Red Cloud could play very well, but he didn't fit. We had five teenagers, plus Red Cloud, and John, who by this stage was always 'merry'. It was beginning to dawn on me that I'd been sold a pup. John suggested we needed a good lead singer, a front-man. He said *"I know a good young lad'een from Manchester who'd be a great addition. His name is Pat Ely"*. I'd serious misgivings, but Pat arrived the following week. It was agreed that he'd bunk down in my room for a few weeks until he found his own place.

A few months earlier, after spotting that John's diary was rather empty, I placed advertisements in *The Western People* seeking a manager to book dates. I got a reply from Eamonn Hughes who had a Monumental Sculptor business in Claremorris, and we subsequently agreed a deal based on him receiving 10% commission. He delivered by getting quite an amount of bookings in the Mayo/Galway area.

Pat was indeed a welcome addition to the band. Red Cloud disappeared. John's days were numbered too, as we'd agreed to go our separate ways. Because John owned the name Savoy Swing Seven, I had to figure out a new name fast, so I came up with Swing 7. Nobody noticed the difference. The mood was much better also, and we got a new lease of life. Pat's couple of weeks bunkering with me stretched into four months. My mother, as usual, never said a word, although it was difficult feeding and washing for another person on her limited budget. Pat always referred to her kindness every time her name was mentioned. A different problem was that Pat had been promised a rosy future and £20 a week by John, neither of which ever materialised. At least I had the 30 shillings from my day job to supplement my band income.

As soon as the dates from Eamonn started to come in, we began earning money again and Pat moved to a flat at The Mall. The first time Eamonn heard the new line-up with Pat was in The Town Hall, Ballinrobe. Afterwards, when he was paying me, he said, *"Pat's a great singer. We won't be able to hold on to him for long"*. He was on the money there.

Smokey Mountain Ramblers

In addition to the ballroom scene there was that other great Irish institution, the Marquee Carnival. Nearly every parish had a carnival which took place between May and September. Parishes would hire a tent, set it up in a field, hook it up for power to the nearest electricity pole and presto, a temporary ballroom. The stage was made from a few planks set up on beer barrels, and the toilets, at best, were a hole in the ground. It worked fine in good weather, but became a nightmare when it rained, as you can imagine. The carnivals were hugely successful, and ran for two or three weeks. You could stuff 1,500 people into a five-pole marquee, and even more when the sides were taken down. One night in October, 1968, we were playing at a carnival in Collooney. What happened next would catapult my life in another direction. Half-way through what was a routine Sunday night dance, I saw two guys coming up the right hand side of the marquee. I recognised one as Des Kelly, the bass player with The Capitol Showband, one of the top five bands in the country. Now what was he was doing in Collooney on a Sunday night? The next day Pat called into *The Sligo Champion* and hit me with a bombshell. He'd had an offer to join a new band in Dublin and was leaving. He said that Bernie was leaving too.... a double whammy. Pat told me Des Kelly had started a five-piece band, the Smokey Mountain Ramblers, to play in pubs and concerts, but now needed three new members to make it a seven-piece that could play in larger venues. In fact they were already making waves with a single called 'Amelia Earhart'. Then Pat hit me with another bombshell, that Des wanted me to join the band!

Pat arranged for Des to call me that night on Hunt's payphone. I was in a tizzy all day, not knowing what to expect. Des rang on the dot of 8 o'clock. He said that Pat had recommended me highly, and invited me to come to Dublin to join the Smokey Mountain Ramblers as a full-time professional musician. I admitted I couldn't play the organ very well, but he said that he had enough good musicians but wanted a band leader. The starting wages would be £25 a week, tax paid, plus expenses, and hopefully more to follow. It was a short conversation as I accepted immediately. I told him I had to serve two weeks' notice in *The Sligo Champion,* which was fine by him. I was on the cusp of a huge increase and a chance to play full-time in a professional band.

Two weeks earlier I'd finished my five-year apprenticeship and collected my first week's salary of £18, before tax. This was at the higher end of the Irish wages chart at the time, and printing was considered to be a very good job. My mother was out when I told my father the good news. He said *"I'm sure you know what you're doing, and good luck with your new career".*

I then headed off to tell the other band members. Naturally it didn't go down well. I told them they could keep the PA system and the van, and could recruit new members and continue. My mother was home when I got back. She said, *"I hear you're leaving us".* I knew she was disappointed with me leaving 'a good pensionable job,' but, as always, she never objected to anything I did and wished me the best, knowing that I had my printing career to fall back on. I gave my notice the next day. It was probably unfair on my boss, as he'd invested five years in my apprenticeship, but Mr. Townsend was very accommodating and offered me his good wishes.

I said goodbye to my parents and sister, and headed off with Bernie on my big adventure on the 8am train from Sligo to Dublin. I was setting out as a 21-year-old on the same journey as thousands of other musicians had done before me, lads who'd set out from small towns across the country, with dreams of hitting the big-time. All I had was a small suitcase with a few clothes, and maybe £20. Bernie's brother-in-law Danny Lehane ran the dining car on the train, and served us a monster fry-up 'to *set ye up'.* Pat had moved to Dublin the previous weekend, and was arranging accommodation for the three of us. Tony O'Donnell had joined the Swing 7 previously, and he brought Bernie's drums, plus my accordion, organ and amplifier, to the Town and Country ballroom in Parnell Square in Dublin where rehearsals were due to start at noon.

I was introduced to my new colleagues, Martin Johnson from Dublin on bass, Dave Kearney, also from Dublin, was on lead guitar, with Lenny Power from Wicklow on rhythm guitar. I then met the fiddle player George Kaye.

George was an exotic creature with long hair, a beard and a posh English accent. Kaye was not his real name, and the story of how he came to Ireland was remarkable. George's father was born in what was then part of Ukraine and was by now in Poland, and his mother came from a corner of Belarus, now also in Poland. After the Russians invaded, George's father was deported to Siberia, a horrible two-week train ride. After Germany invaded Russia, the Poles were told they could walk home! They started on a great trek through Iran, and those who survived joined the Polish Army Corps which eventually became part of General Alexander's 8th Army.

George's father was badly injured and lost an eye at the battle of Monte Cassino in Italy. The Polish Army families had been living in Egypt but were then moved to a refugee camp in India where George was born. His real name was Jerzy Krzynowski, and the family eventually settled in Leicester, England where he was educated there. He started playing in folk groups in the UK with his brother Thadeus. He'd arrived in Ireland to play some gigs and settled there. Somewhere along the line he'd become George Kaye.

Des Kelly was at the rehearsals too, and I was also introduced to Fergus Linnane, our road manager. The rehearsals went extremely well, and I knew immediately we had something special. George was a genius on the fiddle, but in addition to his brilliant playing he had a repertoire of songs like nothing I'd heard before, a mix of country, bluegrass and old-time. His style was unique. Dave was the best guitarist I'd ever heard. He was only 19, and had played in beat groups on the Dublin club scene. Martin was 19, Pat 20, Bernie 22. I was 21 and Lenny the oldest at 26. Most bands in Ireland at the time played pop covers, but Des had a vision for us to be the first band to break through with a country music flavour. We threw in a few pop covers, but that made up only 5% of our set.

On a tight schedule, we had little rehearsal time, and were due to play our first gig at The Longford Arms Hotel four days away. Fergus's father had a building supply company and a two-bedroomed house on Richmond Road, so Fergus arranged for Pat, Bernie, Lenny and me to rent the house at £2.50 each a week. This was heaven, four guys in a house with no worries. Dave and Martin lived at home in Santry and Ballymun Road, while George was married and lived in Raheny.

Next morning we went to Durkin's Menswear in South William Street to be measured for our stage outfits, black trousers, black and gold striped waistcoats, and white shirts. The next few days were frantic. The guys were very good, and we learned around 40 numbers in four days, albeit some might have been a little rough around the edges.

For the gig in Longford we met Fergus and his blue transit van at 4pm at Max Florist, at the junction of Eden Quay and O'Connell Street, and off we went. The five-piece band had performed at The Longford Arms Hotel twice before, and gone down very well. But how would the audience like the new line up? It was not a typical dance hall arrangement, as the gig was to take place in the ballroom set out with tables and chairs. We were due to play two 60-minute sets. We'd agreed the first six numbers, but I had to call the rest of the tunes depending on the mood of the crowd. The first half went very well, although we were very nervous. Des made a few comments at the interval, and the second half was great, resulting in a stack of encores. I knew we'd found something special that night, especially as the band could play in a variety of styles.

It was a hectic week, finishing work at *The Sligo Champion* on the Friday, moving to a house in Dublin, rehearsing a new band and playing what turned out to be a very successful first gig. As a new line-up we had to spend a lot of time patiently rehearsing our show. We had two or three bookings each week for the first month, including a residency every Monday at The Hitching Post in Leixlip organised by two police detectives, Mick Spain and John McGroarty. Later, John carved a very successful career as head of the Drug Squad, one of the top law enforcement positions in Ireland.

About five weeks after our first gig we were booked to play in the Arcadia ballroom in Cork city, one of the largest and most popular venues in the country. This was our first outing in such a top venue. The 'Arc' was owned and managed by a terrific character, Peter Prendergast, who also managed The Dixies, an enormously popular band. The 'Arc' on a Sunday night usually attracted a large crowd, and we were no exception. Peter was a fine host regarding visiting acts. We were invited for drinks upstairs in what is known today as the 'Green Room', a hospitality area for guests. There I was introduced to Eileen Coleman and her friend Margaret Mahoney. Eileen was from Cork, and it would turn out to be a momentous meeting. We were due to play in Middleton, County Cork the following Friday, and as Margaret and Eileen were going to Dublin on that weekend, they asked us if they got to Middleton would we give them a lift to Dublin. Fergus agreed.

Heading outside, I stumbled over some boxes. One of them opened, and I saw it was full of records. I've no doubt somebody had been buying thousands of Dixies' records to boost chart sales. Everybody was at it both in Ireland and in the UK, as a number 1 hit in those days was a very big deal. Welcome to the big time , Tommy!

Eileen and Margaret duly made the gig in Middleton, after which we gave them a lift to Eileen's sister's apartment in Waterloo Road in Dublin. I arranged to call Eileen the following day to arrange a date, but with no phone in Richmond Road, I walked about 400 yards to a coin box on Drumcondra Road. During our first date Eileen mentioned she would be moving to Dublin after Christmas. We agreed to stay in touch, and exchanged letters.

Germany 1969

Eileen moved to Dublin in January, 1969 and started working in Palgrave Murphy in D'Olier Street. Unfortunately, the company went into receivership within a few weeks, but she quickly got another job as a telephonist in the Richmond Hospital, Richmond Street (now a courthouse). We continued to see each other on and off during the following weeks. The band was gaining momentum, and we were now working three-four nights a week. But that would stop on February 20, 1969, Ash Wednesday. Apart from some city venues, there was an almost complete shutdown during the six-and-a-half week period of Lent, ending on Easter Sunday. With not enough work for 500 bands, most went to England and Scotland, a lucky few went to the US and Canada.

In January, we were invited to audition in Cleary's Ballroom on O'Connell Street for a six-week tour of US military bases in Germany. This was important for Des who had to fund our wages during this period and, as a relatively new band, we had no dates booked. We passed the audition, despite a few sharp remarks from the Irish agent, Belfastman Peter Dempsey who told us, *"I'll recommend you, but you have to smarten up and make sure your shoes are polished"*.

So with shoes sufficiently polished we headed off to Germany. Lenny had been there before with a previous band, but it was a big adventure for the rest of us. It was going to be a gruelling trip, eight guys plus equipment cooped up in a transit van, but did we care? We departed Dublin Port for Liverpool early on Monday, February 18, 1969, and drove across England to pick up another ferry at Harwich for the overnight crossing to the Hook of Holland, arriving at 7am. On board the ferry, I met Mickey Brennan from Sligo. He played with The Victors, and was on a similar trip to Germany.

We then had an 8-hour drive to Frankfurt. After we crossed the German border, Lenny asked Fergus to stop at the nearest apotheke, a pharmacy. A veteran of the road, Lenny advised us to stock up on An1 capsules. On questioning him we discovered they were mild 'uppers' used by truck drivers to keep alert. They were harmless over-the counter stimulants, but Lenny claimed they were great for staying up late for drinking sessions.

We arrived in Frankfurt in the late afternoon of February 19, and our first call was to the office of the American Forces Agent to pick up our schedule and directions to our accommodation. The agent was Geoff Patterson, a big wide-eyed Australian guy with a booming voice. *Yeh, abaht taime for ye facking oirish goiys to aroive"*, he jokingly greeted us. Our Fergus had attended a public school and had a very nice Dublin accent. He introduced himself to Geoff as the road manager. *"If you're the facking roid minaja, how come you're not minajin the facking roid?"* So Geoff was a comedian as well!

Germany in 1969 was an entirely different place from what it is today. It was little more than 20 years after the end of WW2, and the Cold War was in full swing. There was a massive deployment of US Air Force and Military personnel in installations throughout the country, as Germany was being used by the US as a staging post for troops coming and going from the Vietnam War. Some of the military installations were massive, and one of the largest, Rhein Main Air Force Base, was about 30k outside Frankfurt. These bases were like towns, with some of them supporting over 30,000 people, including families. They contained shops, housing, and schools, and the currency was the US dollar.

As our first date was not until Friday 22 we were looking forward to some free time. Our accommodation was fine, four twin rooms with cooking facilities in an apartment block close to the central railway station. We divided ourselves in pairs - George and Pat, Lenny and Fergus, Dave and Martin, Bernie and myself. We were not due to be paid until the following Monday, and had to feed ourselves in the meantime. None of us really thought about budgeting, because at home we only had to have breakfast, as we were provided with meals at the venues. Most of us were still very wet behind the ears, in a foreign country with a strange language and with the need to shop for a week. To describe it as a challenge is an understatement.

George volunteered to do the shopping for himself and Pat, but that turned into a disaster. George had a 'different' taste in food, and arrived back with an exotic range of unmentionable foodstuffs, sweet gherkins, pickled onions, octopus in a glass filled with green slimy stuff, cucumber, raw vegetables, and foul-smelling cheese. The only food suitable for Pat was a loaf of dry bread.

I told Bernie we should find a restaurant nearby, have one decent meal a day, and snack the rest of the time, and I found one called the Weinerwald. Of course the menu was in German, but with the help of a waitress we found something to suit our humble Sligo tastes. I learned it off by heart *"Habes hanchen mitt pommes frites und glas milch'*, in other words, half a chicken with fries and a glass of milk. Fed and watered, we hit the town.

Frankfurt was the party town, and boy did they party! I'll never forget the sights and sounds that greeted me. I'd been to cities before, including Dublin and Manchester, but none compared to Frankfurt, teaming with GIs and a noise level that was stupendous. The GIs were either heading to Vietnam and blowing off steam, or coming back from Vietnam and celebrating their return. Every bar, restaurant and pub was packed with revellers. There were thousands of people on the streets. With the noise and the lights, it was as overwhelming as Las Vegas on New Year's Eve. Bernie didn't drink much that night, and after walking around for a few hours open-mouthed, we hit our beds exhausted from the two-day journey.

The other guys didn't fare so well, having loaded up with An1s and hitting the bars. Pat knocked on our door the following morning looking for food. Not being able to eat any of the stuff George had bought, he was broke, having been cleaned out the previous night. I began to realise I'd have my hands full on this trip. In fact it would get worse. I knocked on the other doors, but got no answer. Eventually they all surfaced, but could hardly talk, not being used to XXX-strength German beer. It was not a pretty sight.

All of us played cat and mouse for the next few days, as nobody wanted to share food or cash. It was every man for himself. So it was a relief when Friday came around and our first gig. Rhein-Main Air Force Base was a big place. Every base had entertainment centres for the soldiers, of which there were three types - Enlisted Men, Non-Commissioned Officers, and Officers. The Enlisted Men's rooms were large, with plain tables and chairs. The Non-Commissioned Officers' rooms were far better, with superior quality furniture. The Officers' rooms were sheer luxury, deep pile carpets, and tables set for silver service on crisp linen. Most of our gigs were for the first two categories, but we played a few nights for Officers too. They were genteel affairs, the officers dressed in full military uniform, and their wives in long evening dresses. It was very elegant, but boring for us as we had to play softly. The only consolation was that they had dinner, danced for an hour or so, and then departed for their quarters.

Our first gig was at an Enlisted Men's mess. It operated 24/7, with peak hours between 8pm and midnight when the entertainment is on. As we set up we'd no idea what to expect. Pat was in a bad way, not having eaten for 48 hours, and it didn't help that George was slurping on pickled octopus, licking his lips after every mouthful. He had enough grub as he'd used Pat's budget too. Neither did it help that the stage was close to the kitchens, and as the food wafted past, Pat got weaker by the minute. Food on the bases was subsidised, so a 24oz steak and fries cost a mere 50c. Finally, Pat could take it no more. Yes, desperate men do desperate things. As one of the waiters was returning to the kitchen, Pat grabbed a plate of leftovers and wolfed it down. The manager must have spotted our dilemma because he called me over just as we'd set up our instruments. He said "*I normally don't do this, but you guys seem in pretty bad shape -have a meal on the house*". Pat was ecstatic, as massive steaks were delivered to our dressing room. Although I'd had my "habes hanchen" earlier, I wasn't going to turn down a decent steak. We were scheduled to play four 45-minute sets with 15 minute breaks. Most of the men were from the south, Tennessee,

Arkansas, Mississippi, - and there were no women. The first two sets were uneventful. At the end of the second set, I noticed a couple of GIs talking with George about fiddle tunes, and they asked him to play a specific tune during the next set. George duly obliged, and shortly afterwards, a tray of seven drinks arrived on stage. Then a note came up with another tray asking for some Johnny Cash songs. That was the start of an orgy of music, drinking and revelry. Fergus noticed that there was a spare drink because I didn't drink, and he took advantage of his good fortune.

I actually lost count of the number of drinks that arrived on stage, but the place was hopping. The GIs were dancing on the tables, my guys were on the floor, pissed. Then, after the euphoria, came the emotional stuff. Some of the GIs came up to the stage crying and saying, "*I don't want to go to Vietnam*". Some even flung their dog tags on the floor. Trays of drink continued to arrive, and everybody loved everybody else. I don't know how, but somehow we got through the night. In the middle of this madness was Tommy, stone cold sober. Fergus was wasted, and I packed up all the instruments myself.

Another night we played for Non-Commissioned Officers and their wives. The first set was fine, and we had a good crowd. But when we went back on stage the place was empty except for two people. We couldn't figure it out. I made enquires and discovered that the Division came from New York and they didn't like our music. We assumed the remaining pair would also leave, so we'd have an early night. But nope, they stayed for the next two hours, dancing occasionally while we fumed on stage.

Halfway through our stint, Patterson the Australian announced a special double header for us that would require an overnight drive. We had a Friday night show in Hannover, an afternoon show the following day in Bitburg, close to the Luxemburg border, followed by an evening show in Wiesbaden, and back to Frankfurt that night. It sounded tough, but we were in our twenties and up for any adventure, and Patterson arranged for a larger van with a driver called Wolfgang. Fergus was chuffed with his unexpected "holiday".

The three-hour trip to Hannover and the gig were both uneventful, so we left at 1am for the six-hour trip to Bitburg. I didn't notice the boys had brought on a few crates of beer 'to shorten the road'. We arrived in Bitburg after 7am, but our show wasn't until 2pm, so we'd over 6 hours to kill, and, you guessed it, some of them found a bar. We barely got through the afternoon show, but the evening show was a disaster. I don't know what some of them played, but it wasn't music. I have a recollection of Lenny strumming the banjo with his right hand but, because of the stupor he was in, not having the energy to lift his left hand to play the chords. The result was a rattling, clanging noise.

On the way back to Frankfurt we had two GIs sleeping on the floor of Wolfgang's bus. They'd decided to desert, but quickly changed their minds when they sobered up next morning. Despite all that, the boys in the band were a good bunch and rarely caused serious trouble. There was a great bond between us, and the rest of the tour was fine.

About a week before we were due to go home we were setting up for a gig when the venue manager told us that the former President of the United States, Dwight D Eisenhower, had died, and that all entertainment was cancelled for the next two weeks. We'd been paid the previous day, so we scarpered out of Frankfurt immediately in case they looked for the money back.

We arrived back in Dublin on Sunday, March 30, five days early. Our next date was a week later, Easter Sunday. I called Des to tell him we were home, and learned that interest in the band had exploded while we were away. "*You have no idea what is ahead of you. The diary's full for the next six months*". I'd written to Eileen from Frankfurt, but didn't know if she'd received the letter. I called her that Sunday afternoon, not knowing if she was in Dublin or even if she was still interested, as a lot can happen in six weeks. She was staying with her sister, who was a nurse, and there was a payphone on the landing of their apartment. My luck was in, and we arranged to meet the following night and went out on a regular basis from then on.

Smokey's On A Roll

Easter Sunday was always a special night. The business could get back to normal after Lent, and the longer evenings promised better travelling conditions. Our next gig was at the Cloudland Ballroom, Rooskey on April 6. By this stage, the Smokey Mountain Ramblers had been nicknamed the Smokeys. We duly set up our equipment and then went into Longford to eat. When we arrived back, around 9.30pm, we knew something special was going on by the traffic jam on the bridge at Rooskey, and the throng on the street in front of Cloudland. Our new found status allowed us to hire a support band, so we had to play for only two hours instead of four.

By the time we started at 11 the venue was a sea of people. Bernie kicked off on the drums, followed by George on the fiddle, and a great roar went up. None of us was expecting this reception, and it felt terrific. We got paid on an attendance of 1,600 which the owner, Albert Reynolds, said was a record for Cloudland. The same floor space would have difficulty getting a licence for 500 today, but there were no health and safety issues then. The following night we played in the Silver Sandal in Enniskillen. Same result. A 1,400 sell out.

That began a fabulous run. We had a winning combination, great lead singer, brilliant lead guitarist and in George, a unique singer/musician. Des had called it right too. We played six nights every week, plus Bank Holidays, until we got a break in September. Mondays we had off, so that was date night with Eileen once a week or fortnight. We usually took in a movie, had a meal in the Harp restaurant on O'Connell Bridge, and then hit the TV Club in Harcourt Street. Sometimes we communicated by letter, as the telephone system was very primitive. Calling somebody from Kerry in 1969 was an ordeal, with no guarantee of getting through. But the Monday night dates were always special, and next day I was back on the road.

The money doubled, and doubled again later in the year, and we all bought cars with our new-found fortune. Most people in the entertainment business bought their cars from Brendan Carty in Dublin Motors, Phibsboro. Musicians were notoriously unreliable, but Brendan could arrange finance for serial killers as he was very convincing with insurance companies. I bought a green 1967 Ford Cortina for £100 down, and £400 on the 'drip'. Brendan told me I was a carpenter in case anybody asked! All the other guys splashed out on cars as well - why not? We were all young, with plenty of spending money, and life was great.

My father was at home full time by this stage, and my mother worked at the Connaught Laundry in Castle Street, a dry cleaning establishment. My sister Maura was about to start secondary school. When nurse Maloney retired to County Clare, the McSharry family moved next door. John McSharry was the rent collector for the Church, and when he retired in 1969, the Church sold all their properties for a nominal sum. So my parents bought our home for £300. They immediately bought a front door costing £150!!!!, and built a new bathroom and kitchen. On my first visit home with the new car I brought the first fridge for the house. The innocence of it all!!

During a couple of weeks off in September, Eileen and I and a few band-mates and girlfriends went to Spain. We commenced our first UK tour immediately after our holidays. Friday, Fulham; Saturday, Birmingham; Sunday, Galtymore, Cricklewood, London; Monday, Gresham Holloway Road, London. There were huge crowds everywhere, just like home. The Galtymore was the largest ballroom in the UK/Ireland, and over 5,000 attended our show. But it wasn't all rosy. In order to play the big venues, you had to play the shithouses. The Irish Club in Brixton was nasty, and the worst was the Irish Club in New Cross, a rough area in South London. Even worse, with no elevator, we had to carry our equipment up four flights of stairs. I hated that place, but over-all, the UK tours were very enjoyable.

The success was relentless through the winter of 1969 and spring of 1970. Des tried to link the dates as best as possible, but it was not unusual to play Killarney one night and then drive to Donegal the next. The roads were terrible, and cars unreliable, and I think we changed our cars every six months or so. We could have travelled in a VW Microbus, but opted for the independence of travelling alone.

In the middle of all this, the Northern Ireland political situation erupted. While Belfast was a powder keg, the entertainment business tried to operate as normal, and we played in the Starlight, Belfast in September, 1969 for the very well-known promoter Jim Aiken, The evening itself was fine, but afterwards we could see flames and smoke rising from the rioting. Jim arranged a convoy, and guided us to the safety of the M1 Motorway that led to Dublin. It was a kind act, and we all recognised him as a cut above his rivals. I didn't know it at the time but in later years, Jim, one of the first promoters to bring overseas artists to Ireland, would feature prominently in my life. The band was on a roll, until it all came to a shuddering and unnecessary stop. We were called to a meeting in Des's office in June, 1970. Also present was Des' accountant, Denis Byrne. Denis said that costs were rising, and we'd have to play every Monday night for the rest of the summer for no extra money. This was an insane decision, as we were already close to burnout. Between UK tours and Bank Holidays, we'd just come off a run of 49 consecutive nights, so none of us could believe what we were hearing. Des owned the band, and we were on exceptionally good wages, so I suppose he called the shots. It was quite evident that the money was flowing in, and this was just a basic accountancy exercise.

George hit the roof, and said that under no circumstances would he accept this. He and Pat were married, Bernie and Martin were about to get married, so I knew they could not see this working. I knew the plan was wrong, and raised it with Des and Denis, but they were holding firm. George stormed out, saying he was quitting. Most bands break up because guys can't stand one another, but we enjoyed very good relationships with each other and now it was in danger of disintegrating. Des said that he'd call George and talk to him.

I was very concerned as we had a gig the following night in Drumshanbo. I tried to reason with Des, but he was adamant. I still can't understand why anybody could be so stupid as to break up one of the most successful bands on the circuit. George was one of the biggest attractions in the country. It was not unusual for a throng of fans to stand all night watching him play, and the same for Pat, while Dave had his own following of guitar fans. Des was a nice guy, but he was easily led. Denis had simply looked at a column of numbers and added an extra night with no cost. He never factored in the human element. It was madness. (*Lesson: Accountants are great for advice, but never let them run a business*)

The next day I called George and tried to persuade him to change his mind. He agreed to think it over. We travelled to Drumshanbo, but there was no sign of George. I truly thought he would turn up, but we had to go on stage without him, and I made the excuse that he had the 'flu. The night was horribly flat, both for the band and the audience. I could sense the guys wondering what might happen next. News travelled quickly around the country, but nobody could believe that this had been allowed to happen. Des then suggested replacing George with two saxophonists. It didn't make sense, adding an extra member and changing the sound that had made the band so popular.

So Joe McIntyre from Derry and Tony Cannon from Donegal joined us. They were very good professionals and integrated very well, but it was not the same. We traded on our good name for quite a while because the dates were confirmed, but attendances started to decline.

Canada 1971

We lumbered on through the winter of 1970, but got to play in Canada and the US in March/April, 1971. It was exciting to play somewhere new and escape the downward slide at home. Fergus had left to train as a pilot, so Sean McCabe joined as road manager. He was an ex-cop who loved fast cars.

We flew Aer Lingus to Montreal, and changed for the flight to Toronto where we had a six-week residency at the Maple Leaf

Ballroom. But in between, we had a week playing in New York. The first thing that hit us was the cold. Toronto in winter is unforgiving, with an icy wind whipping up off Lake Ontario. The Maple Leaf was owned by the emigrant Irish builder John Gilligan. He owned a house across the road from the venue and we had it to ourselves, his staff stocking the kitchen with supplies twice a week. The Maple Leaf was fabulous and we played there four nights a week.

The one downside was that the resident band was very good, and we struggled to make an impact. Our playing was fine, but the nights off ended in drinking sessions. That didn't affect me, apart from guys arriving back in the early hours talking shite. I got up early after one of these sessions, only to discover the fridge was practically empty despite having been stocked up the day before. The guys had had a major nosh-up during the night, and fed half the neighbourhood. The next time the food was brought in, some of us hid a few steaks under our mattresses.

It was on this trip when I had my first and last encounter with alcohol. I was invited out to a house for dinner by one of the Maple Leaf staff (I can't remember her name). Her Greek father was there, but, apart from the introduction, he didn't speak a word to me all evening. He was an ignorant git, but her mother and brother were fine and made conversation. When the old guy spoke, it was in Greek. He then proposed a toast for me, and I was handed a drink. It was bottoms up, and I went along with it. Then it hit me. The drink was ouzo, and I became violently sick. Lesson learned, the hard way!

New York 1971

We all looked forward to our week in New York. When we were landing at LaGuardia I got a fright, thinking we were landing in the water! My first night-time glimpse of New York was truly memorable. The promoter Jack Hartigan picked us up in a white van and had booked us in to the Woodward Hotel on Broadway. We did two shows on St. Patrick's Day, a 5pm show at the Jaeger House, and then up to the Irish Club in the Bronx owned by Dan Kiely from Kerry. The club was in a very rough area. We knew Dan, as we'd played in his ballroom in Ballybunion. He and his brother operated in Ireland during the summer and New York in winter. It took us ages to find Dan's club, but eventually located it beneath the overhead railway. It was pitch black outside, with no signage. The door opened and a loud blast of Irish music came out. When the door shut there was total silence....it was very funny!! We enjoyed that week in New York, and went back to Toronto to finish our stint before heading home.

Back in Ireland, the drop in both bookings and crowds were noticeable. Income also dropped, but one night that summer I met Charlie McBrien in Omagh. He was a legendary character in the business, but was the manager of Larry Cunningham and the Mighty Avons, a massive draw at the time. Charlie also booked the bands into the Royal Arms Hotel, a fine venue in Omagh.

An orphan, he'd been raised in various homes, and had left school at 14, and as soon as he was old enough to have a licence, he got a job driving a truck delivering eggs. Barely able to read or write, he spent his spare time going to dances and became friendly with the Clipper Carlton, a big band from Strabane. He then did odd jobs for the Clippers, including carrying their equipment.

But despite the Clippers being a successful band, they still faced the usual challenge of filling dates during Lent. So Charlie enquired about hiring out the Guildhall in Derry for a Clipper Carlton dance during Lent. It was a financial risk, but the place was packed, Charlie cleaned up, and started promoting dances all over Northern Ireland. After he got married, he wanted to buy a house in a very good neighbourhood in Omagh. It was a new development, but he was told he wouldn't get a mortgage. He wasn't wanted in the area because he was a Catholic. But Charlie was made of sterner stuff. He arrived the next day with the price of the house, (£4,000) in cash in a biscuit tin. *"I don't need a mortgage. I have the cash"*. He got the house.

We'd played the Royal Arms with George many times, and he now reckoned that the current line-up without George wasn't making the cut. So he suggested that if I got the old line-up back together, including George, he'd back the venture. I told him I thought it was a long shot, and left it at that.

Proposal

My romance with Eileen was still going strong, and we'd been going out together continuously for over two years. She was working in Fitzwilliam Place at Coopers and Lybrand, one of the largest accountancy firms in the country, where she was receptionist and PA to a group of partners. She was living in 409 North Circular Road. Meanwhile, Mr. Linnane was re-developing his property on Richmond Road, so Pat, Lenny, Bernie and I moved to Santry.

One evening in August, 1971, I collected Eileen from work and as we were driving along Pearse Street she said, *"look, we're going out long enough, it's time we got married"*. She proposed just like that, driving along through the streets of Dublin! I agreed wholeheartedly, and we set the date for February 26, 1972.

The band was struggling, and I was critical of the decisions made the previous year. One night in October we were playing in Glenamaddy, Co. Galway when our then road manager, Jimmy Mulryan, called me to one side to tell me Des was restructuring the band. Martin and I were out. It was a real shock, but although I knew there's no sentiment in the entertainment business, I was disappointed that after all the loyalty I'd shown him, Des didn't tell me himself.

Rocky Tops

So I was not in a good situation, due to get married in four months and no job. Despite making very good money over the previous years, like many of my colleagues in their early 20s, a lot of it went on cars and good living. None of us thought the good times would ever end. However, I had some savings, enough, I estimated, to get me through the winter. So I called Charlie McBrien and told him my story. He said now was the time to get the old band back together. *"I'll back you, but I want you to talk to Maurice Cassidy. He's a right good fellow"*. I didn't know it at the time, but meeting Maurice in October, 1971 was the start of a wonderful 40-year-plus friendship.

I knew little about Maurice, apart from knowing he managed a few bands, and I'd seen him a few years earlier standing beside the stage in Strandhill. He was one of the youngest band managers in the country, managing the Santa Fe, and later, Clipper Carlton Mark 2. Like me, he'd left school early. He'd drifted into the entertainment business in Derry. His girlfriend's father owned the Embassy Ballroom on the Strand in Derry, a very successful venue before it was set on fire during the troubles. Maurice used help out at the box office, one of the best places to make connections at a venue, as the managers ended up there at the end of the night.

Before his ballroom adventures, he and a friend Phil McLoughlin had started selling blankets door to door. They then picked up an agency, and sold items for a catalogue company in London. Their main seller was a line of tea-sets made from Bakelite, a substance very difficult to break. Bakelite was around commercially from the 1920s, but tea-sets made from the stuff were a fad at the time. The guys would call door-to-door to old dears and use their smooth sales pitch....*"look ma'am, these cups and saucers are indestructible, they'll last a lifetime"* as they threw the cups forcefully on the hard floors. It was a winning sales gimmick. Orders were taken and the goods delivered a few weeks later. If Maurice every gets around to writing a book, I have a title for him: *"From Unbreakable Tea-sets To Carnegie Hall"*.

I met Maurice in his Dublin apartment in Merrion Square. I thought he must be loaded as the apartment was so luxurious. I stepped on the deepest red carpet I'd ever seen and looked at shelves stacked with books. Maurice wasn't really loaded, he was just like myself, hustling to get on the next step of the ladder. He just wore a better disguise than me. He confirmed he'd talked to Charlie, and they'd agreed to joint-manage the band if I could get it together. We agreed to talk weekly after that. But getting the band together was not going to be easy. Lenny wasn't interested. Naturally, the others were reluctant to jump ship without security, as they were all married and had commitments. But eventually we reached an agreement and started rehearsing on March 1, 1972, a few days after Eileen and I married.

Wedding 1972

Although I wasn't working, I had a busy few months getting the band together and preparing for the wedding. Eileen and I rented a one-bed apartment on St Mary's Road and moved there a few weeks before the big day. It was a much better apartment than anything either of us had lived in previously. We were married at St Joseph's Church, Berkeley Road, on Friday, February 26, 1972, a very special day for me. Neither of us wanted a large wedding, so it was confined to family and close friends, about 30 in all. As far as I can remember, this was the first and only time that both sets of parents met.

My cousin Sean was groomsman and Eileen's sister Margaret bridesmaid. The reception was held in the Crofton Hotel, on the airport road. As the income-free winter had taken a toll on my savings, I was concerned I'd not have enough money to pay for the reception. It's funny looking back to that day and reflecting on the cost of modern weddings. The reception, including musicians, cost £73! We left Dublin for our honeymoon, a few days in the Manor House Hotel, outside Enniskillen. We started out not knowing what was in store for us, just like the song Christy Moore sings, 'The Voyage', written by Johnny Duhan. It compares life to a voyage with two people setting out on an ocean trip full of adventure and the unpredictable. I reckon marriage is probably the greatest leap of faith two people will ever commit to.

We started rehearsing the new band with the original line-up, apart from Lenny who was tired of the travelling. Tony

Cannon replaced him. Des owned the name Smokey Mountain Ramblers, so we couldn't use it, and opted for The Rocky Tops. Charlie and Maurice funded the start-up, and we played out first gig at the Royal Arms Hotel in Omagh. It was great to be earning again. But even though we had the same line-up, it was never quite the same as the previous band.

The first six months were fine, but it was very difficult to earn big money, and we had to accept moderate fees. There was also a major shift in the business, with cabaret rooms springing up as the ballroom era was coming to an end. Most of our gigs were in Northern Ireland which was in turmoil. The British Government had introduced internment which only inflamed the situation, and every day had bombings, shootings, and killings. Yet, despite the mayhem, people still went out dancing. Travelling in Northern Ireland was very dangerous, especially at night, but we continued to work there as we'd little choice.

Then Eileen announced that she was expecting a baby in late May, 1973. By this time we were really struggling with the band, and income was very patchy. I'd bought a Ford Granada which was constantly breaking down, and Eileen had her Mini stolen outside our apartment in St Mary's Road. One night after a gig in Ballykelly, Co Derry, I discovered my car was missing. It was found later not far away, but the engine had been blown. I bought an Austin A60 the next day in Omagh for £15. It was a wreck with bald tires, but it was all I could afford.

Meanwhile, Maurice had moved to a new apartment in Serpentine Avenue, and was managing the Irish singer Tony Kenny who was making waves in the UK. Maurice intended moving to the UK for a period, and asked Eileen and I to move into his apartment while he was away. We moved to Serpentine Avenue about six weeks before the baby was due. We'd also arranged for Eileen's younger sister Toni to move to Dublin to look after the baby when Eileen returned to work.

I dropped Eileen at The Coombe Maternity Hospital on May 22 before driving to a gig in Fintona, Co, Tyrone, a 250-mile round trip. My main concern was that the A60 wouldn't make the journey, but I arrived back safely in the early hours. I called the hospital at 5.45, and the nurse told me to call back in 30 minutes.

The next time I called she told me I was the father of a healthy baby girl and that I could come to the hospital after an hour. Clodagh was born just after 6am on May 23. When I arrived, Eileen was sitting up in bed, make-up on as if nothing had happened. It was a wonderful experience holding Clodagh and being a father for the first time. My mother and father came to Dublin on the following Monday to see their grand-daughter for the first time.

We stayed for about six months in Serpentine Avenue, and as Maurice was returning home we moved to a house in Santry as a temporary arrangement. It was time we put down some roots, and I'd put down a deposit on a house just off the Malahide Road that was due to be finished early in 1974. Then came a very serious incident. One day, as I was changing Clodagh's nappy in the Santry house, some coals fell out of the fireplace and the rug caught fire. I rushed Clodagh into the car outside, and frantically doused the fire with water. It was a close thing, but our baby was unhurt.

The bookings continued to decline. Eileen was working, but it was clear that I had to do something about our future. The industry was changing too. The new cabaret venues were licensed, thereby providing a much better option for customers. At the same time, DJ's were becoming acceptable. Ballroom owners could hire a DJ for £50 instead of paying a band 50% of the door receipts. The winter of 1973/74 was grim, as we trudged up and down the country for little money. It had become a chore. Bernie became very unreliable, and started missing gigs. The first night he didn't turn up I sat behind the drums and tapped out a simple beat for the night. It was the start of a very short career as a drummer.

A few years earlier, I'd run into Padraic Fox, one of my old band mates in Sligo. He'd bought a plot of land on Cairns Road in Sligo, and said there was another plot beside it. He advised me to have a chat with the farmer who owned the land. I did, and we struck a deal - £500 for a quarter-acre site, including a £100 deposit. Two years later, I still hadn't completed the paperwork (because the farmer's lawyer hadn't contacted me) when I got a message from Francis Kelly in Tadley Estates in Sligo. He offered me £1,000 if I'd sell the plot. Since I didn't have the necessary £400 to complete the original deal, it sounded very attractive. Inflation was beginning to take off in Ireland at the time, so I sold him the plot for £1,100, a profit of £600, not bad, given that I'd only paid £100 in all.

While all this was happening, Eileen and I were discussing what to do next. It was not an option for me to continue playing music professionally. I could play a bit of piano, organ, drums and accordion, but I wasn't good enough really. I also knew that life on the road had to end sometime. One day while we were in Sligo I mentioned to Eileen that we might fare better by moving there. I'd nothing specific lined up, but felt that I'd a chance of starting up something in my home town. There was also a possibility of a job in *The Sligo Champion*. I'd also spotted an advertisement in the *Champion* for a four-bedroom house under construction on the Green Road, and we now had a deposit from the sale of the plot. The house would cost £5,600. Eileen was hesitant about moving to Sligo, understandably, as she'd always lived in cities. After further discussion, she agreed it was worth a try, so in June 1974, our babysitter Toni moved back to Cork and Eileen, Clodagh and I re-located to Sligo. We put down the deposit on the Green Road house which was due to be finished at the end of the year. In the interim we lived with my parents in Upper John Street. My sister Maura was now living in Dublin as she'd starting teacher training in Blackrock. Putting down the deposit was the easy bit, but getting a mortgage was very difficult. I was still playing music but very infrequently. I tried numerous banks and institutions but was turned down by them all, as banks were 'closed' for mortgages. As a last resort I contacted Brendan Carty, the car dealer, who told me about a broker in College Green who might be able to arrange a mortgage, but I'd have to drop him £100.

I forget the broker's name, but I remember the company - *Invest and Prosper*. I delivered the £100 and the broker delivered the goods, and within a month the Irish Permanent Building Society approved a mortgage of £5,000. And yes, my profession had been listed as carpenter! I had opened an account at the Bank of Ireland in Grattan Street, Sligo, and deposited the approval letter with the manager, Ray Mullen. He said he'd advance the cheque for the sale of the house as soon as he received the paperwork from our solicitors. Perhaps better times were on the way?

3

BUSINESS BEGINS

Star Records

By now I'd known Maurice for almost three years and we'd struck up a very good relationship. He was managing Tommy Makem and Liam Clancy, as well as Colm Wilkinson. We'd discussed starting a business together but nothing came to hand. In any case we'd no capital. I really don't know when I got the idea of starting up a record store, but I suppose it was a natural extension of what I'd been doing. A new shopping centre was opening in the centre of Sligo, and the units were due to be completed in October, 1974. The developers were the Williams Group from Tullamore who owned the Five Star supermarket. They were clients of Coopers and Lybrand's, Eileen's former employers, and through her connections Maurice and I obtained a 35-year lease on Unit 7, Sligo Shopping Centre.

We had no business plan, no clue what to do, and no money! While living in Dublin I'd become a regular customer of Golden Discs, the largest record chain in the country with their head office over their small outlet in Tara Street. I'd gotten to know the owner Jack Fitzgerald, and I told him I was opening a record store in Sligo. He said he'd help us, since he had no plans to open in Sligo. So it was going to be a busy six months, opening the store, moving into a new house and trying to scratch out a living with the band.

Then Maurice came up with a plan. We were friendly with the music producer and band manager Brian Molloy. Brian was interested in how record stores worked, and said he'd invest. The deal was that I'd buy into the business as soon as I could get some capital. So, we were over the first hurdle. Next we tackled the record companies from whom we'd need to buy stock. It was relatively easy to get credit from them in those days. I think we needed £250 or £500 to open an account with most companies with 30 days credit terms. But EMI wanted £1,000, so Jack Fitzgerald agreed to supply me with EMI product. To learn the business I spent a week in Golden Discs in Henry Street, the busiest store in Dublin at the time. It was a terrific experience, and it helped me to understand that the key ingredient for a successful store was buying the right inventory.

There were four record stores in Sligo at the time. Fitzgerald's (not related to Jack) was the only dedicated record shop. Broderick's had a music department over their newsagents business, and Morahan's carried a small selection in their electrical store. Woolworth's also had a record section. I reckoned that a smart new record store would do well if it stocked a better variety of music. I also believed that a good modern fit-out would attract customers from the other stores.

So I basically copied the layout of one of the Golden Discs stores, and hired a few carpenters to build it. Thus, Star Records opened for business in October, 1974, and was very successful from day one. I worked the shop myself, and Eileen helped out at lunchtime. As we grew the business, Carmel Mahon, John Feeney, Kathleen McDonald, Danny McCarthy and Richie Barry contributed greatly at different times over the years.

In sharp contrast to the rise of Star Records, the band was coming to an end. Some of the Rocky Tops had moved to more secure employment, and it was a constant struggle to recruit new members as we couldn't offer decent money. So I played my last date as a professional musician in November, 1974. Sadly, as I write this in 2015, of the seven original Smokey Mountain Ramblers, plus Fergus, who headed out for Longford in November, 1968, only three of us are still alive, George, Pat and myself.

Moving in

The house was nearing completion. The builder said he needed the final payment, but added that his costs had increased and he wanted an additional £500. It might as well have been £50,000. I'd paid the deposit of £600, and had loan approval for £5,000, but the builder was looking for £5,500. I'd just started Star Records and agreed to pay myself a wage, but I had to pay the builder's balance at the end of the week.

I called to the bank on Friday afternoon. Ray Mullen, the bank manager, wasn't there, but I spoke to his assistant manager Gerry Barry. I told him I'd called to collect the bank draft for the final payment of the house. *"Oh yes"*, Gerry said. *"You have approval. How much is the final amount?"* With a straight face and taking a deep breath, I told him it was £5,500. *"I'll be back in a minute"*, said Gerry. The next five minutes dragged out like an eternity. If he goes to check the file I'll be sunk. But he came back with the draft for £5,500 and wished me luck. I took it and ran as fast as I could to the solicitors Argue and Phibbs (what a great name!). I was worried that the bank would realise their mistake and deny the payment. But I got the contract signed, so we owned the house! As it was late on Friday I had the weekend free before I might get the call from the bank.

True enough, on the following Monday, I got the call from the manager. I was expecting a bollocking, and really had no answer ready. To my surprise, Ray said *"Tommy, you went over by a few bob, but you'll probably need to buy things for the house. We'll add another £500, and you can pay back the additional £1,000 over 3 years"*. Ray is retired now, and lives not too far away from me, but I see him regularly, and will always regard him as a gentleman.

We moved into our new house on Green Road on January 1, 1975 with just the basics, a bed, a cot for Clodagh and two chairs. There were no carpets, curtains, or central heating, but it was our first house and we were delighted. Although the business had only started and we'd no track record, Ray Mullen next gave me a £3,000 loan to buy out Brian Molloy. It seems a small amount now, but you could buy a decent house on its own land in Sligo for £6,000 then. £3,000 would be the equivalent of maybe €150,000 today. I'm not sure if any bank would lend a newcomer €150,000 to start up a business these days.

Now Maurice and I now owned the business, the first of many businesses and partnerships we were to be involved with over the next 40 years and we're still going strong.

Eileen's father had been unwell for over a year and died in April, 1975, a very sad occasion as he was only 54. Eileen was particularly upset that he'd never had the opportunity to come to Sligo to see our new house and our new life.

Star Records grew stronger every month as I learned more about the business and the location was much better than I envisaged. The store was under cover, and as we always had plenty of rain in the West of Ireland, young people congregated outside the shop. I also had a fabulous sound system, the best in town, so there was always a buzz in the store and in the covered Mall outside. If the '60s belonged to the English scene, the US in the '70s produced remarkable talent, The Eagles, Neil Young, Joni Mitchell, Fleetwood Mac (the later version). The phenomenal disco scene also produced multi-million selling albums like *Saturday Night Fever*. I stocked everything possible in the shop, including back catalogue material never seen in Sligo before.

Tommy the DJ

With the demise of the ballroom scene, discos sprouted up in hotel function rooms, and I fancied I might break into this scene as a DJ. After all, I had all the latest records and knew exactly what the local people liked musically from observing their purchasing trends. In the summer of 1975, I noticed a big advertisement in *The Sligo Champion* announcing a new disco called Barbarellas was opening on the following Friday in Jury's Hotel (now Sligo Park Hotel). There was a big buzz about this new venture run by Seamus Monaghan and Chris Murphy. The advertisement also stated that one of Dublin's top DJ's would be spinning the records. I was disappointed, as I figured that this might spoil my chances of breaking into the scene locally.

So that Friday night I went down to Jury's and sat outside in my car. The place was jammed, but the music I could hear was diabolical. The Dublin DJ must have mistakenly reckoned that Sligo yokels would be only interested in country music and waltzes. He threw in the odd chart hit, but got back quickly to the junk stuff. I spotted a gap, and it was time to make my move.

Seamus Monaghan owned a clothes boutique in Market Street, and I was waiting for him the next morning when he opened up. I congratulated him on his venture, but said the music was terrible. He agreed, and said he couldn't believe how bad the night turned out, with people leaving early. Although they had a three-month deal, they fired the DJ on the spot. So I made a pitch to Seamus, saying I'd all the latest chart disco music and could do a much better job than the Dublin guy. He said he'd consult with his partner Chris, so we agreed to meet again at Jury's after work. Seamus and Chris had invested a lot of money in this venture and must have had further negative feedback during the day, because when I met them they were very concerned. Somehow I convinced them that I could do the job. They offered me a trial for the following Friday, and, if it worked out, I had the gig long term.

This was great news, but I had three major challenges to overcome:

1. I'd never worked as a DJ before

2. I had no DJ equipment

3. I'd only six days to get a show together.

I decided to go for broke, as I saw this as a wonderful opportunity. I had some advantages, including the experience of appearing before large crowds with the band. I'd called all the songs, so I knew how to work a crowd. The same basic formula works everywhere - start strong, pace the programme well during the middle section, and finish up with the best six tunes.

I'd also heard that Jim Melly was selling his disco equipment. He'd done some DJ'ing around town but was packing it in. I called to his house and he told me, "*I'll sell you the equipment,*

Tommy, but there's no money in being a DJ". I thanked him for his honesty, but to retreat now was not an option. I loaded the car with twin turntables, an amplifier, a couple of speakers and 3 projector lights.....£40 the lot. I set it up at home, and practised changing records and putting a programme together over the next few evenings. Eileen's uncle was visiting at the time, and he had a small cine projector with cartoons. I thought I might try showing the cartoons on a wall during the disco, a mad idea that just might work and give people something to talk about.

I'd a few spare amplifiers and a bass speaker and hooked them all up together. My first stint as a DJ was a terrific success, and the night went off without a hitch. The cartoons were a big hit too. I noticed that on the previous week, the Dublin DJ finished on the dot of 2am, so I threw in a few good numbers at the end and played on until 2.15. It was a night I really didn't want to end.

Jim Aiken

I hadn't talked to Jim Aiken since I played at the Starlight in 1969, but I got a call from him in March, 1976. He was promoting a nationwide tour for harpist Mary O'Hara, and asked me to help out with the local promotion for her concert at the Silver Slipper in Strandhill by putting up the posters, placing the advertisements, selling the tickets and so on. The Byrnes were adding a new function room at The Silver Slipper, and the refurbished complex was to be known as The Baymount Entertainment Centre. Jim had become the number one promoter in Ireland, with a wonderful reputation for promoting overseas artists both in Northern Ireland and in the Republic. I was to get to know him really well in later years.

After Jim left school, he joined the Seminary in Maynooth, but after a few years realised the priesthood was not for him and became a teacher in Belfast. He started promoting music events in the Belfast area, including the Royal Showband in the Ulster Hall in 1962. The Royal were the number one band then, and the night was a great success. Jim had to teach classes the next day, but having made a lot of money with the Royal gig, found it difficult to concentrate. So after his pupils went home, he did the accounts on the blackboard. He'd made £1,100 for one night, exactly the same amount he earned as a teacher for a whole year. His father told him that it was the Devil's money and there was something wrong with a business where he could earn a year's salary in one night!

So that was the end of Jim's teaching career, and he was hooked on music promotion instead. The Mary O'Hara concert went very well too, and I met Jim at Jury's Hotel afterwards to settle the money. Neither of us had eaten much all day, so we ordered from room service. At 1am we did the settlement, with the bed covered in cash, receipts, dockets, sandwiches, buns and pots of tea. Although we'd agreed no specific deal, Jim was extremely generous when paying me for my work.

We had a successful year in Barbarellas too, with every Friday packed, but after about a year, Seamus and Chris decided to end the gig as the hotel couldn't guarantee continuous availability of the room. Between weddings and black-tie dinner dances, we were pushed to the margins. This was understandable, as such functions were the hotel's core business. So it was a short, but very worthwhile, venture.

When the Baymount Entertainment Centre was complete, Sean Byrne engaged me as resident DJ every Friday and Sunday. Within months, Sligo Rugby Club asked me to move from the Baymount to DJ at their club up the road. For years the Rugby Club had a disco or band every Friday night, but as soon as the Baymount opened, their crowds dwindled. I told them that there was no point in competing directly with the Baymount, so why not switch to Saturday night instead? Game on. I started spinning records for them, so now had three nights in Strandhill, every Friday and Sunday in the Baymount, plus Saturday in the Rugby Club, where before long house full signs went up every week.

Star Records was doing very well too. Then, spotting an empty unit in the shopping centre, Eileen opened a boutique called Lucky Strike Fashions. It was reasonably successful for a while, and just about breaking even after the first year. In 1977 we had an approach from Edmund Waters. He owned a bakery in Bridge Street, and believed the Lucky Strike unit would suit a bakery because it had very good footfall. Eileen was expecting again, so it made sense to sell the shop to Edmond.

Daughter No 2

1978 turned out to be a very busy year, and we were looking forward to having a sister/brother for Clodagh. The baby was due in May, but when I first dropped Eileen at Sligo General Hospital, it was a false alarm. She was admitted again six days later. I decided I'd attend the birth, and everything was fine until I saw gynaecologist Billy Donovan putting on his white wellingtons. My wuss gene kicked in, so I implemented plan 'B' ... .the exit, a coward to the last. Melanie was born on Thursday, May 11, 1978. Now I had no chance, surrounded by three women!

Star Records continued to prosper through what was a truly wonderful period to be in the entertainment business. We'd sold thousands of units of *Saturday Night Fever* followed quickly by *Grease*. But competition was far more intense too. Woolworth's opened a new record department, and Fitzgerald's moved to a high profile shop in O'Connell St. It meant I had to work harder. Home video became a big attraction, so I hooked up one of the first VCR players to a TV in the shop, and record companies gave me lots of promotional videos to play in the shop. I know it seems quaint now, but this was a big deal at the time. Kids from college stopped by a lunch time and stood open-mouthed watching Pink Floyd's *The Wall*.

Silver Swan

I was having lunch in the Hotel Silver Swan when the owner Michael Higgins (no relation) asked me would I be interested in spinning the records there. He offered me a percentage of the door takings, a very attractive offer as I was getting a flat fee elsewhere. I gave it some serious thought. By this stage, the Baymount opened on Saturday nights for live bands. Strandhill had only a handful of houses at the time, but every Saturday night over 2,000 people attended entertainment events there. We added up the figures. 1,200 in the Baymount, 400 at the Rugby Club and over 400 in Nace O'Dowd's and Patsy Byrne's venue down at the shore. Nearly all of the revellers travelled out from Sligo, so Michael and I figured it should not be a major task to entice some of them to stay in Sligo.

The Rugby Club was not too happy about this development, but it was well established, so I told them it didn't matter who spun the records. That proved to be true, and they were still going strong 10 years later. We put out a substantial advertising campaign for Valentinos, the Saturday night disco at the Swan, and it took off from day one. This was definitely my most enjoyable stint as a DJ. We had a great team. I looked after the music, Michael managed the overall event and our mutual friend Charlie Townsend collected the cash at the box office. Every night was a barrel of laughs.

The centre of Sligo could be very rough on a Saturday night it was crucial that we attracted the right clientele, so we hired three bouncers to keep the peace. These were tough guys. One had worked in East End London nightclubs, another was an ex-boxer, and a third had worked at the Baymount. Today everything is done to set standards, doormen are licensed and equipped with earpieces linked to radios and CCTV monitors. Back then, a bouncer could almost do what he liked. I shudder now to think what they got up to outside, but our three lads simply went into three monkeys mode... 'see no evil' etc.

Nearly every Saturday night the packed event produced some incident or another. One night a young guy was annoying me by constantly coming up to the DJ booth and asking me to play his favourite songs. One of the bouncers arrived on the scene, and I soon saw two dirty fingers disappearing up the young guy's nostrils. He was led by the nose through the crowd and then outside, where he was dispatched ungracefully down the stairs.

One night during the disco I looked out the window and spotted a car owned by one of the bouncers. It was moving, and looking more closely I realised it was full of sheep. The owner said *"Never mind...they're just going on their holidays"*. Apparently, his farm straddled the border with County Fermanagh and he was collecting grants for his sheep from both the British and Irish Governments. He'd collect the sheep on one side, drive to Sligo for the disco, then dispatch the sheep on the other side in the early hours of the morning. I now understood what he meant by the sheep "going on holidays".

With *Saturday Night Fever* all the rage, we arranged our own Fever night with a disco dancing competition. We had 10 heats, with the winners going on to the Grand Final. The heat winners won £100, and the outright winner £1,000. This was a considerable sum at the time, and the 11 weeks were crazy. On the final night, people started lining up at 6pm. It was mayhem, but a marvellous publicity stunt. We thoroughly enjoyed a fabulous few years, but had to call it a day when Michael re-furbishing his hotel and turned the function room into bedrooms.

In September 1978, Eileen and I had our first proper holiday since we got married. Clodagh was going to school, and my mother looked after both children. We spent two weeks in Florida, did the whole Disney thing, went to Palm Beach, drove down to the Keys, and had a wonderful trip. Eileen went home while I went on a musical road trip for another week, ending up in Austin, Texas at a concert by the Texas swing band Asleep at the Wheel at the Armadillo World Headquarters. The legendary venue has since closed, but the band is still going strong and I try to catch them whenever I'm in the US.

Sean Byrne then asked me to help him book bands in the Baymount. I suppose it was a natural development, and was not such a big deal. We had a good run for a few years, but most of these ventures are cyclical, and eventually the Baymount closed. I remember booking U2 for one of their early Irish tours in 1980, way before they became a major international attraction. They played on a Friday night and 400 people attended, surprisingly good for a relatively unknown band.

Galway

As Star Records was well established in Sligo I suggested to Maurice that we open a store in Galway. Danno Heaslip was a well-known Galway auctioneer, and he said "*I have the perfect place for you*" I had learned through experience that every salesman has "a perfect place" for every client just as every horse dealer has "a perfect horse" for you! Anyway, Danno hooked me up with the O'Malley brothers who were developing a small number of units at The Olde Malt in Quay Street, Galway. I signed a lease and opened for business in November, 1978.

I'd advertised for a manager, but the response was disappointing. One evening in Galway I met up with Frank Clancy who originally came from Sligo but was living in Tuam. He introduced me to Joe Bernie who agreed to manage Star Records, Galway. Joe was also a musician with the Swingtime Aces, but no longer wanted to do the travel bit, so this worked out fine. (He still plays the saxophone with big bands in Galway.) This was an exceptionally busy time for me, and the weekends were especially manic. I'd spend a few days in Galway setting up the shop, travel back to Sligo on Friday evening, grab something to eat, spin the records at the Baymount, and catch a few hours' sleep. Then back to Galway early on Saturday morning and home again in time for the Swan on Saturday night. Phew!

The year ended with a family wedding. At the end of December my sister Maura married Kevin Sweeney and the reception was in Rosses Point. Clodagh was a flower girl. Maura had qualified as a teacher, and was living in Dublin. Kevin was also a teacher, and they moved to a new house in Clondalkin, Dublin after they got married.

1980 - 1989 Shop Street, Galway

The shop in the Olde Malt was doing fine, but the location wasn't ideal, and the opportunity arose to move to Shop Street in 1980. Although a smaller space, business doubled overnight, and we now had the two best record stores in the West of Ireland. The concert business in Ireland steadily increased too, as more and more overseas artists toured here. Star Records in Sligo and Galway were recognised as the best places to buy tickets, and Jim Aiken was well established as a major concert promoter.

Denis Desmond was an up and coming promoter, and he started sending tickets for us to sell. I'd met Denis in 1978 when he promoted the Australian rock band Rose Tattoo in Strandhill. He was the Entertainments Officer in Cork University and partnered with Eamonn McCann, his counterpart in Queens University, Belfast. After both graduated, they formed a promotions company MCD (McCann/Desmond). In time, Aiken Promotions and MCD became two of the most successful concert promoters in the world.

In those days, promoters were responsible for all the ticketing for concerts, using a much different process than applies today. Back then they'd provide a printed plan of the concert venue to a printer who'd print books of tickets as had been done for hundreds of years. This worked well for a box office, but for major events the promoter had to physically distribute tickets to various outlets around the country. The outlets had to return the tickets by post about three days before the concert so that all the money for the show could be settled on the night. As a result, no tickets were available in rural locations in the two or three days immediately before an event, very frustrating for customers. Most of our business was done by phone, but occasionally Jim called in person to distribute or collect tickets.

Refereeing

After I returned to live in Sligo and had finished with the band, I started to play football again, Gaelic football for St. John's in Carraroe, and soccer for Merville. It was not very serious, but it was good for keeping the muscles oiled. But by 1981 I was 34 and could feel my legs going. My tackles were going in late and it was time to stop.

I still wanted to keep an interest in the game, but didn't fancy coaching. Then I noticed a newspaper article about the need to recruit local soccer referees. I still don't know why this appealed to me, but a few weeks later, I was coming out of the Bus Stop newsagents when I bumped into Willie Bradley, secretary of the local branch of the Irish Soccer Referees Society. I asked him about the article.

Willie had an impressive career with Sligo Rovers and was the leading referee in the area. He asked me to call to his house the following week and I think he was surprised when I turned up. He was very blunt, and said that refereeing required 100% commitment. I promised such commitment, and started a new career that lasted 23 years.

Willie tutored me on the Laws of the Game, and I passed the entrance exam after a few sessions. I refereed my first game in October, 1981 in Riverstown between Arrow Harps Reserves and Cornagon Celtic. Cornagon were a bunch of mountain men from Leitrim who hunted the ball in packs and had no pattern or game plan. It was a bewildering experience, but I only dished out three yellow cards. I was exhausted, instead of enjoying a pleasant stroll around a field that I'd expected.

Nobody told me that a referee runs an average of eight miles during a game. Despite that, I thoroughly enjoyed the experience and was immediately looking forward to the next game. Willie was a wonderful mentor, and we enjoyed a great relationship through my career and beyond. Refereeing suited me perfectly. After a game, players usually socialise in a pub, and if I'd taken up coaching I'd have to go along with the crowd. But as a referee I'd no such obligations and could go straight home.

Refereeing is about man management. You have no friends, but must rely on a whistle and your demeanour. You have to handle 22 players, 10 substitutes on the bench, and the management team, maybe 40 people in all. That's the size of a small company. In later years, I would use the experience I gained as a referee to great advantage in the business world.

1. A referee has to stay calm in a crisis....same for a business leader

2. Make clear and decisive decisions

3. Don't be afraid of taking responsibility for a decision

4. Don't dwell on a wrong decision. You can't undo the past, but can learn from it.

5. Be fair to the players, same to employees

6. Don't accept abuse from players. I never tolerated abuse from anybody in business.

7. A referee has to think quickly on his feet...same for a business leader.

8. Anticipation...refereeing is about anticipation, where the play is going next and were the trouble might take place.
A business leader should anticipate potential trouble and deal with it before it festers

9. Encourage teamwork and loyalty. A referee and his assistants have to work as a team.

10. Most important....develop a thick skin!

Willie mentioned that sometimes *"you have to take the long way around"* when making a decision close to the penalty area. A player might be fouled, but it might not be clear if it was inside or outside the area. Usually, all hell breaks loose in such situations. The defending team claim innocence, the attackers scream for a penalty, and both sides try to put pressure on the referee. Willie advised me that sometimes it's better to take a slight detour when running to the scene of the offence, and that I should run slightly slower in an arc to buy a vital second or two.
I often applied this advice in the business world. Sometimes delaying a decision by a second or two can work to your advantage. With the emphasis on teamwork and loyalty, referees

need help from their assistants many times during a game, and also the other way around. We always backed each other, and I believe team loyalty is very important in business too.

Of course refereeing is not suited to everybody, as many people can't handle the rollicking from the side-lines. But I thrived on it. There's something very endearing when you hear a big crowd shouting *"the referee's a bollox"!* I developed a very thick skin which helped me greatly in later years. I moved through the ranks, and within five years was promoted to the League of Ireland panel, the premier group for referees in the country. I'd a mixed time on that panel given my problem with fitness. Between travelling up and down to Galway and Dublin on Star Records business, I was also spinning the records at disco's three nights a week, so it was extremely difficult to devote the training time necessary for refereeing at that level. We were also required to participate in annual fitness tests, and failure meant you couldn't referee in the League for 12 months. I failed the test twice in the 12 years I was on the senor panel, but, overall, the experience was invaluable.

I next moved Star Records to a larger unit within Sligo Shopping Centre in 1982. It was a very deceptive space, as the previous owner hadn't utilised all the available square footage. After opening up all the available space it became a very fine store. I didn't want to sell the old shop, and it became Sweets And Things, a tidy little business that was further enhanced when I got the license to sell newspapers, then a 'closed shop' just like the taxi business. A limited number of newspaper vendors were licensed in each area. There were two newspaper/ magazine distributors at the time, Eason's and Newspread. I went through the normal channels, but was refused, and found my way to the Managing Director of Eason's. He listened to my story, and agreed to supply my shop with newspapers and magazines. Newspread followed immediately.

I was by now a DJ at the Great Southern Hotel which had recently been bought by a group of local businessmen who started a nightclub. This was to be my swan song as a DJ, as I had more than enough on my plate, two shops in Sligo and one in Galway, and taking every game available as a referee, at least two at the weekends and schoolboy games during the week.

I was always a little conscious that having left school at 16 I'd missed out on the education front. I'd started buying the *Sunday Times* when I was 18 when only a handful were sold in Sligo. I used it keep up-to-date on key world events. I read that a new invention called the CD was about to be launched, and record companies were due to bring a small range of them to the market. I saw this as a potential game changer, and became the owner of the first CD player in Sligo. It cost £800, a whopping amount at the time, (equal to about €3,500 today). Similar players can now be picked up for under €100! The superior sound of CDs was a big boost to the record industry, and many collectors started replacing their vinyl collections with CDs.

Around this time I read another article in *The Sunday Times* that made me think seriously about the future. The article outlined how much money people would need in their later years. I found it sobering. I was only 35, and never thought much about the future. That was for old people. I had no pension and had made no provisions for the future. Yes, I had three shops on the go, but they were only breaking even or making modest profits. I was making a decent living, but saw there was no great fortune to be made from such small stores in the West of Ireland. I knew I must do something, and stored the article in the back of my mind.

I was renting videos through the record stores, but I was really not at the races. Three or four competitors were doing a much better job by opening for longer hours and stocking a much wider range. So I opened a proper video rental store in Castle Street, 11am-11pm, seven days a week. I had a considerably larger overhead, but it was the right move. Danny McCarthy was the manager, and Eileen and I put in a lot of hours too.

My father died in August, 1984. About 10 years earlier, he'd become a motoring instructor, a job he loved, and numerous pupils passed through his hands. He was also involved with the Rehabilitation Association, a local branch of a national charity. They organised a fundraising walk around Ireland, and my father drove the helpers on the trip. There was a knock on the door at 3am. There's never good news at that hour, and I knew something was wrong when a policeman and Mrs McGurrin, whom I recognised from the Rehabilitation Association, delivered the bad news. Sadly, he'd had a heart attack and died in Cork. He was just 70, and had problems with various illnesses over the previous 20 years. But I can never forget that he gave me a start in the entertainment business by buying me my first accordion back in 1956.

HMV v Virgin

1985 was a massive year in the record business. Bruce Springsteen released *Born in the USA* in 1984, and it was still selling massively a year later. He played Slane Castle in 1985, the largest crowd of his career so far. The phenomenally successful *Live Aid* telecast also produced a huge surge in record sales.

Late that year, I attended a meeting in Belfast with Maurice, Jim Aiken and Noel Harrison. Noel owned Harrison Records in Belfast, and sold all the tickets for Jim's shows in Northern Ireland and also provided the box office services for Jim's Slane Castle concerts. Golden Discs was the largest record chain in Ireland, but with relatively small outlets. Jim sold his tickets through Golden Discs for all his Dublin shows. At the meeting we agreed that we'd move forward with the aim of opening a large record store in Dublin on a scale not seen before. The fact that the country was in the middle of a deep recession did not deter us, and Maurice volunteered to look for a suitable property, while Noel and I would research the logistics of running such a store.

Within a few weeks, Maurice came up with not one location but two. Woolworths were exiting the market and putting all their stores in Ireland up for sale, and these stores were in attractive high street locations. The one on Henry Street was due to come on the market in 1986, and their Grafton Street store in early 1987. The properties were snapped up by pension funds who would refurbish them and offer them on a leasehold basis. We debated for a few weeks which one to go for. There were rumours that Richard Branson was looking at Ireland for a Virgin Megastore, but nothing concrete. But our dilemma was that if we leased one store, our competitor might plump for the other.

Maurice argued that if we were going to go seriously into this business, we should be brave and take the two stores. The four brave horsemen said why not, and we signed two very expensive leases for both stores without thinking of the consequences. Nobody had mentioned money or a business plan at this stage, but Jim said *"keep going until we're stopped"*. On reflection it was madness but it never stopped us before.

We met up in New York one weekend to look closely at the scene there. We visited the two Tower Records stores in Greenwich Village and Columbus Circle on a Friday night. I was knocked out by the level of activity in the stores at such a late hour, not just the number of people but the volume of purchases. Customers seemed to spend over $200, and the range of choice of inventory was equally impressive. There was nothing like this in Ireland, and we were all buoyed up when discussing our venture over dinner. Jim was in fine form, and said *"if nothing comes of this venture, at least we had a couple of good dinners and a weekend in New York"*.

Our upbeat mood didn't last long. Next morning Jim arrived for breakfast and said he'd talked to his wife Ann who told him that Richard Branson had been on the *Late Late Show* the previous night and announced he was opening a Virgin Megastore in Dublin on the site of the old McBirney's department store on Aston Quay. This was right in the middle of our two stores! This was a serious blow. Branson was a major name and the Virgin brand was internationally recognisable. Up to now, there had been no large record stores in Dublin, now three would open up within 12 months.

It was time for a serious rethink. We might be brave and foolish, but not that foolish. We needed help here, so I suggested contacting HMV. They were going head to head with Virgin in the UK and might fancy a similar joust in Ireland. Maurice contacted David Landsman, a lawyer in London who specialised in the entertainment industry. We were in luck. Landsman came back and said that HMV had looked at Ireland, although it was not a priority. But now that Virgin had announced they were coming here, HMV were interested in talking to us.

Brian McLoughlin, Managing Director of HMV, arrived in Dublin with two other executives. We took them to both locations, and explained that Dublin had two major downtown retail locations, Henry Street for Northsiders and Grafton Street for Southsiders. The HMV team were very impressed with the locations, and felt that the size of both stores, around 7,000 square feet on three floors, was just perfect. We then moved to the offices of Farrell-Grant-Sparks nearby to continue the negotiations.

Ten years earlier, Pearse Farrell had qualified as an accountant and set up his own company FGS from an office he shared with Maurice. His practice had grown substantially to become one of the leading accountancy firms in Ireland. We'd all used FGS at various times and were very comfortable having Pearse involved in these negotiations. That first meeting with HMV proved to be very productive. They admitted we had two excellent trading sites, and with their brand and our local knowledge we could make a very successful business. It was near the end of the year, and they promised to come back early in 1986 with a business plan and a proposal for a deal.

The HMV suits duly arrived back in January, 1986. They were still very enthusiastic about the project and especially about taking on Richard Branson. They proposed we enter into a joint venture, 50% equity to HMV and 50% to the Irish investors. Jim, Maurice, Noel and I stepped outside for a huddle, and agreed we'd go ahead in principle and the lawyers could work out the details. The HMV guys produced a business plan, and said the project would require £750,000 in capital plus bank financing. We put on our best poker faces and nodded confidently, as if money was no object, and we shook hands on the deal. But when they left the room we fell about laughing. *"Where the fuck will we get the money from?"*

In reality this was a good deal. HMV was one of the best brands in the world. They would do the heavy lifting, manage the business, and, if everything went to plan, we'd get a very good return on our investment. HMV had a considerable management resource, and it was obvious that had we proceeded with the project ourselves, we'd have drowned. Contracts were drawn up, with us having to find the money by April. So Pearse arranged a meeting at the Bank of Ireland head office in Baggot Street with a view to borrowing funds.

The meeting with the bank officials was a circus. We each had individual interviews at which the officials asked about our net worth and all the usual shite. When they started asking about personal guarantees, we headed for the hills. I asked Jim how he got on at his interview and he said *"I told them I was 52, two stone overweight, and that's all they needed to know"*......classic answer! Talking to the banks was a waste of time.

Jim was fine, but the rest of us had to scramble to find the funds. I sold Sweets and Things, re-mortgaged the house, plundered everything else, and somehow scrambled across the line. On the day of the signing the HMV guys were very formal and proper, and I don't know what they made of us ragbags writing cheques and throwing them in a pile on the table.

The next six months passed very quickly. The HMV team took over the project and they clearly knew what they were at. Jim said he'd move his ticket sales from Golden Discs to HMV which would help build footfall. Walking up Grafton Street one day I bumped into Jack Fitzgerald, still owner of Golden Discs. It was clear that the landscape was about to change and he was understandably upset. He proceeded to give me a lecture in a doorway, and told me I'd lose all my money. I just listened. Jack had been decent to me when I started out, so there was no point in being nasty or falling out with him now.

Ticketshop

There was a big build up to the Grand Opening of the Henry Street store in November, 1986, and MD Brian McLoughlin said it was the best opening day's receipts for any HMV store ever. Having a good opening was important, especially with Virgin about to enter the market. Our Grafton Street store was due to open in April, 1987.

As it happened, HMV had no interest in ticketing. They were happy to get the footfall, so the Irish investors set up a separate company to manage that side of the business. As Noel had the most experience we agreed he'd oversee this area and I'd assist him. So we formed Ticketshop. It was never meant to be a commercial entity, as our primary goal was to provide footfall to HMV which hopefully would enhance our main investment.

Eamonn O'Connor came on board as Ticketshop's General Manager. He'd previously worked for the Revenue Commissioners and Companies Office. A few months earlier, Jim's son Peter had reason to visit the Companies Office. While waiting for documentation he struck up a conversation with Eamonn, and this resulted in Eamonn working for Aiken Promotions at a gig in the National Stadium. Before long, Eamonn was in charge of hiring the part-time staff for Aiken Promotions in Dublin, a great gig for Eamonn's colleagues in the Revenue. By day they were doing boring paperwork, then at night, they were in the rock 'n roll business.

Ticketshop opened for business in December, 1986 with Eamonn as General Mananger and Mary Kelly as Operations Manager. Our total investment was a float of £40, and the first few payments on a couple of leased cash registers. HMV provided the counter, signage and a windowless office in the basement that we used for administration. It may well have been a record for a low-cost start-up business, but what began that day in that dingy basement became one of the best known and most successful companies in Ireland.

One of our first ticket on-sale was for Norwegian band AHA. When I went down to Henry Street the street was over-run with screaming kids. It was chaos. I spotted Noel inside, but no sign of Eamonn. The screams became even more deafening. As soon as the doors opened, the kids rushed in, knocked over the counter and I found Eamonn on the floor underneath. Eventually order was restored, and we sold out the concert. The low-low cost Ticketshop was up and running.

The race was also on between us and Virgin to see who would open the next store. We beat them to it by a couple of weeks, when HMV Grafton Street opened as planned in April, 1987 with a ticket desk inside the front door. Although the space was tiny, the desk was right on Grafton Street with tremendous footfall. Soon, Virgin opened a massive 20,000 sq. ft. store on Aston Quay. We had a combined 15,000 sq. ft., more than the combined space of all the other record retailers in Dublin. But it was clear that there was one large store too many, and there was going to be a bloody battle between us and Virgin over the coming years.

Great days in Slane

David Bowie was the headline act at Slane Castle in 1987, Queen having appeared there the previous year. Ticket sales leading up to the 1986 concert were sluggish, but there was a substantial walk-up. Remember there was still virtually no nationwide ticket distribution system. Those outlets that had tickets had to return them a few days earlier, so nobody could buy tickets for the last 2-3 days apart from a handful of outlets. Nobody was prepared for the massive walk-up on the day. It was chaotic. The promoter's ticket inventory ran out, so we started hand-writing tickets on the Castle's stationery. When the stationary ran out, we turned to hand-writing on the dining room menu cards and anything we could lay our hands on. We'd no time to count the cash which was stuffed in black bin liners, stored in a secure location and banked the following Monday.

Unfortunately, tragedies blighted the early days at Slane, including a number who drowned trying to swim across the River Boyne. I've never understood why people put their lives at risk to save the admission price of £20. So before the 1987 concert a new safety plan was put in place, and extra security drafted in. The police provided two amphibious crafts to patrol the river and prevent people from crossing.

In addition to being set in a most picturesque location, the concert area in Slane is one of the best in the world, a natural amphitheatre with a capacity of 80,000 and the stage set against the backdrop of the river. Further backstage are the dressing rooms, production area, hospitality space for the artists, and a helipad for VIP guests.

There's a wooded area at the back of the Castle, and that's where we had the aggravation. In previous years, the gurriers swam across the river and headed for the cover of the woods which would put them inside the arena. But in 1987 we were waiting for them, having set up a sort of box office right in the middle of the wood. The 'box office' was the trunk of a car, a box of tickets and a cash float. I volunteered to look after it, and if the gurriers managed to escape detection swimming across the river, we'd extract entrance admission from them in the woods.

Eamonn provided 12 security guys on a day out from the Revenue, plus two Alsatian dogs. The rabble took us on early, and there were hundreds on the hill on the far side of the river. They waited for the police patrol to go upstream, and some then dashed across. We'd a few easy pickings at the start, rounding up the dripping victims, and extracted £20 for a ticket. One of the Revenue guys, Brendan Lynch, had even turned up dressed in camouflage fatigues. He handled one of the alsatians, and really looked the part. When the rocks starting flying someone shouted *"duck"*, but Brendan got nailed on the head. Boy was he mad, as we bandaged him up and put him back in action.

The rabble kept coming. It was like a scene from a Vietnam movie, with helicopters whirring over the trees, dogs barking, rocks flying and our guys pulling the gurriers out of the water. Brendan could be seen in the thick of the action with a bloodied bandage around his head. Some of the gurriers were scared shitless by the dogs. Brendan had dripping wet, white-faced gurriers up against a tree with the dog on a lead barking menacingly, while one of Brendan's mates took their money. I think I "sold" over 250 tickets in the woods that day, and had a box of wet money in the trunk. It wasn't about the sales as such, but a point was made. We never had any further aggravation at Slane after that.

Enniskillen Bombing

I had a refereeing appointment in Monaghan on November 8 the same year. Driving through Enniskillen on my way to the game, it became obvious something was seriously wrong. There was a lot of police activity, diverting traffic away from the centre of the town. I could see a huge pall of smoke up ahead, with scores of people running away from what I assumed was a big fire, and ambulances and fire tenders dashing towards it. It wasn't until I turned on the 1 o'clock radio news that I learned that a bomb had been set off at a Remembrance Day ceremony and eleven innocent people had been killed. I was never in any danger myself, although my route passed within a few hundred yards of the bombing. It was a very sobering sight.

Xtra-vision was the largest video rental company in Ireland, and they'd recently gone public. They were on an acquisition binge, and approached me about purchasing the store in Castle Street which was barely breaking even, and the hours were decidedly anti-social. Xtra-vision had no interest in due diligence, they simply wanted a presence in the town and needed to move fast. So I sold up in 1989, immediately investing the money in a new record store in Eyre Square, Galway. At the end of 1989, we moved to a much larger store in Shop Street.

1990 -1999 "Tickets at HMV"

The battle with Virgin was indeed like a war of attrition. The country was still in recession, with massive unemployment. We were behind in our projections, although HMV assured us it would come good if we stuck it out. They were right. We had one crucial weapon in the battle with Virgin ... tickets sales.

The radio industry had changed radically in the mid-eighties with de-regulation, and numerous commercial stations opened up in Dublin and around the country. This was an attractive way for promoters to advertise shows. Soon it was virtually impossible to tune into a radio station anywhere in the country without hearing a commercial for *"Tickets at HMV"*. It was relentless wall-to-wall promotion for shows, but HMV rode on the slipstream of this promotion. The same applied to TV. I've no doubt the ticketing made the difference, and our rivals Virgin never could achieve the same profile. But it didn't last for either of us. Later, HMV encountered some serious difficulties and went into liquidation around 2009. Virgin also disappeared from the high streets.

In early 1990, at a Ticketshop director's meeting, Noel said he could no longer devote sufficient time to ticketing. He'd expanded his record business in Northern Ireland and was about to open a big new store in the Isle of Man. So it was agreed that I'd become Managing Director of Ticketshop. We'd started out this business not as a commercial venture, but to assist and enhance our HMV investment, but the business was now turning over a lot of money. Despite this, Ticketshop was losing money, the problem being the gross profit margin. We were operating on wafer thin margins and it could not continue in the same vein. In effect, we were 'busy fools', just turning over money for no serious gain.

A new player had entered the market who would impact hugely on the landscape of the entertainment business in Ireland. Harry Crosbie, among other things, was a property developer with considerable property interests along Dublin's North quays. At the end of the East Wall quay, there stood an old stone building that had been used for repairing train engines. It had been lying idle for a long time when Harry decided to convert it into a multi-purpose arena.

This was The Point, and it would become one of the busiest venues in the world. Up to then, concerts in Dublin were usually held in the National Stadium, capacity 2,200, and the RDS, capacity 5,000. The Point could hold 6,000 seated and up to 8,500 seated/standing. It was like a line from the movie Field of Dreams- *"If you build it, they will come"*. Well Harry built it and they came in droves. He then entered into a joint venture with Apollo Leisure, a major UK entertainment company who owned and managed over 30 venues. Apollo Leisure became the managing partners for The Point.

Disney On Ice

It was time for a serious assessment about what we had to do next. There was no doubt that a proper ticketing market existed, but we needed to figure out how to bring it to the next stage. We faced a number of challenges. Aiken Promotions was our largest client by far, and Jim was a shareholder in Ticketshop. We also received an allocation of tickets from MCD, but they still sold most of their tickets through Golden Discs. MCD boss Denis Desmond was understandably wary of supplying us with more tickets since his main competitor was Jim. We had some other clients, but they were smaller.

The exception was the Feld Corporation who promoted *Disney On Ice*. We'd provided a service for Disney for years. In addition to selling tickets, Eamonn had a crew to lay down the ice for the show. This was a laborious task, with a number of guys pouring water on a refrigerated floor, and building up the ice inch by inch over a few days. Although *Disney* sold a lot of tickets, the selling process was excruciating. They had about 25 performances over 10 days, with 3 different price points as well as concessions for children and OAPs. It was a nightmare to control, and the settlement took days. We were supplied with books of tickets with two perforated stubs, one for a full-price ticket and one for concessions. We had to keep all the stubs for the settlement, so our staff had to count 75 bundles of stubs and compare them with the cash collected, an almost impossible task.

In the late 1980s, *Disney* decided to mount shows in both Belfast and Dublin. Belfast was a major risk with the city was gripped by major sectarian conflict. Because the city was/is divided along tribal lines, Nationalist/Catholic or Unionist/Protestant, shows usually took place in the King's Hall, a major exhibition venue in neutral territory. However, that venue not being available, *Disney* decided to erect a large tent for the week's performance in a park in east Belfast, the predominately Unionist/Protestant area. Local turf in Belfast was controlled by paramilitaries, the IRA in Nationalist areas and UDA in Unionist territory. Both organisations operated a "security service" for local businesses, in other words, an extortion racket. Pay up, or have your business burned down.

There was much goodwill when *Disney* announced they were coming to east Belfast. Nothing serious happened in the area, and it was an opportunity, especially for the kids, to enjoy some light entertainment. It was also understood that the UDA would not enforce the usual "security service" for the period. Unfortunately, a bunch of hoods could not resist the opportunity to make easy money and decided on a solo run. They figured that a pile of money would be collected, so the venue needed their "security". The day before the opening performance some guys approached the tent and asked to speak to the management. "*We are doing security*", they declared, and named their price. Well, they'd come to the wrong place and the wrong man.

Art Ricker was a legendary *Disney* operator, tough as nails and who'd been in the worst hellholes you could imagine. There was virtually no threatening situation that Art hadn't encountered before. *Disney* having already performed in over 70 countries, from Chile to Egypt. So Art politely said, "*We're fine, sir, we have our own security*". The extortionists were not expecting this attitude. "*You don't understand.... we will be doing security for the week and you will pay us*". Art stood firm, and asked the hoods to leave. "*We'll be back tomorrow*", they said, and showed Art they were packing guns.

So Art went to the police and outlined the scenario. Although there was widespread extortion in Belfast then, nobody would testify for fear of losing their lives. The police explained to Art that they could never get evidence for a conviction. Art said he'd testify, much to the delight of the police. They knew who the criminals were, but so far couldn't nail them. Now it was game on.

The following day the police arrived early and set up a trap. They hid up trees and placed directional microphones in strategic areas to pick up the criminals' conversations as they neared the tent, chatting away about how much they'd earn from the shake down. They were caught red-handed trying to extort money from *Disney*, and a few months later were brought to trial. Most of them had previous convictions, so were shown no mercy and sentenced to multiple years in prison.....ouch!

But there was a sequel to the story. The criminals were brought to a prison which was segregated so as to keep the IRA and UDA apart. The exercise yard was separated by a wire fence, and when the convicted hoods came out for exercise they were spotted by some of the IRA guys who dropped down on their knees and started to sing *"Hi ho, hi ho....it's off to jail we go"*....very funny, if not so for the guys serving 12 years.

Meanwhile, Eamonn and I continued trying to figure out a strategy for moving forward. Bringing this business to the next level was going to be a long and torturous process, and the first big battle was negotiating a new commission deal with our clients. After exhausting negotiations that lasted weeks, we agreed new terms with Jim that considerably increased our gross profit margin. We also negotiated an annual increase for subsequent years. Eamonn developed a working relationship with Denis who slowly began to trust Ticketshop, and we gradually received bigger allocations for his MCD events. At least 90% of our sales were over the counter, as promoters still used printed tickets.

We had a call centre for telephone bookings. Well, I'm exaggerating. The 'call centre' was whoever answered the phone and wrote the details on a piece of paper. We charged a fee for posting out tickets, but we had a major problem in that there was behind-the-times guy running Visa Ireland who wouldn't deal with us because we were charging an additional service fee on top of the ticket price. We banked with Bank of Ireland, who had the MasterCard franchise, so we'd no problems with their card. Visa had the biggest market share by a long way, yet our phone business was limited to MasterCard customers.

A short time later, the banking conditions changed so that all banks could offer Visa or MasterCard services. As soon as this happened, Visa capitulated and the old guy was shipped out. It was a sweet day when we could process both cards. We even bought a couple of answering machines at £29.99 each, a big splash out!! When the 'call centre' staff went home, we linked the machines to the telephone lines. Customers could leave details overnight, and we'd process the tickets the following day. But some of the recordings on these machines were hilarious. People would have conversations with the machine, thinking somebody was on the other side. *"We bought two tickets last night, but Mary's sister now wants to go to the concert, so can you send out two more"*....no credit card details, no address.....nothing!

I know it sounds very primitive now, but nothing else was available. What we did have was unlimited drive and energy. Eamonn was the heartbeat of the company, and we'd a really good working relationship. He was front of house and liaised with the promoters, I did all the office stuff and worked on strategy, with Mary Kelly still in charge of operations. We even moved our office from the basement in Henry Street to the top floor of the HMV store in Grafton Street. What a relief to work in daylight again!

Those early start-up days were really exciting, and anybody involved with a start-up will know what I mean. Time didn't matter, and 12-16 hour days were the norm. Most of the time you're flying blind, but you have total belief that you'll make it happen. We never had a business plan, budget, or main goal, but somewhere deep down we were convinced the business would succeed. I had my weekly routine. I worked at Star Records in Sligo or Galway on Monday, and the rest of the week in Dublin. I worked Saturday's back in Sligo. Eamonn used to say, *"This is far better than stamping documents in a Government Office"*. We were delighted that The Point had opened as it allowed promoters to bring additional concerts to Ireland. The capacity was also a factor, as it now made financial sense for top touring artists to visit Ireland. What we hadn't bargained for was Apollo getting into the ticketing business. They wanted to adopt the UK model, where the venue box office controlled the ticketing and allocated some tickets to agents. The promoters were happy with our service, but had no choice but to leave some of the tickets with The Point box office which employed a large staff. But we still had a significant advantage. *"Tickets at HMV"* continued to thunder out across the airwaves, so customers continued buying tickets from Ticketshop. We were also receiving enquiries from outlets all over the country looking for tickets to sell. We supplied these outlets from our allocation, and split the commission with them. It was very risky, because if outlets didn't pay up, we took the hit. The other major problem was managing and controlling these tickets, and Eamonn must have driven over 1,200 miles a week with tickets in the trunk of his car. It was a continuous cycle, distributing the tickets and then circling back to collect the money.

We had to abandon our £29.99 "call centre", as business was growing too fast. Golden Pages, a semi-State company, had a serious call centre in Waterloo Road. So they started selling tickets for us, but it was always a battle with them. They only operated Mon-Friday from 9-5pm. Our busiest on-sale day was Saturday, and we'd major confrontations trying to get them to staff up on Saturdays. Every time Eamonn and I arrived in the building we could see the "oh Jesus" looks ...... *"I have to work on my day off?"!*

Neville was the MD, a nice man who was not at home with the rock 'roll business as we upset his neat 9-5, Monday to Friday operation. But the problem for Golden Pages was that they'd signed a contract with us. I remember one particular busy on-sale, a Neil Diamond concert at Croke Park promoted by Jim. Telephone traffic was so heavy the exchange in Dublin 4 crashed. There was uproar....hospitals, banks, and businesses for miles around had no service for most of the day. Of course promoters love this kind of stuff. Within hours Jim had a newspaper headline *NEIL DIAMOND CRASHES TELEPHONE EXCHANGE*. Of course, Eamonn and I had to face the music, and Telecom Eireann threatened to withdraw our number altogether. Eamonn told the suits that they'd be better employed beefing up their Exchange!! We compromised by promising to inform TE of any future heavy traffic events so that they could divert calls through different exchanges.

The first major West End show to come to the Point was *CATS*. I think it was scheduled to perform for 8 weeks, and over 200,000 tickets had to be sold. This was an enormous undertaking, and a logistical nightmare, with 8 shows a week for 8 weeks, 3 different prices for mid-weeks, weekends and matinees. Paul Latham was the General Manager of The Point, and a few weeks before *CATS* was due to go on sale, he installed a computer system in The Point. He also arranged for a computer terminal at our Henry Street and Grafton Street stores so we could sell the shows from The Point system.

Computer systems had become common to all UK box offices, but were comparatively new for us. We were actually dreading having to manage the different ticket prices and stubs. We'd some experience of this with *Disney On Ice* and that was a nightmare, and *CATS* would be on a much larger scale. The computer terminals were duly installed, and staff trained to sell the tickets. But there was one problem, the system wouldn't function properly. The system, called RITA, was designed for the Royal Shakespeare Company box office and British Telecom provided the telecommunications support. The system worked reasonably well at the Point box office, but hadn't been designed for remote access or very heavy traffic. It was fine for day-to-day sales, but once the system came under pressure, it would simply lie down. It was very frustrating, compounded by the fact that all the support was in the UK.

One Saturday morning the system crashed yet again, and Eamonn had no luck getting hold of a BT engineer. Determined to resolve the problem, he tracked down at his home a senior executive in BT with responsibility for RITA, and chewed his arse off. The guy had been mowing his lawn, and was indignant that we'd the nerve to call him at home. It was becomingly increasingly obvious this system wouldn't work, but The Point insisted on staying with it.

I happened to be in Dublin on the following Saturday when the system crashed again, with a huge line stretching around the corner into Chatham Street. Some had been in the line for hours.

Eamonn and I went down the line apologising for the hold-up, noting that some customers had travelled long distances. So we were savaged in a variety of accents from around the country. That experience would have a bearing on our later strategy.

"Mista La Conna"

Calling to the Grafton Street office one day I spotted a limousine parked outside flying the Chinese flag....W.T.F? Inside, I heard Eamonn deep in discussion with a couple of Chinese guys in suits. On the table was a suitcase full of cash. Shortly afterwards they left with the suitcase. It turned out that they were part of a cultural group on a five-year World tour. They'd arrive in a city, hire a venue, and put on a Chinese cultural show. They'd a neat scheme for funding this activity, as it had been arranged that in every city the local Chinese Embassy provided a suitcase full of cash with which to promote the event. Sound good so far?

Somebody had advised them to contact Mr. O'Connor in Dublin, so every morning the limo would arrive at 10 am sharp with the Chinese man looking for 'Mista La Conna'. They wanted to put on a show in the National Stadium, eight times a day, seven days a week, for a whole month. That worked out at over 220 performances, 500,000 tickets. To us this was madness, but they wouldn't take no for an answer, so Eamonn told them who to contact and who to hire.

It turned out that hardly anybody was interested in Chinese Culture. For some performances fewer than 10 people showed up, but these guys didn't care, and the show went on. I think they gave up after two weeks having sold no more than 3,000 tickets. But before they left town they invited Eamonn and his wife Breda to a reception in the Chinese Embassy. The reception was especially for Eamonn and Breda only. They were the sole guests! They had to sit in a large room with only two chairs and endure a two-hour performance of Chinese Culture. For all I know, these guys are still circling the world collecting suitcases full of cash from their local embassies.

Nationwide computer system

We soldiered on for another year or so, but there came a point when we had to do something. We were still losing money, although the losses were narrowing. I thought we should go for broke and computerise the business with a proper nationwide system. Tickets at the time were primarily sold in Dublin, and a few other urban locations. I remembered that with *Cats* people travelled from all over to buy tickets in Dublin. I was convinced that if we could bring the tickets to the customers, we'd grow the market. I also had first-hand experience of having to send back tickets two or three days before an event when there might still be people willing to buy them. But they wouldn't risk travelling 150-200 miles with no guarantee of admission. As I saw it, promoters and event organisers were losing out because of a flawed distribution system. Somebody would eventually set up a proper system in Ireland, so it might as well be Ticketshop.

I outlined our plan to my partners over dinner, although I'd no facts, figures or research data. I said that after four years trading and turning over millions of pounds, we were still carrying a loss. We should either get out of the business or go for it. I argued that Ticketron and Ticketmaster in the United States had a model we should copy. If it worked there, it'd work here. Maurice and Noel were happy to go along with it, but Jim had reservations, although he accepted that we had to do something. The old Ticketshop had been set up as a non-profit operation, but if we were to move forward with a full commercial operation, he felt he might be compromised in his role as promoter. He'd prefer to be independent as a promoter, and would resign from Ticketshop. But giving his blessing to the project, he promised he'd commit his tickets to Ticketshop. But he had a sting in the tail. With a wry smile he said, *"Now that I'm a client, I can give you a hard time"*.

It would take over 18 months to get the new system up and running.

Blockbuster

I was at home one evening in 1990 when Maurice called from New York. He'd seen a fabulous video store on 3rd Avenue that I should check out, so I flew to New York the next morning. The store was called Blockbuster, and it was massive. There were only small video stores in Ireland, so Blockbuster was in a different class. Instead of six copies of each top 10 movie, Blockbuster had 50 and across a much broader range. It was very impressive. We'd recently changed the model in Ireland by introducing large record stores, so why not do the same in the video rental business? If it worked for one, it'll work for the other.

Blockbuster was the brainchild of Wayne Huizenga. He'd started out with a single truck in 1968 and built his Waste Management Company into the largest in the US before selling it in the 1980s for over $2billion. He then took the same team that made Waste Management so successful and rolled out Blockbuster across the US.

Our Dublin accountant Pearse Farrell arranged a meeting for us with one of Blockbuster's executives, the Iraqi Saeed Hammam in London where Blockbuster had recently opened their first store on Walworth Road. Pearse, Maurice and I met Saeed at the Carlton Towers Hotel in Sloane Street. After becoming a franchisee of Blockbuster, in two years Saeed had rolled out over 100 stores in the greater Chicago area, and then sold them back to the parent company. It was a staggering achievement. He was now part of the Blockbuster Executive Management with the task of growing the company rapidly, and we discussed the possibility of getting the Blockbuster franchise for Ireland. We'd a good calling card in having brought HMV to Ireland. Saeed was enthusiastic, and we agreed to move forward.

Within a few weeks we received the paperwork from Blockbuster granting us the master franchise for the Island of Ireland, North and South. Jim, Maurice, Noel, Pearse and I threw in some seed money to get the ball rolling, but, as usual, we kicked the serious financial issues down the road. I started on the research, and Pearse and I attended a Blockbuster Conference in Orlando, Florida. The scale of the operation was enormous. Blockbuster had grown from zero to 3,000 stores in a few years and was the hottest company in the US. The numbers were staggering, and for the first time I realised the sheer size of the US retail market. Some of the stores were company-owned, but the majority were franchisees, some of whom had done well with Wayne at his Waste Management business. Most of the others had McDonalds or Kentucky Fried Chicken franchises. One guy had a Blockbuster store in the tiny island of Guam in the Pacific.

There was a lot of testosterone in the room, and I loved the buzz. Wayne made it clear he wanted to roll out the stores at a fast rate in Ireland. Pearse and I bullshitted our way through the meeting, and gave assurances that we'd deliver. But it was really another case of *"where the fuck will we get the money?"!* I did however leave Orlando with the Blockbuster playbook, a fabulous document based on the legendary McDonalds playbook. It outlined in great detail how to choose a location, the layout of the store, staffing, everything down to where to buy the doormat. It was a dummy's guide to opening a store.

Back in Dublin the serious work began. I was already in the early stages of planning to computerise the Ticketshop business which was enough work on its own. There was a follow up meeting with the guys who provided the seed money for the Blockbuster plan, and I offered to help with the development plan but said we should hire a Chief Executive to run it.

We came up with an inventive plan. Although engaged in a brutal retail battle with Virgin Records, HMV was trading very well. But Virgin matched us pound for pound like real heavyweights. One of the reasons Virgin was so successful was their excellent Chief Executive, Dermot Hanrahan, and we approached him to see if he'd be interested in becoming CEO of Blockbuster Ireland. We had a double motive in this. (1) Hire one of the best retailer experts in the country. (2)

Weaken the opposition to the advantage of HMV. It was akin to taking out the best playmaker or quarterback in the game. After a few months' negotiations, Dermot came on board. We were delighted with this coup. I'd already started working on the plan. I'd source locations, Dermot would negotiate with the real estate agents, hire staff, prepare for the launch etc. It was envisaged that I'd hand over to Dermot as the project progressed.

The playbook was a brilliant source of advice and information. Choosing a location was great fun as well as a science. In retail "Location, Location, Location" is paramount, but Blockbuster had additional dimensions. First off, I had to adapt the US model to the Irish retail landscape. Everything in the US is fairly orderly. The cities are laid out in a grid, usually avenues north/south, streets east/west. The ideal US store would be on an intersection with 20 or so car parking spaces. In the US nearly everybody drives everywhere, except maybe in Manhattan. The European system is entirely different. Most businesses are on High Streets, with parking some distance away. The model I had to follow said that a Blockbuster Superstore would work in a population of 25,000 - 50,000 people, so I divided up the Greater Dublin area into 20 neighbourhoods of 50,000 people. We'd start with 12 stores and then move to the outskirts.

I hired the research company Behaviour and Attitudes to research a few sample neighbourhoods, and the results were fascinating, giving me such information as the various age groups in the area, their income, spend per head, how much they spent on leisure and food, how many times they went to the cinema and so on. I'd never done this stuff before and found it riveting. I sent the data to Blockbuster who matched it with their data, and came back with the turnover we could expect from each location. They also asked me to re-check some of the numbers. The neighbourhood of Tallaght had a median age of 21, while the figure for Walworth Road in the UK was 34. But then Ireland had one of the youngest populations in Europe.

Dermot and I were working very well together. I'd spend a half day in Ticketshop and the other half working on Blockbuster. It was manic. Dermot produced a fabulous business plan, and we were ready to roll. As we needed to raise a lot of money we did various roadshows to potential investors. It was tough, as money was very tight in 1991. Some people were very interested, but we were running into a problem as there was no way the original seed guys could fund the entire capital sum required.

In June we attended a meeting with Wayne Huizenga in London where he was enjoying a few weeks doing "The Season", horse racing at Ascot, Wimbledon for the tennis, British Open Golf etc. He invited some clients for an evening cruise on the Thames, but although it was a social occasion, Wayne found time for business, and expressed his concern over the delay in rolling out the Irish operation. We kicked to touch on the night. He had recently secured the franchise for the Florida Marlins team in Major League Baseball which was expanding by two teams. The start-up cost was $100m, and another $100m was required annually to run the team. I struggled to get my head around these numbers. I had great respect for Wayne who'd started with one truck, worked 20-hour days and became one of those great US entrepreneurs who emerge from time to time.

It was getting close to crunch time. We suggested we should open one store to test the market, but they were very unhappy with this. One store was no good. It was all or nothing. In the end we decided to fold the cards, as we simply couldn't raise the money. It was disappointing, but I found the experience invaluable. I learned how a major US Corporation worked, how an operation scaled, and what made the whole business tick. It is funny how these things work out. Although one door closed, another opportunity would come from an unexpected source.

Wayne later sold Blockbuster at the top of the market. He also owned the Miami Dolphins football team, and the Florida Panthers ice hockey team, and the last I heard of him he'd started Auto Nation, another huge network of second-hand car dealerships. Wayne was a winner.

FM104

The radio business in Ireland had been completely State-controlled for decades. There was only one English language and one Irish language station for the Republic of Ireland up to 1978. The situation then loosened up a bit with the launch of what is now 2FM, primarily a Top 40 music station. Up to then, we had to listen to pirate stations and the occasional leakage from the UK and Northern Ireland, or Radio Luxemburg.

This absurd situation had spun out of control in the early 1980s with pirate stations popping up everywhere. The inevitable happened, and the Government deregulated the market, issuing licenses for stations all over the country. Pearse, Maurice and Jim were part of a consortium that obtained one of the licenses for Dublin. It was called Capitol Radio, later re-named Rock104. But by 1991, the station had very poor ratings and was also bleeding money. Dermot Hanrahan was available since we'd folded the Blockbuster project, so Maurice and Pearse asked him to see if he thought Rock104 could be salvaged.

Dermot came back within a few months with a radical business plan, proposing that the station be rebranded and the music format changed. A major injection of funds was also required. Some of the original investors had no stomach to stay in, and indicated that they'd pull out. Dermot's plan was very convincing. He argued that the previous format was too heavily geared towards males, and although it was attracting listeners, advertising was way below what was required to break even.

Dermot retained a radio consultant from Los Angeles to format the playlist, and the re-launch would be backed by a huge advertising campaign. Maurice asked me to go in with him on the new investment. Although I knew nothing much about the workings of radio stations, I was very comfortable with my colleagues. In addition, Dermot was a first class operator with a proven track record. So I scraped up the money and dived in. It was a 'Hail Mary' investment, not unlike a casino. The re-branded station FM104 cranked out in May, 1992. It would turn out to be a very interesting investment.

Sweet Shops

While all this was going on, in 1990/91 I became involved in another madcap scheme. Noel Harrison called me one day saying he'd spotted a fabulous retail store in Cork called Sweets, so I went down to have a look. It was based on an old fashioned sweet shop with a most unusual design. With Noel's other friend from Belfast, Willie McArthur, I went to see the owner John Prendergast. We discussed a deal whereby we'd invest and roll out a chain of such stores. John was well up for it. He'd be Managing Director, the other three piled in and I quickly found a suitable shop in O'Connell Street, Sligo. It was a huge success from the start, selling six tons of sweets in 10 days. I reckoned we were onto a winner.

The stores didn't cost much to set up, and there was a wide gross profit margin. Within a few months we had six, all funded on cash flow, in Cork, Sligo, Belfast, Galway, Omagh plus one John owned in Dublin. There was no stopping us as we discussed opening 100 stores. Sadly, it didn't last long. The pattern was the same in all the stores, impressive openings and then a settling down to a moderate turnover. Basically it was a fad with no long-term future, and we folded the business promptly. I lost money on the venture, not much, but it hurt all the same. We should've put one store on trial for a few months before rolling out the others. It was a mad few months, if great fun. *(Lesson: Research, research and research again before you roll out any product)*

Eileen took over the Sligo store, and got the franchise for Leonidas Belgian chocolate. I reckon I was her best customer! The store did fine for a year, but hardly broke even. The potential market was too narrow. *(Lesson: You need population for a niche business)*

Ticketshop: the next phase

We were employing only 6/7 people in the company in early 1992, and our foray into computerisation was really amateur hour. I knew nothing about technology, Eamonn even less. But we both believed we had to find a way to distribute tickets to a wider market, to areas that didn't have access before. Eamonn had been to the US a few years earlier and somehow got hold of the Ticketron Operations Manual. We read it many times, but it might as well have been written in Swahili.

During those early days we also tried to do business with the GAA, but without success. The organisation hadn't changed the way it sold tickets since forming in 1884. We invited their Chief Financial Officer to lunch every year, hoping to get some allocation of tickets, but it was always "thanks but no thanks".

GAA tickets were printed by Alluset, a Dublin company who specialised in secure ticket printing. One of their representatives, Vincent Byrne, was in our office purchasing tickets for some of his clients when I struck up a conversation with him about our intention to computerise the business. He said he attended the Europe Talks Tickets conference every year, and that I should register for the next conference in Edinburgh in May, 1992. He advised me to talk to Hill Arts & Entertainment, a US company with an office in London (It's now *tickets.com*). I took a call from Stacia Smailes, and we arranged to discuss our project in Dublin. I gave her an outline of what we wanted, and she demonstrated some very impressive software which she could supply, but we'd have to find a local hardware supplier. She submitted a proposal within a few weeks.

Digital Equipment Corporation (DEC) was the largest player in the hardware game in Ireland in 1992, and provided most of the computer services for the Government. I met them and they were happy to work with Hill Arts in providing a joint service for Ticketshop. We'd purchase the hardware from DEC, and license the software from Hill Arts.

Our plan was to connect about 20 outlets around the country to our central system. Dermot O'Sullivan, was the chief sales person for DEC who'd come back with the costs that included project managing everything, which suited us fine. Eamonn and I went on the road for discussions with the outlets. This was not an easy task, as some of them had affiliations with promoters going back years. But most of them were enthusiastic, as they'd suffered the same frustrations I had in having to send back unsold tickets early, or not having tickets at all. But some adapted a 'wait and see' policy which was a nuisance for us. It was essential for Ticketshop to have a geographic spread in order to launch a real nationwide service, and eventually we got commitments from 20 outlets.

Then DEC came back looking for £900,000 upfront for the equipment, plus an annual management fee. Their guys continued with the presentation, but I'd tuned out after I heard the words *'nine hundred thousand'*. There was another problem. Telecom Eireann was the only serious telecommunications company at the time, and their estimate for providing leased lines for the outlets was outrageous. There was no way we could make this work, and it was all starting to unravel. We'd hired two finance people, Frank Rourke and Stephen Kavanagh, and had a basic business plan for the first time since we started Ticketshop, but the plan would now have to be completed revamped.

We did the usual rounds of the banks but nobody was interested, and a particularly nasty piece of work in Ulster Bank openly ridiculed the proposal. He couldn't see any need for such a ticketing service in a small country. It was looking very bleak. I told Dermot O'Sullivan in DEC we were having difficulty raising finance, and would have to shelve the project until financial conditions improved. I was very concerned that if The Point got their act together, they'd gain a foothold in the market. I'd no doubt that whoever grabbed this opportunity first would dominate the market, so we were very vulnerable.

About 10 days later Dermot called me for a lunch appointment, and, much to my surprise, said that DEC was prepared to finance everything and provide a turnkey service. He said DEC liked what we were attempting to put in place, and if the model worked, they could offer a similar service to other clients. He proposed a five-year deal, with quarterly payments in arrears. They had all the necessary resources, so this was a terrific opportunity. We were back in the game.

Then we had another stroke of luck. A few days after the meeting with Dermot, I spotted a promotional piece in the *Sunday Tribune* featuring husband and wife team Susan and Nick Wheeler. They'd returned from the UK and started a call centre called Telepages, offering a 24-hour sales support service for clients. Eamonn and I were at the Telepages office first thing the next morning. The difference between Telepages and Golden Pages was remarkable. Golden Pages was a unionised house riddled with unhelpful practices, whereas Susan and Nick were hungry for our business, and had a proposal on my desk within 24 hours. It was a perfect opportunity for both companies, so we immediately transferred our business to Telepages. Eamonn took great pleasure in cancelling the Golden Pages contract because of all the grief they'd given him. But we agreed to hold off announcing the new 24-hour service until we could launch the nationwide computerised service. I was thrilled that we were making progress, and could see exciting possibilities ahead.

As can often be the case, it was two steps forward and one back. Dermot told me DEC had reservations about Hill Arts and Entertainment whose software was fine but with so few staff in the UK they couldn't service our business and we should look at another software supplier. I should have checked this. I really knew nothing about software or systems, so I did some more research. There were only two companies that provided the software and technical support that met our ambitions, Ticketmaster and BOCS (Box Office Computer System). Ticketmaster were a US company with a poor reputation, but a good presence in the UK. I felt there was no point in approaching them as our two main suppliers, Aiken Promotions and MCD, would have serious difficulty with this arrangement.

Furthermore, if I approached Ticketmaster they'd figure out how vulnerable we were, and deal directly with our clients. We were sitting ducks, with zero leverage. So it had to be BOCS who had an extensive list of clients in the UK and elsewhere. I met them at Europe Talks Tickets conference in Edinburgh and we shook hands on a deal, subject to DEC giving the ok. DEC did due diligence on BOCS and admitted they were in a different class. The launch of Ticketshop's new computerised nationwide service, including a 24-hour telephone booking service, was set for September, 1992.

Meanwhile, we had a business to run. We had a sizeable reputation, and the distribution part of the business continued to grow, as more and more outlets throughout the country hooked up with Ticketshop. HMV was flying too. We'd won the battle with Virgin who never recovered from us poaching Dermot Hanrahan.

Most people assumed that HMV ran the tickets, but in reality Ticketshop and HMV were joined at the hip with one difference. HMV was profitable, but Ticketshop was running on empty. We were making very little money from distribution, and collecting money was a nightmare. We gave the promoters sales figures weekly, including outlet sales. We had to pay for all tickets sales, then hit the road in a desperate effort to collect the money before the cheques were banked. Fortunately it took two days to clear a cheque in 1992.

We never announced we were calling to outlets in case the owners went missing. I vividly remember one particularly hairy trip with Eamonn in his old clapped-out BMW. We set out at dawn and hit Athlone, then Galway, Limerick, and Cork. We had two more calls to make before the stores shut at 6pm. So it was after 5.30 when we left Portlaoise for Carlow. The recommended time for this trip was 45 minutes on a hazardous road over a mountain. We were bombing along when I saw the speedometer was tipping 105mph. I said, *"Eamonn, we'll get killed!"* He replied, *"We'll be dead anyway if we don't get our money from Rainbow Records"*. We arrived just as the owner Paddy Carroll was pulling down the shutters. He paid up. But every week was the same knife-edge, writing cheques to promoters, then scrambling to get the cash in time.

Big Gus

Occasionally we had to call in reinforcements to help collect the money. Our favourite guy was Fergus Leinster. Big Gus was a huge man, 6ft 7ins, 300lbs, the head docker in Dublin docks who also did security at concerts. Word travelled through the network about the giant collecting money for Ticketshop. A few inches were added to his height. *"He must be over 7ft and weigh 400lbs"!* Despite his size he was extremely gentle, soft-spoken, and always immaculately dressed. Gus would head out in one direction, Eamonn the other. It was wonderful. Gus always collected. He never had to get nasty, his massive size was enough. When you see a guy having to stoop coming through a door, it's probably best not to argue.

Only once did he have to use his 'influence'. A shop owed us £5,000, the owner was missing and the assistant was annoying Gus with lame excuses. Enough was enough. Gus reached over the counter, unplugged the cash register and went out the door with it. Within 10 minutes we received a frantic phone from the owner blubbering apologies. The £5,000 appeared, and the cash register was returned.

Another particularly difficult guy owed over £12,000 and was paying us very slowly. Eamonn and Gus headed off from Dublin at 3.30am to visit the guy who lived in a remote area 15 miles from his outlet. When he opened his front door in his dressing gown to collect the milk at 7.30am he was greeted with a polite *"good morning"* from the boys. He paid up. Mission accomplished. £5,000 and £12,000 might seem like small change today, but back then four or five outlets could put your lights out. We were walking a tightrope...without a rope!

The big gig in 1992 was the annual *Trip To Tipp* three-day festival in Thurles, County Tipperary, started by Denis Desmond in 1990. We'd built up enough confidence with Denis so that he increased our allocations of tickets. When we offered to provide a full box office for the festival he accepted.

We bunked up in caravans for the weekend. I remember the event mostly for the final night when Van Morrison topped the bill. While Van sang 'Moondance' a full moon filled the sky. It was a fabulous sight, *"a marvellous night for a Moondance."* Denis may have lost money on that first outing in Thurles, but he hit the jackpot in 1991 with a 50,000 sell-out every night. He'd arrived in Thurles in an old second-hand car, dumped it the day after the festival and drove back to Dublin in a brand new Mercedes. He never looked back after that. He'd hit the big-time, and now we had two world class promoters in Ireland.

1992 was another sell-out for him. This time we rented holiday homes for the weekend at Holycross, five miles from Thurles, much more comfortable for staff than caravans. We opened the box offices at 11 am and closed at midnight or later. The days were long, but we loved the buzz, and our strategy was to give the promoters the best possible service so they'd have difficulty in leaving us.

As soon it was confirmed that we were proceeding with a new computerised system, Jim resigned from Ticketshop. Our projections depended on very high monthly ticket sales, but we hit a wall before we started. Jim and MCD wanted to wait before committing to the new system. This was a big blow, as I was counting on having every ticket. This was getting complicated, as there were now three different distribution models. The promoters sold and distributed the old 'hard' printed ticket, the Point had their system, and we were about to launch.

DEC and BOCS worked very well together, and had everything installed on time, and we completed training during the first week in September. We had 24 outlets, 23 in the Republic and

Noel Harrison's outlet in Belfast. We had a 24-position call centre ready.

Everything was fine, all that was missing was a flagship event to launch the new system. Christy Moore was due to put three shows on sale at The Point, so I met Christy's manager Mattie Fox at the Longford Arms Hotel, (yes, the same place where I'd played my first professional gig in 1969.) Mattie was very positive. He understood the concept, and agreed to put the three shows for Christy on sale through us, 15,000 tickets. We were in business.

		Child's Name	Birth	Address
of Admission Reg No				
. 4. 51	148	John Giblin	29 May. 44 Dr.	Doorly Park
5. 51	149	Joseph Carter	25.1.46	Knappaghmore
5. 51	150	Paul C. F. Elliot	31. 7. 45	31 Doorly Park
4. 51	133	Vincent McGuinn	3.7.44	5 St. Patrick's Te
. "	134	Michael Gilmartin	9.12.44	Harmony Hill
. .	135	Joseph Mc Donagh	27.10.44	Chapel St.
. 4. 51	136	Patrick James Mc Gowan	6. 1. 46	
. .	137	Gervase McDermot	13. 8.44	15 St. Annes Terr
. 4. 51	138	Patrick Mc Nally	4.4.47	17 Doorly Park
. . .	139	James Vincent Lynch	12. 7.46	St. Joseph's Terr
" . .	140	Joseph Delaney	9.11.44	St. Brigids Pl
2. 4. 51	141	Anthony O'Hara	7.1.47	Pound St.
. 7. 4. 51	142	Patrick Ambrose Tighe	7. 10 46	Garavogue
7. 5. 51	154	Emor James B. Sheelan	28. 7. 45	Larkhill
5. 4. 51	153	Damian Leyden	14.10.45	5 St. Brigids Pla
2. 4. 51	147	James Myddleton	24. 4. 47	Old Market St.
3. 4. 51	12. X. 44	Anthony Renrick	12. 6.46	Connelly St.
. 4. 51	28. X. 44	James Foley	28.1.46	Tracey Avenue
8. 5. 51	155	Francis Mc Sharry	10. 9 46	St. Patrick's T
15. 5. 51	156	Thomas Downes	28.3.46	Shannon
15. 5. 51	157	James Harte	13. 5.44	Gallows Hill
20. 5. 51	158	Michael Leo Vokes	21. 8. 45	Chapel St.
21. 5. 51	159	Gérard Dilworth	19.5.47	
22 .	160	Thomas P. Higgins	2.5.47	John St.
22.5.51	161	Patrick Smullen	26.4.45	O'Connell St
29. 5. 51	162	Columba McGowan	12. 2.47	Castle St.
1. 5. 51	163	George Downey	30. 4. 46	Garavogue
. .	164	James V. McLaren	10. 10. 44	Pearse Rd X
. .	62	William Rooney	29. 6. 44	Garavogue

Scoil Fatima Roll, 1951

Parents William and Mary

with Mother, 1969

St. Mary's Ceili Band

*L/R: Padraig McManus, John Bray, Ray Wickam,
T H, Andy Healy seated. 1965*

*L/R P McManus, A Healy, T H, S Devins, P Fox,
B Fallon (front), 1966*

St Mary's Band with Texas King. Back Row:
M Feeney (Texas King), T H, B. Fallon, P.McManus,
Front Row: P. Fox, T. O'Donnell, S. Devins, 1967

John McGivern, Rainbow Ballroom

Baymount Hotel and Silver Slipper Ballroom

with Eileen, 1969

Smokey Mountain Ramblers, 1969

Wedding Day, February 1972

Wedding Day, 1972, with my parents

Our box office, Thurles, Trip to Tipp 1994

Refereeing Days with David Wogan and Hugh Kerins

Glasgow Celtic vs Sligo Rovers

China, 2003

Riverdance flashmob, Great Wall, China 2003

60th birthday photo with Eileen, Melanie & Clodagh

Band reunion, 2012. L/R: Francie Lenihan, Gene Berrill, Pat Ely, George Kaye, Liam Gilmartin, T H, Gerry Gallagher, Tom Jamieson (not in photo)

*with Maurice Cassidy,
friend for over 40 years*

*Eamonn O'Connor
(1961 - 2013)*

2 hats, 4 hands...
with Simone

Terry Barnes, John Pleasants, Sean Moriarty, T H.,
San Francisco, 2015

Accent Media auction night

Accent Media launch, Soho House, Los Angeles 2014.
L/R: Gary Fisher, Steve Machin, T H.

4

FROM TICKETSHOP TO TICKETMASTER

Ticketshop's Grand Opening

In September, 1992 Ticketshop entered a new era with a glitzy launch in the National Concert Hall to which we invited key players in the entertainment industry, including clients from Northern Ireland. We'd originally intended opening more outlets in Northern Ireland but for budgetary and logistical reasons, we deferred this. We introduced a new logo inspired by the Ticketmaster logo, thinking we might as well be inspired by the best!

Our innovative 24-hour service caused quite an impact. Admittedly, we were taking some liberty pushing the 24-hour concept, as only two people manned the phones between 10pm and 8am, but it was the perception that mattered.

We put Christy's tickets on sale a few days later. Despite being an entirely new concept, the launch went smoothly with few hitches. The outlets were delighted, as they now had access to every ticket for every performance in all price categories, and we sold out the three shows in a few days. Mattie was delighted, and added three more shows. We appreciated very much that he gave us that start.

Turmoil

Our next big show was *Disney On Ice* which we'd ticketed for a number of years. They were pleased we had a computer system as they were used to this elsewhere. Bu the cat and mouse game continued with the main promoters who only put a few smaller events on our system.

A couple of weeks after the launch, Eileen and I attended the wedding of a friend in the US. By the time I got back, the sky had begun to fall in. Several countries in the European Exchange Rate Mechanism, including Ireland, were in crisis, causing turmoil in the money market. The Irish Pound was devalued, and interest rates rose to 35%-40% overnight. A meeting with my bank manager went on for ages as he was constantly interrupted with phone calls from customers. Most were demanding to know why AIB were offering 35% for overnight deposits, when other institutions were offering 40%. Happy days for those with money on deposit, but I was at the bank for a lecture about my overdraft. These were unprecedented times, and promoters were understandably very cautious since consumers had reduced their spending.

Business practically came to a halt, with serious repercussions for Ticketshop. When your supply of customers dries up, trouble looms. I knew things were getting tight since we didn't have many shows on sale, but hoped the climate would improve and the crisis would end. But not this time. I was in my office one Friday in November when one of our finance people Frank said, *"Tommy, we don't have enough money to pay Disney"*. 20 years later I can still picture Frank standing over my desk giving me the horrible news.

We were staring into the abyss. If we didn't pay Disney, the word would go out and we'd be toast. I was devastated. After all, it had been my idea to computerise the business, and I had to take responsibility for the situation. I organised a crisis meeting with my two partners and offered my resignation. The problem was that we were hopelessly under-capitalised. We'd some losses, and always believed we could trade out of them. But not this time. In addition to the Disney problem, we also had a whopping first quarter invoice coming from DEC.

My colleagues turned down my resignation offer, so we had to look for a way out of this very serious situation. Our options were: 1) Find money to pay Disney somehow. 2) Get some fresh capital. 3) Draw up a new business plan with realistic goals.

Everybody in the office knew we'd a serious problem, and were naturally very concerned. Eamonn was terrific as always, and offered 100% support no matter what we decided to do. We hired a Financial Manager, Michael O'Reilly, to manage the day-to-day finances and draw up a business plan that would flush some money from a bank. The Disney shows were due to end in two days, and we'd have to transfer their money the following day. The Disney accountant gave Eamonn the figures on the Sunday night. We now had to wire funds to Wells Fargo Bank in San Francisco but we were well short. I estimated that we needed 2-3 weeks in order to sort something out. We had new shows coming on stream, but the cash flow crisis needed immediate action.

Disney had moved to Sheffield for the next leg of their tour, so I reckoned it might be three or four days before they'd call. Also, back then transfers of overseas funds could take up to a week. I then resorted to one of the oldest tricks in the book, and inserted a wrong digit on the wire instructions to Wells Fargo. I'm not proud of this, but we had our backs to the wall. This manoeuvre bought us a week before the wire was returned. I detailed our predicament to our very sympathetic bank manager who said he couldn't give me funds or extend an overdraft, but he'd help by bending the rules. He advised me to go missing for a few days.

The Disney accountant was jumping up and down by now, but I told him we'd transferred the money and that he could contact our bank to verify that. He called our bank manager who duly took the hit, apologising for making a mistake with the digits. Between delays and shuffling about, we got almost three week's grace. That bank manager had saved our skins.

I told Jim Aiken about our problem. He wasn't pleased, but left a cheque on my desk for a considerable amount of money. It was extremely generous, and typical of the man. Assuming it was pointless approaching the mainstream banks for funds, we applied to Anglo Irish Bank who had a reputation for lending to mavericks. The wait was torture, but, unexpectedly, they came through after a week.

We re-wired the money to Disney with a day to spare. We then had to face DEC who were entitled to pull the plug as we hadn't made the first payment. I suppose they reckoned they were better off sticking with Ticketshop for a few quarters than pulling the plug early on. Although still in business, Ticketshop was really on life support. We approached our partners from HMV about financing, but they declined. This was disappointing, as our ticketing contributed substantially to the success of HMV in Ireland. (*Lesson: Never start a business without being fully funded...next lesson, ignore previous lesson!!*)

The Comeback

In the middle of this crisis, I received my first European football appointment, a EUFA Cup game, Club Brugge v Stuttgart in Bruges, Belgium. Unfortunately there was no way I could leave the office and, besides, I was in no fit state of mind to officiate in an important European game. It was an extraordinarily stressful time. I think I went four nights without sleep during the first week, with many sleepless nights thereafter. With Christmas coming, the future looked very bleak. Without question, it was the worst time of my life. We'd a miserable Christmas, very difficult for my family, but Eileen was extremely supportive. Eamonn was also immense, standing shoulder to shoulder with me, and I must credit our staff who also dug deep.

On December 26, I went into a room with a sheet of paper and mapped out a plan. There was no question that this crisis would beat me.....failure was not an option. Despite the ongoing crisis, I'd great belief in what we were doing. The positive signs were there, but we needed to persevere and to increase the gross margin and ticket volume. If we could stick to this plan, I firmly believed we'd come good. The next 12 months would be make or break, and I must keep everything going while dealing with the Ticketshop crisis. Joe Carroll, who owned Zhivago Records, had asked me if I'd sell the Galway shops. It was time.

1993 started off slowly, and we managed the situation on a day-by-day basis. One day a politician called to my office. (I won't mention his name, but he later became a Government Minister). He said he was very unhappy about the fees we charged on ticket sales, and that we should consider dropping all charges. I was sitting there with a tray-full of bills while this cretin lectured me about our business practices, a guy who never took a risk in his life! I'm normally very calm, but I let rip and ran him down the stairs.

Through sheer willpower we kept the show on the road, and after about three months the siege began to lift as promoters relented and put more shows on our system. I was actually able to pay Jim's loan back that Summer. He seemed pleased and more than surprised that we'd turned the corner so quickly. The system was now working very well, and we ended the year showing only a small loss. Selling Star Records Galway also meant I could concentrate more on Ticketshop.

1994 was a very busy year for a variety of reasons. Our good luck continued, and although we were not completely out of the woods, business increased month by month. We'd sharpened our financial discipline, and there was no going back to the old ways. The Point gave up on RITA and agreed to install our system at their venue, a very sweet victory, although the contract negotiations were arduous. David Rogers, the Financial Controller for Apollo, had a reputation for stringing out negotiations and wearing people down. However, we had the promoters firmly in our camp, giving us serious leverage in the negotiations with Rogers, so we let him stew.

Their local lawyer was pregnant at the time. She'd had her baby and taken time off work afterwards, but the baby was already walking and the contract was still unsigned. The Point shouldn't have allowed us to flourish. They held all the aces in owning the largest venue in the country. Had they been more aggressive they could've dominated the market. I guess they weren't hungry enough.

Wimbledon F.C.

I then received a brochure from property developer Owen O'Callaghan who was developing a new multi-purpose stadium and shopping centre at Liffey Valley in West Dublin. He had a full complement of tenants for the shopping centre, but no team for the stadium. He was courting the Soccer and Rugby associations, as their stadium in Lansdowne Road badly needed

refurbishment. The GAA had a plan for their own stadium at Croke Park, and were unlikely to share with the other associations. Naturally,
I was very interested in this new project as it could involve a ticketing contract, so I visited Owen at his office in Cork in May, 1994. He had projections for a number of sporting events, as well as concerts, every year. I thought his concert projections were very optimistic, but the main weakness was that he had no anchor tenant. There would also be a question mark over concerts. For outdoor events, promoters could choose Croke Park, Lansdowne Road, RDS and other facilities, but increased venue competition created a better situation for the promoters. Owen and I agreed to stay in touch.

In August, 1994 I read an article about Wimbledon Football Club in the sports section of the *Sunday Times*. It was actually more a rant than an article. The Premier Soccer League in England had been formed in 1992 out of the old League Division One. It was becoming a serious money-spinner, with terrestrial TV stations being outgunned by the new pay-per-view satellite stations. Clubs were awash with funds. The colourful owner of Wimbledon, Sam Hammam had bought the club years back when it played in a semi-professional league. They gained promotion every year for 10 seasons and now were playing in the Premier League, a massive achievement carried out on a shoestring. Wimbledon, nick-named "The Crazy Gang", had won the FA Cup in 1988 by defeating Liverpool, then England and European Champions. It was a remarkable story.

Sam came to the UK from Lebanon and was in the construction business. In the article he was ranting against Merton Council's refusal to grant him planning permission to redevelop his stadium at Plough Lane, a ramshackle stadium Sam inherited when he bought Wimbledon Football Club. It had a capacity of only 12,000, completely inadequate for the Premier League.

Sam loved talking to the media. He was a dream for reporters who could rely on him supplying a colourful quote. In the *Sunday Times* article he said that if he couldn't get planning permission for Plough Lane, he wouldn't hesitate to move the club outside the borough, or even outside London if necessary. Now this was interesting. Owen O'Callaghan had a stadium without a team, and Sam might have a team without a stadium. And there was another factor. Dublin was a city with no Premiership team. This was a perfect fit. I mentioned my thoughts to Maurice, but then let it sit for a few weeks.

HMV buyout
Outside Ticketshop, matters were moving along nicely. Dermot Hanrahan had turned FM104 around to become the top radio station in Dublin. We received an offer from the HMV board to buy us out , and we agreed, subject to some conditions:

1. Ticketshop administration would move out of the HMV building on Grafton Street.

2. HMV would grant a licence for Ticketshop to continue selling tickets at HMV stores.

Although it took a few years longer than we expected, HMV came good in the end, and it was heartening to get a decent payday at last. We joked about needing to go to school to learn how to cope with being ahead rather than struggling from day to day. Ticketshop moved to a new office that was ideal, close to the main action on Grafton Street, but with the independence of our own office.

Sam Hammam
I wrote to Sam Hammam on September 1, 1994 requesting a meeting to discuss a proposal but not mentioning my idea of a Wimbledon move to Dublin. I didn't really expect a response, but a few days later our receptionist told me there was a Mr. Hammam on the line. It was Sam's brother Ned, and we spoke briefly. He asked about the purpose of the proposed meeting, and I gave him a brief outline. He said, *"It's a crazy idea, crazy,*

but it might work". We arranged to meet at the Dorchester Hotel in London on Friday, September 10, and Maurice and I headed over for what turned out to be a great adventure.

Ned arrived promptly and told us Sam couldn't attend, which we assumed was an old Arabic tactic ...... send a scout to see if a deal was worth it, and then spring the main man to seal the deal. Ned was surprisingly open, admitting that both he and Sam thought the idea, although crazy, was worth discussing. He kept shaking his head and repeating the word 'crazy', but we could see he was interested, and we invited him and Sam to Dublin for further discussions.

However, our optimism was misplaced, and I received a letter from Ned the following week thanking us for our 'brave idea', but he didn't think the proposal was realistic. He invited us to stay in touch, but it seemed the door was closed on what I thought would be a viable and exciting prospect.

A few months later, in February, 1995, Maurice was walking up Baggot Street when he met U2 manager Paul McGuinness and journalist/broadcaster, Eamon Dunphy. Over coffee, the Wimbledon project was discussed. Eamon was very friendly with Wimbledon manager, Joe Kinnear, an ex-Ireland International footballer, who was very enthusiastic about our project and could see the wider picture. Apparently, Sam had sounded Joe out about our approach and he'd had a re-think. Joe told Eamon that moving Wimbledon to Dublin was a fantastic idea that should be pursued with vigour.

Paul was a heavyweight in the worldwide music industry, and his involvement would lend extra credibility to the project. So Paul, Eamon, Maurice, Paul's number 2 Trevor Bowen, and I gathered in U2's office a few days later. We discussed the project for some time, and agreed that we should progress the idea. As a journalist, Eamon said he couldn't participate in an equity position, but would be very pleased to act as an advisor/facilitator. So it was agreed we would invite Sam Hammam to Dublin.

In March, 1995, Sam and Ned arrived in Dublin to meet the consortium at Paul's office in Hanover Quay. Owen O'Callaghan was invited by Eamon. That meeting was hilarious. It was the first time I'd seen Sam who launched into a long speech extolling the virtues of Wimbledon and giving us a history lesson. He grabbed his crotch, and thumped his chest. He talked about his passion for the club, passion for the fans, passion for the tea lady, passion for everything. We looked at one another. This guy is as mad as a bag of cats. He then said he'd be hung from the highest lamppost by the fans if he moved the club to Dublin. But in the next breadth he proposed to talk to the Chairmen of the other Premiership clubs, the EU governing body UEFA, BskyB TV, politicians, whoever. This soliloquy lasted about 45 minutes and he ended by repeating that the idea was crazy but he'd like to explore it further. We looked at each other again .... Sam might be bonkers, but behind all the theatrics was a very shrewd operator.

He said that it was not like the US where franchise teams are moved from city to city. I pointed out there were lots of examples in Europe where teams don't play within their national borders. Berwick is in England, but Berwick Rangers play in the Scottish League. FC Vaduz from Liechtenstein play in the Swiss League, AC Monaco, in the French League, Derry City from Northern Ireland, a UK jurisdiction, play in the League of Ireland, and so on.

The latest controversy in football at the time was the Bosman Ruling. The European Court of Justice had ruled that workers were free to move within the EU after the Belgian footballer, Jean-Marc Bosman took a case to the Court. This had a profound effect, as players were now free to move to another club anywhere within the European Union at the end of their contract, without any transfer fee being paid, with major ramifications for the soccer fraternity. On the issue of Wimbledon being allowed to play in Dublin, we thought this might also be an issue for the European Court of Justice, and reckoned we'd win.

We continued the discussion over lunch. Despite Sam's rant, he was clearly very interested. He now had an alternative to Plough Lane, albeit a very challenging task. Owen O'Callaghan's plan was for a stadium with 42,000 seats, but designed so it could be enlarged to 55,000 without any short-term reduction in capacity. Sam's eyes lit up. *"Before we build the stadium, we must build an inter-denominational church so the fans can pray before the games"*. This prompted more awkward glances all around. O'Callaghan nodded, *"Sure Sam, we'll build a church"*. Knowing O'Callaghan, I reckon he'd build anything, as long as the stadium itself went up!

It wasn't really such a madcap idea either. In the 1950s the Brazilian Government decided to build Brasilia, a new capital city in the jungle and a very futuristic concept at the time. They carved out the city in the shape of an aeroplane. I was in Brasilia for Brazil v Chile and saw the spectacular buildings, mostly designed by Oscar Niemeyer, a legendary architect. But they'd first built a church for the workers shaped like a nun's headgear, so Sam was not entirely on the wrong trail.

We were confident that a Premiership team in Dublin would attract capacity crowds from all over the country. I'd seen the statistics. Fans travelled from all over for Ireland's home international games. Indeed, thousands of Irish football fans travel weekly to the UK for football matches. Dunphy mentioned that Joe Kinnear had said he'd sign Irish International players to give the club an Irish flavour. We all agreed to reflect on our deliberations.

We met again the following month, with two additional attendees. Paul introduced us to David Maher, a friend of his who owned a land bank beside the proposed stadium in Liffey Valley. Owen O'Callaghan brought his architect, Ambrose Kelly, who designed the stadium. Sam was very excited, and said he'd talked to over 10 of the Premiership Chairmen and they promised they'd vote for allowing Wimbledon to move to Dublin. But he repeatedly expressed his serious concern about Wimbledon's fans, and dramatically claimed he'd fear for his life as the team had a rough following. We also accepted that it would not be long before the media got wind of our plans.

Sam estimated it could take at least a year, maybe two, to make it happen. We were under no illusions either. The odds for pulling this off were very low, but nothing ventured, nothing gained.

Considerable lobbying needed to be undertaken, and we agreed that this had to be done slowly and carefully. In summary, we needed the approval of the Premier League, at least 75% of Premier League Chairmen, the European Soccer body, (UEFA), and the Football Association of Ireland (FAI). We also had to have relevant Government departments and local authorities on our side.

Our initial thoughts were that if both the FAI and PL agreed, UEFA would rubber stamp the move. We also believed that the FAI would strenuously object. At the time, they were hoping to build a stadium at Citywest as soon as they got funds. But our plan would give them a free stadium, saving them over £50m.

I suggested another initiative. The League of Ireland was dying on its feet, mainly down to very poor management, although we couldn't say this to the governing body, the FAI. I proposed that we'd levy £1 per ticket sold for the Premiership games to be placed in a fund to promote local football. I was confident this initiative would raise over £1m a year, and with the right lobbying, matching funds could be obtained. There was a huge benefit for the FAI in this.

Ten years later, the FAI and the rugby body (IRFU) jointly redeveloped Lansdowne Road, now The Aviva Stadium. The FAI's attempt to raise €70m was a disaster, and they're still in serious debt. Had they gone with our plan, the money gained from international revenues could have been channelled towards the domestic game. It was a wasted opportunity.

The story hit the media in May, 1995. *The Star* was first and others followed with what was a massive story. I've over 50 press cuttings covering different angles. The vast majority supported the move, although there was negative feedback from the FAI. Dunphy was very familiar with the journalists, and briefed them on progress to date. Meanwhile, Wimbledon ended the season mid-way in the table, a superb result for a team with small resources.

Nothing much happened over the next six months. Paul stayed in touch with Sam, and Joe Kinnear kept Dunphy in the loop. Then Sam got cold feet and started procrastinating. I've seen this many times ... people change their minds, other priorities take precedence. Sam's team was still doing very well. They'd beaten Manchester United 4-1 at Old Trafford and were fifth in the Premier League. The Irish group met in Paul's office, and we agreed that Paul should write to Sam again, showing lots of love. We were still 100% committed to the project and we needed Sam back on board.

Sam returns

Sam and Ned arrived back at the end of April, 1996 for a meeting in Paul's office, and the project was full-on again. Sam said he'd prefer if we invested in his club and play the games in London for a few years. He said it'd be easier to make the move if we showed commitment. We were not particularly interested in this, but would go along with it if there was a clear plan to move to Dublin within two years. O'Callaghan couldn't proceed with the stadium until Sam committed. He could easily finance £50m with a Premiership team on board, but needed the signature. We also discussed the possibility of playing some games in Lansdowne Road for a year or so while the stadium was under construction. This was all do-able.

Sam agreed to allow the accountancy firm KPMG to access his books. He could account for 96% of the shares, which he bought 12 years earlier, but nobody knew who owned the other 4%. We were satisfied it'd be no problem. Then negotiations focused on the price. Sam and Ned went into a huddle in the corner and talking Arabic. We were laughing in the other corner, scrambling to find a few words of Gaelic, but with little success. Sam said he valued the club at £8m sterling and would require £6m sterling for 75%. We then went into a huddle, discussed the proposal for about five minutes, and accepted the price. I think Sam and Ned were surprised at our quick response. Handshakes all around, the deal was done. Paul McGuinness and Dave Maher would have 25%, Maurice and I 25%, O'Callaghan 25%, and Sam the rest. It was Sam's problem to deal with the mystery 4%.

Dunphy contacted a former Government Attorney General who put him in touch with a top legal guy in Brussels. But we preferred not to go the legal route, as matters could get bogged down in Brussels for years. Consensus was a better way forward. KPMG's report was more or less as Sam had revealed. Sam personally owned the ground in Plough Lane but this was not included in the proposed sale. Surprisingly, there was £2m stg in the bank. Compared with the astronomical sums and massive debt in the game today, £2m in the black 20 years ago was a fabulous achievement. Sam clearly ran a very tight ship. The advice from KPMG was that from their examination of the affairs of the club, it was reasonable to proceed with the deal subject to further due diligence.

Media interest was running rampant. Virtually all the major soccer writers, including Hugh McIlvanney and Brian Glanville (*Sunday Times*), Henry Winter (*Daily Telegraph*) and scores of others supported the project. The same applied to the Irish media, apart from Cathal Dervan who said it would never happen. Sky Sports also supported the move. This was understandable, because if a Premiership team was based in Ireland, Sky would sign up tens of thousands of new subscribers.

We retained Cormac Gordon from Ivor Fitzpatrick Solicitors to draft the Heads of Agreement to buy 75% of the Club for £6m sterling. Maurice and I adopted our usual approach, agree the deal and then try to figure out where we'd get the money. The contract was sent to Sam who replied that the deal was for 74% not 75%. This was odd, but we decided we'd deal with it later. Sam then invited Owen, Maurice, Paul and I to attend the opening day of the 1996/97 season on August 17. We also dined at his house on the preceding night so as to tie up any loose ends in the deal.

Sam goes AWOL

That dinner provided my first inkling that something was askew. Despite all the talk of millions/billions from Sam, he lived in a fairly modest house in St John's Wood. His brother Ned lived a few doors away. The dinner was pretty ordinary too, but the conversation consisted of positive talk about the move to Dublin and the plans for the future.

Ned offered to drive us back to our hotel in a 15-year old battered Volvo. As we were leaving, O'Callaghan asked Sam for a private conversation. As we bounced our way back to the hotel, Ned said Wimbledon's next match was the following Wednesday in Newcastle and that he intended driving there and back on the day. I looked at Maurice ... a 600-mile round trip in a wreck of a car?

We attended the match the next day at Selhurst Park as Wimbledon were now having to play their home matches at Crystal Palace's ground. Sam had tickets for us in the Directors' box. The opening day of the season is always full of expectation, new players, new kits, new targets. The occasion was filled with even more expectation as Manchester United provided the opposition. David Beckham scored a fabulous goal from inside his own half and Wimbledon lost 0-3, but nobody was concerned as this was an exceptional Man U side. We were spotted too, sparking a media frenzy about the 'imminent' move of Wimbledon to Dublin.

Soon after that trip it began to unravel. We tried to make an appointment to start the due diligence process, but various excuses were made. I was then alarmed to hear that Sam and Owen had undertaken a tour of League of Ireland clubs lobbying for their support. This was a bad move. Owen knew very little about League of Ireland teams, and Sam would surely piss them off ... which he duly did. It was even more alarming that two members of the consortium did a solo run without consulting the rest of us. Maybe the private conversation between Sam and Owen in Sam's house had something to do with it. It's water under the bridge now, but I have my suspicions.

Next, Sam tried to change the deal. He said the £8m stg valuation was merely nominal, and the real valuation was £24m. I have all the notes from those meetings and £24m stg was never mentioned. Sam said another £18m stg would have to be put into the club over a period, and then he'd start contributing to his share. In effect, Sam wanted a 'carry' on his share, but hadn't mentioned this before. This threw everything out the window. Sam and Ned went underground, ignoring all communications, letters, and phone calls. We now had to accept the deal with Sam was over.

Norway

Sam had behaved badly, and there was more to come. I was passing through London City Airport in March, 1997 when I saw a TV report that Sam had sold a majority stake in his club to Kjell Inge Rokke, a Norwegian billionaire. I stood open-mouthed listening to Sam giving the same spiel to the Sky Sports reporter as he'd given us in the U2 office. The difference was that he got £30m from Kjell Inge. Fair enough, he got more money, but I believe he would have had greater long-term value with the Irish consortium. The club had the potential to be a major European force operating out of Dublin, and would be the only game in town.

Shortly afterwards, Sam sold the Plough Lane stadium to Sainsbury's supermarket chain for £22m stg. He was on a roll, until it too began to fall apart, and difficulties arose between him and Mr. Rokke. Matters had deteriorated to the point that Rokke announced that he would never attend a Wimbledon game again. This was no surprise, given our dealings with Sam. Naturally, we monitored the unfolding story, and I called a meeting with Paul, Maurice, Eamonn and our lawyer Cormac Gordon. Now that Rokke was a majority shareholder in Wimbledon, he might be easier to deal with. The team was still playing at Selhurst Park, but starting to struggle on the pitch. Nothing had changed with our Grand Plan, but the team was going nowhere and had a very poor following. They badly needed a new home, and we had the solution.

We wrote to Rokke requesting a meeting to discuss our proposal. He agreed to the meeting, but he couldn't attend himself and sent his Managing Director. The meeting took place on Sunday, December 7, 1997 at the Aker Solutions office in Oslo. Cormac Gordon, Maurice and I travelled on the Saturday and had a drink with Norway's No 1 concert promoter, Rune Lumb who gave us the background on Mr. Rokke.

The Aker Solutions office was within walking distance of our hotel. The Managing Director (I think his name was Bjorn) arrived bang on time, and the offices were stunning, overlooking the harbour. Bjorn unloaded his troubles, and was scathing about Sam. Norway is a very modern liberal country, but Sam refused to deal with any female executive, and openly insulted them. Every time he called and a female answered, he insisted on talking to a male. Bjorn said Mr. Rokke was exasperated, and confirmed that Rokke was not talking to Sam and would not attend Wimbledon games. Bjorn was so animated about Sam I thought he'd have a seizure. We discussed the Dublin proposal and he thanked us for our interest, but he believed Mr. Rokke would sell his majority stake in Wimbledon at the earliest opportunity.

Mr. Rokke eventually sold his shares in 2000 to Pete Winkelman, a property developer and former record producer. Sam was toast. Winkelman changed the team's name to MK Dons and re-located to Milton Keynes, about 60 miles from Wimbledon, where they still play. Sam then gained a majority shareholding in Cardiff City Football Club, where he was Chairman from 2000-2006.

By chance one evening I was watching a documentary on Channel 4 about football hooliganism, a terrible scourge for a time, but largely eliminated now. The reporter had secretly filmed a meeting with fascist football troublemakers. Who was orchestrating the meeting but Sam Hammam's bodyguard, with Sam standing beside him! Here was the Chairman of Cardiff City supporting a fascist thug. This guy was severely twisted, and, not surprisingly, he had to resign as Chairman after the programme was broadcast.

Cardiff City F.C. was eventually acquired by Malaysian businessman Vincent Tan and the team promoted to the Premier League in April, 2013. I watched the final day celebrations on TV and at the end of the game, the camera panned up to the back of the grandstand. And who was there but Mr Sam Hammam. He'd been made honorary President of the Club!

Riverdance

While all this Wimbledon stuff was going on, another big adventure was about to take off. In late October, 1994 I got a call from Maurice who was down at The Point with Moya Doherty and asking if I was available for a meeting. I was, and he joined me in less than an hour. It would be a momentous meeting, although I didn't know it at the time.

Moya was a TV producer in RTE, and earlier that year had produced the Eurovision Song Contest in Dublin. It was a huge occasion, with an estimated TV audience of over 300m viewers. The show turned out to be an outstanding success for Moya and for the country. Ireland won the song contest with 'Rock 'n Roll Kids' sung by Charlie McGettigan and Paul Harrington. However, their win was completely overshadowed by the phenomenon of Riverdance. During each Eurovision, it was customary for the host country to present a set-piece interlude while the participating countries were preparing to vote. Traditionally, it featured music/dance with a theme relevant to the host country, and most of these productions had been bland, forgettable affairs designed primarily to fill up airtime.

The previous year Moya had seen Michael Flatley and Jean Butler dance at a concert and decided to fill the Eurovision spot with a contemporary Irish dance piece featuring them plus a large supporting cast. Bill Whelan was commissioned to write the music. Nobody knew what to expect, but the reaction was truly extraordinary, arguably the most sensational seven minutes of Irish music and dance ever seen. 5,000 people leapt to their feet for a standing ovation in the hall, while tens of millions were transfixed in front of the television sets.

That was merely the start, and Riverdance fever continued for days. Every talk show was dominated by expressions of delight at the performance. At the bank on the following Monday people were gathered around a TV set on which Riverdance was playing on a loop all day. Such was the demand, RTE aired the full seven minutes on the prime time 6 o'clock news. I know of nothing else that lifted the spirits of the nation as much as *Riverdance* did. The video was released a few months later, and it became the biggest selling Irish video of all time. People bought them six at a time and sent them to relatives all over the world.

I'd heard on the grapevine that Moya intended building a show around *Riverdance,* although the details were very sketchy. So I assumed that's what the meeting would be about, and Maurice, Moya and her assistant Breda Cash arrived at my office as arranged. The mood wasn't terribly upbeat when they arrived. Their earlier meeting at The Point hadn't gone as well as expected, hence Maurice had suggested that she have a chat with Ticketshop.

Moya outlined her plans. She'd produce the show, her husband John McColgan would be director, and Maurice would be the promoter. Normally a show like this would be produced for a traditional theatre of around 1,000-1,200 seats, but Moya ambitiously wanted to present a show on a much larger scale for larger venues. In that, she faced a number of major challenges. Due to scheduling and availability, the show had to be ready by February. She'd only about 14 weeks to her preferred opening night, and the show was nowhere near completion. Bill Whelan was in the studios, still writing and recording pieces. On the surface it seemed to me that it might be better to wait. But waiting was not an option.

There were a number of different seating configurations at The Point, and the venue suggested a seating plan of 2,700, normal for theatre shows in the venue. Moya didn't want the top priced ticket to exceed £22.50. There was a major problem with this model, as it was a very expensive show to produce. If priced on the £22.50/2,700 model, in order to break even the show would have to sell 85% of the tickets for every performance for four weeks.

We discussed this at length. It was an unacceptable risk for Moya who was a house producer for RTE on a salary. She had already mortgaged her house for this show, so everything was on the line. The general consensus is that a producer should never take risks over 50%, so 85% was madness by comparison.

I asked our Operations Manager Mary Kelly to look at the configuration. Mary was a wizard on the system, and came back after 30 minutes with a different plan. By moving the configuration she said that we could get 3,200 tickets at a push. This was a considerable improvement. It reduced the risk, but was still too high. Maurice said, *"The show will be strong. I believe it's priced too low. We should go for a top price of £27.50"*. But Moya was very reluctant to bump the price. Maurice argued again that the ticket price would be fine, but Moya's personal risk was still too much. I agreed.

The top theatre ticket price in 1994 was about £25, but I also felt that £27.50 was not unreasonable. Mary went back to re-jig the gross for the four-week run. We knew the figures would be much better, but not enough. Maurice suggested Moya needed investors. She replied that Paul McGuinness and RTE had put in some seed money, and they might invest. Harry Crosbie had also expressed an interest and she said she'd contact him.

While all this was going on, The Point's General Manager Paul Latham called for Maurice. Maurice had provisionally booked four weeks at The Point for *Riverdance,* and Latham was under severe pressure from other promoters for some of those dates. He needed a decision before the end of the day, otherwise he'd have to release the dates. He was not being unreasonable. He had a venue to rent and the other promoters had artists on hold too.

We spent a very pressurised few hours. It was touch and go if the show would go ahead with so much up in the air. Maurice said he'd invest in the show and undertook to call Paul McGuinness and RTE. I was seriously thinking that Ticketshop should invest, but decided to think it through thoroughly, and we discussed everything again for nearly an hour. The clock was running down and Latham called again. Moya said with luck we'll get the investment, and nodded her approval. Maurice confirmed he'd take the dates and sign the contract the following morning. Tickets would have to go on sale as soon as possible, and we set the on-sale date for Saturday week, only 10 days away.

I figured that Ticketshop should take the risk and invest in the show. I reckoned we'd make some money on commissions and fees, and if it flopped we might lose £20,000. If it did decent business, we'd do reasonably well. We were really putting in some sweat equity, so I was not primarily focusing on the investment. It was more important that the show went ahead so we'd earn money from ticket sales. After all, our core business was selling tickets, and Eamonn agreed it was worth the risk. Even though Ticketshop was still in recovery mode and almost breaking even, we could take a £20,000 loss.

I called Maurice and told him Ticketshop would go in. He'd talked to McGuinness who confirmed he'd invest too. The decision-makers in RTE had gone home, but we were confident that they'd row in with us. It was a momentous few hours, with more to follow. Moya called next day thanking me for having faith in the production. She said she'd try to get the contracts sorted, but it was unlikely that everything would be agreed before tickets went on sale. In essence it was a handshake deal on an investment for five years. I'd have been very happy to get our money back, plus a small profit, and earn fees of the sale of 45,000 tickets for the four-week run, about 50% of the venue capacity.

There was considerable interest in the show in the days leading up to the on-sale on Saturday morning, and our phones had been busy all week with enquiries. We were expecting a busy day. This was before the Internet, and our soundings came via outlets and phone enquiries. The 24-hours before a big on-sale is the most nerve-wracking time for promoters and producers all over the world. Advertisements have been placed in newspapers, TV slots booked, and DJs cajoled into plugging the show on radio. You've done all you can, but nobody knows if the tickets will actually sell. With rare exceptions, you get a good indication of how the show will do in the first few hours. We opened the sales at 9am and the reaction was tremendous. Nobody had anticipated the tsunami of interest, or that we would break the record for a single day's takings for a theatre show in Ireland. The four-week run was completely sold out five days later, so Maurice added an extra week, and that also sold out. This was remarkable, since nobody really knew what the show was about. They simply wanted to see the seven minutes of *Riverdance* live. After another three weeks we got the contract signed. This was like placing a bet after the horse had won at very long odds. I don't mean to be glib here, as we would have invested the money even if the show was a flop, but it was exhilarating to be involved in a smash hit. We had our money back, plus profit, after five days.

As 1994 came to an end, it was good to reflect on a very successful year. Ticketshop finally turned a profit, and we could give staff a decent Christmas bonus. It was a great year for the country also, as the economy was coming out of a horrible 12-year recession. The Taoiseach Albert Reynolds secured an £8b stimulus package from the EU which would later propel the economy to greater heights. Ireland beat Italy at the World Cup in Giants Stadium, USA. The IRA declared a ceasefire, and we had the *Riverdance* phenomenon. There was an air of optimism everywhere.

Opening Night

Riverdance had its premiere in The Point on February 9, 1995. It was a phenomenal success for lead dancers Michael Flatley and Jean Butler. Not too many had seen Michael dance live before, although I'd seen him years earlier when he guested with The Chieftains in Carnegie Hall. He was so different that night in New York, dancing in a tailored suit which was quite unusual. Having sold out the five-week run, plans were underway for the show to return to The Point later in the summer.

Crowd reaction was incredible, with standing ovations every night. Promoters from all over the world came to Dublin to see the show, and offers poured in from all corners. Maurice was in a wonderful position, and his role was to ensure the show went to the right venues with the right promoters in each territory.

After the subsequent eight-week sell-out in The Point, the show was set to open in Hammersmith Apollo in London. Advance sales were massive, and it too was heading for a sell-out. But just days before the opening, reports appeared in the media about contractual differences between Flatley and Moya. Flatley guested on ITV's *Morning Show,* and when quizzed about the difficulties he replied *"we're working on it and I expect it'll be sorted".* It wasn't sorted. Moya couldn't agree to Michael's demands and gave him an ultimatum.

What happened next was hard to believe. Moya fired Michael the day before the London premiere. That took enormous courage, and Maurice called the investors to tell them the news. I thought it was the end, as the hottest show in the world could hardly continue without the lead dancer. Moya replaced Michael with his understudy, Colin Dunne. Eileen and I travelled to the premiere in London, and when Colin appeared on the stage, I was disappointed. Michael had everything, brilliance, flair, and buckets of star quality, but though Colin was a brilliant technical dancer I didn't think he had that star quality. In this I was totally wrong.

There was a standing ovation at the end of the first half, and more standing ovations at the end. At the after-show party in the Natural History Museum in Kensington we were all elated, although anxiously waiting for the critics reviews. For anybody associated with an opening night, the most nerve-racking hours are those between the curtain coming down and the newspapers hitting the stands. As we all waited under the dinosaur skeletons, the tension was palpable. Eventually, first editions arrived with stunning reviews all around. The show was a major hit in one of the most demanding markets in the world. The next day, ticket sales were enormous, and the run sold out in a very short time. It's funny sometimes how things work out. Had Moya not fired Michael, his demands would have eventually caused problems and reduced profits all round. She courageously replaced a high-earning dancer with a moderately-paid performer to the benefit of the investors. The other lesson learned was that *Riverdance* did not need a star. The show itself was the star. Indeed, such was the demand that eventually there were three productions performing world-wide simultaneously.

Michael Flatley set up his own company and enjoyed much international success with his *Lord Of The Dance*. So, one seven-minute Eurovision filler spawned two of the most successful entertainment shows ever and triggered an enormously positive worldwide interest in Irish music and dance that continues to this day. But it's often overlooked that Bill Whelan wrote a brilliant score, an outstanding piece of work. The entertainment industry is a funny business, full of surprises and the unexpected. (*Lesson: There are no rules...the unexpected can be the norm*)

Ticketshop, Northern Ireland

Once we had financial stability at Ticketshop, everything clicked into place. We had the wind in our sails and could do no wrong. When we started computerising the business in late 1992, we had one outlet in Northern Ireland, the Virgin Megastore in Belfast. But we were vulnerable, as UK ticket operators could set up there and outflank us. On the other hand, the cost of setting up a Northern Ireland network was considerable, and ticket volume was low in comparison to the Republic. Our business required volume to operate profitably, and it was doubtful if we could achieve the numbers required in Northern Ireland.

But if we didn't make a move, we'd leave the door open for a competitor who could set up in Belfast and eventually attack our position in the Republic. Eamonn and I discussed this at length. Despite the risk we decided to establish a proper operation in Northern Ireland. Noel Harrison had a small office in Queen Street, so we did a deal with him for rent and staff, and opened 12 outlets across the province. This expansion in the network meant considerable increases in costs of equipment and other expenses.

The additional logistical problems caused difficulties for our financial team. We were now dealing in two currencies, Irish punts and British sterling. An added problem was the almost daily fluctuation of the exchange rate. We had to set a rate on our system, but because we operated on tight margins, it'd be very costly if we got it wrong. Promoters quite rightly expected to be paid in the currency where shows took place.

So the first year was very hairy, and we lost money in Northern Ireland. However, as often happens, once we had the wind in our backs we got lucky. *Riverdance* was coming to the King's Hall in Belfast for a four week run that sold out, and within a few weeks from ticket commission alone we'd recovered all our set-up costs and losses. It was equally interesting to observe the demographics. Northern Ireland is a very polarised society, yet *Riverdance* audiences crossed all divides, and it was not unusual to have three generations of the same family in the audience. It was equally encouraging to see politicians who normally would not bid each other time of day, mingling amicably at the show. Over the next few years we could do no wrong. *Riverdance* was in massive demand worldwide, and there were many memorable opening nights. The New York premiere in Radio City Music Hall was exceptional, followed by a terrific after-show party in the Plaza Hotel on Central Park. The run had sold out and the show was to embark on an extensive tour across the US that lasted for years.

Mother passed away

My mother died in April, 1995. Her illness had been diagnosed the previous September when she went for tests. We didn't realise she hadn't been feeling well for some time. Like many of her generation, she didn't wish to make a fuss, and so neglected her health. I believe that had she flagged her concerns earlier, the illness might have been treated. She was a remarkable woman who'd led a very simple life with great style and dignity. She had a terrific relationship with Eileen, unusual for a mother and daughter-in-law. In truth, they were best friends.

Ticketmaster

Sometime around October 1996, I received a call from the manager of the Gaiety Theatre saying that two executives from Ticketmaster UK had called there touting for business and giving the impression they were about to set up in Ireland. This could be trouble we didn't need. I'd always been concerned that Ticketmaster would arrive in Ireland with the potential to seriously damage Ticketshop. It didn't take long to track down the two executives and meet them later in the afternoon.

Jules Boardman was Managing Director of Ticketmaster UK, and he was accompanied by Nick Blackburn, General Manager. We hit it off straight away. Jules's background was in English theatre, and Nick had a previous career in the rock 'n roll business. They'd had the Ticketmaster franchise for a number of years, but it was about to be bought back by the Ticketmaster Corporation in Los Angeles. Jules would continue to run the UK operation and was looking to expand the business into Ireland. I didn't want to hear this. I told them that I had long-term contracts with all the major promoters (a white lie!), so it would be difficult for Ticketmaster to secure enough tickets in the market to justify an investment here. We circled one another for a while, and I broached the subject of how we might work together. Jules was expecting some executives from Los Angeles on a routine visit, and suggested I come to London for a meeting.

Two weeks later, I arrived at the Ticketmaster UK headquarters in Leicester Square. Compared to our puny operation, it was very impressive. I met Bob Leonard and Marc Bension, part of the Ticketmaster executive team in Los Angeles. Marc was a very combative person who'd previously been involved in building entertainment arenas for MCA. Bob was a former professional footballer who was highly successful in the entertainment business. It was clear he had tremendous knowledge of the ticketing industry.

The meeting was hilarious. Marc started out pontificating on how he'd blow us out of the water.... *"You don't stand a fucking chance"*. I combated by bluffing *"With what? I have all the tickets and promoters signed"*. Bob then cleared his throat and launched a huge spit which landed six feet away in a waste paper basket. I can still recall the pained look on Jules's face. He was a perfect English gentleman and this disgusted him. Yet, despite the posturing on both sides, we built up a rapport. Bob said it was worth exploring further, and invited me to Los Angeles to see if there were grounds for co-operation.

The Ticketmaster Story

The Ticketmaster story is fascinating. The company was started in 1975 by Albert Leffler, Gordon Gunn and Peter Gadwa. Albert had graduated from Arizona State University, and was doing an internship as box office manager in the Santa Fe Opera in New Mexico and wondering what he would do next. He already had a fascination for computerised ticketing which was relatively new. His wife Kathy had a brother who put him in in touch with his friend Gordon Gunn who had started a business as a re-seller for Digital Equipment Corporation (Yes DEC, the same company that helped me out in 1992).

Albert and Gordon knew of a brilliant mathematics student called Peter Gadwa. They invited him to dinner and during the course of the evening decided to start up a computerised ticketing business. These were simply enthusiastic young people with a dream and no business plan. They had no name for the company either, but sometime later, Albert's wife recalled the name of a dry cleaning business in El Paso, Texas called Master Cleaners. She suggested they call their new venture Ticketmaster, an appropriate choice since the three partners wanted to create a better experience than existing systems.

The first US Company to make inroads as a nationwide computerisation system was Ticketron. There were other systems, but usually operated only on a regional or city-wide basis. It could be argued that BASS (Bay Area Seating Service) in San Francisco created what is now the Ticketmaster model, but the nationwide Ticketron system was the best at the time. However it had major flaws. It took 2 months of training, and had to charge high fees to venues for providing their service.

Steve Wozniak was a founder of Apple, with Steve Jobs. He had a passion for the rock 'n roll business and ran a festival called US Festival outside San Francisco. It was a monumental disaster. Steve lost $millions over that weekend, a colossal loss even today, but completely off the scale in 1976. Part of the problem was the ticketing. Steve had a contract with Ticketron, but something went drastically wrong and they couldn't reconcile the event. Ticketron was struggling in other markets too, most likely because the system couldn't cope with heavy demand.

In the meantime, Albert, Peter and Gordon spent the year developing their Ticketmaster system and raising finance. It was a tortuous time for the fledgling company, with finance a constant worry. An investor, Charley Hamby came on board, allowing the company to set up an office and providing some breathing space. In January, 1977, Ticketmaster debuted with a concert by the Electric Light Orchestra at the University of New Mexico in Albuquerque. The company proceeded to ticket events in three markets in the South West: Phoenix, El Paso and Albuquerque.

An opportunity then arose to provide a ticketing system for the New Orleans Superdome, a major catch that required an upfront investment of $250,000. Hamby was done, and had no option but to sell his investment in Ticketmaster. The Pritzker family from Chicago who owned the Hyatt Hotel chain also managed the New Orleans Superdome. In return for advancing the funds to complete the installation in the Superdome, they acquired a substantial stake in Ticketmaster from Hamby.

For a few years the Pritzkers continued to invest in Ticketmaster, but by early 1980 concluded it was a losing proposition and were unwilling to sink any more money into the company. They instructed their tax advisor Burt Kantor to find a buyer, and he contacted his friend, a lawyer in New York who said the Pritzkers should talk to Fred Rosen who *"is sitting here in my office"*. It was to be a momentous call. Fred was a lawyer and a sometime stand-up comedian....his favourite quip was: *"You haven't lived until you've died on stage"!* Kanter hired Rosen as a special advisor to Ticketmaster, and charged him with either finding a way to make Ticketmaster profitable or to sell the company.

Fred spent 12 months traversing the country looking at systems and financial models, and examined existing Ticketmaster contracts with venues and sports teams. He discovered that Ticketmaster imposed the same $1 service charge for a $5 ticket as a $40 ticket. It didn't make financial sense. He immediately changed the model to multiple service charges for each price point, instantly increasing the bottom line.

By this stage Fred had figured that if he could scale the company and go nationwide, he would succeed. His vision was to develop the best ticketing system in the world, and he made major investments in software and hardware. He also believed he could challenge Ticketron whom everybody saw as giants, but Fred saw them as dinosaurs. In order to implement his plan, he needed an investment of $4m. Although Pritzkers intended to sell the company, Jay Pritzker said he would go in for $1m as Fred said he had another $3m lined up. In the end, Pritzkers took up all of the $4m, and a new era began.

The Pritzker family had clout in the Chicago area, so favours were called in and Fred was able to sign major clients, giving Ticketmaster a foothold in a big market. He then moved the headquarters to California, a massive market too. Terry Barnes, originally from Indiana, ran the mid-west business out of Chicago and also moved with Fred to become General Manager. Fred then came up with a financial model that changed the ticketing game forever. We hear today about disruptive technology, but Fred had the ultimate disruptive model in the early 1980s. Historically, a box office was an expensive overhead. It required staff, and each venue needed a mini phone room, all expensive. The box office charged the promoter 5%-7% of gross receipts, plus credit card charges. There were no extra charges to the public.

Fred then came up with a master plan and approached some of the venues with a deal. The venue would close their box office on the opening day of a show on-sale. Ticketmaster would add on a service charge, and share some of this service charge with the venue. It was a huge if controversial move. Overnight the box office became a profit centre, rather than a cost centre.

Fred then came up with another coup. He provided free computer equipment for venues, and entered long-term exclusive contracts so venues only allowed tickets to be sold through Ticketmaster. Some venues closed their box offices completely, apart from show night, and just took the rebates. He enhanced the deals by offering upfront cash sums against future ticket rebates.

The venues could not believe their luck, but there was uproar in the industry and promoters went crazy. The venues, buoyant with new-found liquidity, said to the promoters, *"If you want to play in our venues, these are the rules"*. What could the promoters do? They had to book artists into the best venues, otherwise they'd face an inquest from the artist's management. Then promoters turned on Fred. He had an answer for them. *"I'll cut you in on the deal too"*. When the vitriol and shouting died down, the landscape had changed, and everybody seemed to win, except the competing ticketing companies.

1. The promoters didn't have a 5% box office cost and had extra money in the kitty from Ticketmaster's rebate deal

2. Artists got better deals as promoters had more funds to play with

3. Venues reduced costs and enjoyed the deal rebate

4. Ticketmaster was the real winner. They got a constant flow of tickets with guaranteed income over minimum five-year contracts.

This new model resulted in an overall ticket price increase, but it could be argued that the promoter hadn't priced the gig correctly in the first place. It wasn't all bad news for the consumer either. Previously, fans seeking tickets had to queue for days at a venue. Now, Ticketmaster flooded each market they entered with ticket outlets. Instead of one purchase point, the consumer had up to 50 outlets, and a much better phone service through which to purchase tickets. Yes, consumers had to pay more, but the convenience made buying tickets a better experience. Of course the press was scathing, and still is, but they forget that

Ticketmaster takes the hit, while much of the service charge rebate goes back to the artist, venue and promoter.

So Fred had hit the jackpot. Venues lined up to adopt the new model, and soon Ticketmaster had signed up every major venue in every major market across the US and Canada. Ticketron tried to counteract by offering a cheaper service, but they were dead in the water. The venues said *"Ok, you'll charge us less but it's still a cost, while Fred is giving us an income stream and free equipment"*. Ticketron struggled on for a few years, but Fred eventually bought them out for a nominal sum. In 1984 Ticketmaster had revenues of $200m, in 1987 it was $400m, and after the Ticketron takeover in 1991, revenues blew through $1b.

Yet it was not all plain sailing within the industry. Aerosmith manager Tim Smith called a meeting with Fred. The band was about to embark on a major tour, expecting to sell 1 million tickets in the US alone. Tim ranted and raved for 15 minutes... *"No fucking way will I agree to your charges and fees. I want a discount"*. Fred stared silently for a while. Then he said *"We'll raise the fee an additional $1 and split the extra between us"* The manager did the math; his band would earn an extra $500,000 for the tour. Smith said he turned down the offer, Fred said he took the deal....... I don't know, but my hunch is that Fred won that round.

There's no doubt that Fred completely changed the industry through his belief in the technology. He'd seen that Ticketron and other systems couldn't hack it when major events went on sale. It was, and still is a controversial play, but his model is now the industry standard almost worldwide. The only difference is that the upfront demands are greater all round. Of course, the real winners are the artists. In the 1960s, the split was 60/40 in favour of the artist, but today it's not uncommon for the artist to take 90% or more of the receipts after expenses.

The model has extended to other industries, but is disguised in a different language. Supermarkets charge "hello" money to suppliers who want their merchandise on the shelves, but it's usually termed a "marketing" fee.

It's totally deflating when a major show goes on sale and the computer system fails, as I saw myself many times in our early computer days. Promoters have done the advertising, thousands of customers eagerly want to purchase, and then the system goes down. It's a horrible feeling. Fred knew that if the Ticketmaster system could stay solid under pressure, he'd outsell his competitors. And that's exactly what happened.

Into the mouth of the lion

I didn't know what to expect when I arrived in Los Angeles for the Ticketmaster meeting in November, 1996. They had offices on the top three floors above a bank on Wilshire Boulevard, close to Koreatown. CEO Fred Rosen was out of town, so I was met by Chief Operating Officer, Gene Cobuzzi, and Chief Technology Officer, Tom Hogg. Bob Leonard and Marc Bension from the London meeting were there too.

The meeting started awkwardly in a room through the window of which I was looking directly at the famous Hollywood sign on the Hollywood Hills. I had no plan, apart from wanting to keep them out of Ireland. This was a bit silly, as Ticketmaster had the resources to do what they liked. If they arrived in Dublin and wrote big cheques it would be game over for Ticketshop. I was even thinking the meeting was a big mistake and going nowhere. These guys were sharks and could gobble me up. It was an uneven playing field, Inter Cert Summerhill College v University degrees from Stanford and Harvard. However, I had one ace. I'll reckoned none of these guys had refereed a match in front of 10,000 in the Brandywell, hearing the crowd bellow *"Who's the bollox in the black?"* That toughens you!

Some music industry people would sell their first born for a deal. I was once at a conference in London when the question of loyalty came up. One aggrieved promoter from Egypt was complaining he got no loyalty from an agent when trying to book an act. *"If you want loyalty, buy a fucking dog!"* came the response, in front of 200 people.

Then I got a lucky break. Another executive, Tim Wood, who ran the Western Division, popped in and I was introduced as the guy from Ireland. Tim said *"I have an Irish passport, but I've never been to Ireland"*. Everybody laughed, and the whole atmosphere in the room changed. The other guys started teasing Tim about not visiting Ireland, so I invited them all to Dublin for pints of Guinness.

Now we talked about how we could work together, and within an hour had the bones of a deal in place. Ticketmaster proposed a deal they'd recently executed in another North American market. They'd buy 50% of Ticketshop now, and the other 50% five years later on a profit multiple. It was suggested that Tim would go to Dublin to give us the once over, and get his passport stamped.

The deal was very attractive for Ticketshop on a number of fronts:

1. Ticketmaster had the best technology in the world and we'd have access to their expertise.

2. At a stroke, we'd eliminate a potential major competitor and secure our position in the market.

3. Eamonn and I would continue to run the business

4. It would eventually provide a financial exit for the Ticketmaster partners.

Tom Hogg gave me a tour of their wonderful premises, including the computer room bristling with the latest technology. I was like a kid in Toys R Us. I had to have these goodies!! Tom said *"we power everything here from Seattle to Denver to Mexico City"*. I only wanted a system to power everything from Donegal to Dublin to Dingle. I was realising then that our computer system was completely inadequate when compared to Ticketmaster's. Tom also showed me the gigantic phone room with maybe 500 people taking calls on two floors. He said, *"We have 12 other call centres like this spread across the US"*. It was difficult to take in the scale of it.

There was no going back. I had to do the deal with Ticketmaster as I could see multiple opportunities opening up in Ireland. We'd have a world class technology platform, and a new Internet channel ready to launch. We shook hands, and over dinner that evening we continued learning about each other.

I learned that when we started Ticketshop the model we adopted was very similar to the US Ticketmaster model, apart from its scale. They told me a very funny story too. When Ticketmaster had launched their Internet service a few months earlier, they decided to call up the person who bought the first ticket. The media were called in, and they made a big deal about it. Fred called the guy who actually turned out to be a bit of a recluse. *"What made you decide to buy tickets on the Internet rather than from an outlet or our call centre?"* asked Fred. The recluse answered *"I don't like talking to people and I'm not talking to you"*, and then hung up! So much for the big PR story.

On my return journey I dropped into Ticketmaster's New York office. One of their executives raved about the Internet, like someone straight out of central casting, all animation and a broad New Jersey accent. *"Have you got the Internet yet, Tommy? It's just wonderful. It's the opposite to robbery. They come in the middle of the night, steal the tickets and leave the fuckin' money!"*

Closing the deal

Shaking hands on a deal is one thing, but getting the deal across the line is another, and I now had to get approval from my partners. Some say equity is blood, and selling part of a company is a major decision. Although we owned 100% of Ticketshop, we were vulnerable to competitors entering the market. My view was that if we had a good run, even after selling 50% of Ticketshop, the other 50% would be worth a lot more than the existing 100%.

And there was another challenge. The Internet was becoming a factor in the market, and my instincts told me this new medium was perfect for selling tickets. It would require major investment and specialist skills which we didn't have. I outlined this to my partners, and we agreed that getting under the umbrella of Ticketmaster would be a smart move. I knew there were risks, as a big multi-national could destroy a partner, and the business world is riddled with fractured relationships and dashed dreams. However, this was a risk worth taking, and I felt we were in a strong position to overcome any potential problems, having learned much from the Blockbuster and HMV experience.

The paperwork arrived in January, 1997 and Ticketmaster sent a guy to go through our books. I was upfront with everything, believing there's no point in trying to hide stuff as you'll be found out. There were no issues, and it was agreed to go to contract. But as soon as the lawyers started churning out paper, the trouble started, and bogged us down for months. Ticketmaster disappeared off my radar, and I thought the deal was dead.

In June, I went on a boat trip on the River Shannon with Eileen. There was no mobile coverage on the river, and when I called our lawyers from a coin box in Ballinamore, Co. Leitrim, there was still no news from Ticketmaster. My concern was that we were coming to the end of our software license agreement with BOCS, and they were pressing me to extend for another five years. So I got a bag of coins from a bank and called Marc Bension in Los Angeles from Ballinamore at 50p for every 30 seconds. I said, *"Marc, you have to shit or get off the potty"*. He apologised for the delay, but assured me there was nothing sinister. Ticketmaster people were stretched, and Ireland was not a priority.

There was a flurry of activity over the next few weeks, until we hit another roadblock. Jules Boardman wanted to retain Northern Ireland as part of the UK market. I jokingly told him that the UK had Northern Ireland for 800 years, and I was reclaiming it for this deal. I told the Americans it was a deal-breaker. Our major clients operated in both Northern Ireland and the Republic, and it would be stupid to disrupt what was a successful operation. I was also watching the bottom line. Business in Northern Ireland was increasing every year, with more new venues coming on stream.

When the Americans agreed that the contract was for the island of Ireland we were back on track, and Marc Bension arrived in Dublin on July 26 with Ticketmaster's in-house lawyer Danny Goodman. The legal process was horrendous. We negotiated crap for 5 days, including what would happen if I got the Ebola virus (I'm not kidding!). The final document (84 signatures on each side) was signed at 11pm on Friday, July 31, 1997.

The Cavalry arrive

Our contract with BOCS was due to expire on August 31, so we'd one month to migrate to the Ticketmaster system, a monumental task. Converting one venue is normally a challenge, but we were converting the whole country, including Northern Ireland with its different currency. But Americans are brilliant at logistics, and a team of 20 arrived from the US and at least another 10 from the UK. Keith English would be our new Head of Technology. This was a great break for us, as he was originally from Dublin and had worked in London with Ticketmaster UK for some years. He and his family wanted to re-locate to Dublin, so it worked out fine for all concerned.

It was a testing time, because in addition to planning for the new system, we had to keep our existing clients happy. On August 31, we transferred all the data from the old system to the Ticketmaster system. It was an all-night affair. In the early hours, I noticed a message coming through on a computer screen, *"Dodi dead, Diana dying"*. It was the night Princess Diana died in Paris.

I knew the next few months would be equally difficult. Learning to operate a new system is very challenging, and there's always somebody who'll claim *"the old system was better"*. Clients were jumping up and down, and everybody was exhausted. Ticketmaster sent over Dave Henderson, a veteran of the Ticketron migration, from Phoenix. He was extremely helpful and calmed everybody down. Within a few months, everything had settled down and we had a fabulous new system. Where once we had a Honda 50 2-stroke engine, we now had a Rolls Royce v12.

All roads pointed to the Internet. Sales through this medium were growing rapidly in the US, and it had recently launched in the UK. We launched www.ticketmaster.ie in 1999, and I remember Keith informing me that we'd sold the first ticket. Within a few weeks, he told me *"We sold over 100 tickets on the Internet yesterday"*. It was the start of a revolution. Ticketmaster in Ireland today sells over 8,000 internet tickets on an average day, and sometimes over 50,000 on a day when a big stadium show goes on sale.

The Internet brought explosive growth to the industry. Before, we sold tickets in outlets and by phone. But logistically and financially we could only hire so many people in a phone centre. Besides, maybe one in three calls resulted in a sale, and it was physically impossible for phone agents to sell more than a certain number of tickets per hour. On the morning of a busy show on-sale, the phones could go crazy at 9am, and we brought the network down on several occasions. The minimum shift for a telephone operator was four hours, yet a show could sell out in 10 minutes and they've nothing left to sell.

The difficulty for a promoter had been lack of information. It was worse in the old 'hard' ticket days where tickets were sold only at outlets. It was impossible to distribute the tickets evenly. A shop in Dundalk might have too few tickets, a shop in Sligo might have too many. Sometimes it took a few days for the promoter to gather information, and sales suffered as a result. Computer selling changed all that. All outlets and the phone room accessed tickets from a single database, and it didn't matter where the tickets were sold.

The Internet led to further advances. Tens of thousands of customers could buy tickets online simultaneously. Five minutes after a show went on sale, we could tell the promoter how many people were trying to buy tickets. This is vital information, as the promoting business is hazardous. When an artist embarks on a world tour, and can only perform a limited number of shows, his agent tries to extract as much money as possible for each show. The European leg of a world tour might contain 40 dates, yet there might be 60 promoters or more wanting to promote the act. The ideal situation is for an artist to perform two or three dates in one city for economies of scale. It means less travelling, and the promoter can spread costs over multiple nights.

Information is vital so promoters can gauge demand in each city. In the old days, a promoter might have to wait for days to see if it might be worth putting an additional show on sale. Now he can add a show at the press of a computer key. This opened up numerous possibilities for promoters who could now grow their business with confidence, using vital information and using a ticketing company that could handle it. These advances also resulted in better choices for the consumer/fan.

Rosses Point

I was invited to attend the Ticketmaster annual conference in Chicago starting on April 4, 1999. The previous Saturday was a beautiful morning, and I went to Rosses Point to read the papers. I noticed they'd widened the road during the winter, and the houses had some trees and new stone gateways. I also noted that it looked as if somebody was going to build on a plot of land.

It was a fabulous location, south-facing and with panoramic views over the water. I knew the owner of the house next to the plot, Dr. Paddy Henry, as he attended my mother when she was ill. I called to his house enquiring about the plot, but it wasn't convenient as the Henrys had just returned from holiday. I suggested I'd write to Paddy as he owned the plot in question.

The flight to Chicago on Monday was due to depart at 3pm, so I spent the morning in my office. Just before I left for the airport, I dropped Paddy a note enquiring if he'd sell me the plot. I thought it was a very long shot. But a few days later, Eileen told me that Paddy had replied that he was about to put up the 'for sale' sign. He said I should talk to his auctioneer.

After discussing this with Eileen, I called the auctioneer on my return but said I wouldn't get into a 'Dutch auction' with others. He named a price and I agreed, and within 10 days we'd exchanged contracts. We'd had no intention of leaving our Green Road house until my chance visit to Rosses Point. Also, since all US flights, except Chicago depart in the morning. If I'd been travelling to another city I'd not have had time to write the letter and Paddy might have sold the plot to somebody else.

First Ticketmaster conference

The Ticketmaster conference was an eye-opener, with around 300 employees from all over the US in attendance. Apart from UK and Ireland, Ticketmaster had only one other European market, Norway. The company also operated in Australia, where the Managing Director was Maria O'Connor. Maria was from Belfast, but her family moved to Australia in the late 1970s to escape the Northern Ireland 'troubles'. She'd started as a phone operator with Ticketmaster and worked her way to the top. We swapped stories and developed a great friendship over the years.

There was a module in the conference for International attendees. It looked thin with only UK, Ireland, Norway and Australia, so they added Canada to make up the numbers. I gave the delegates an outline of how we do business in Ireland. Everybody was very friendly and receptive, and I was warmly welcomed into the Ticketmaster family. I knew we'd made the right decision in hitching our wagon to Ticketmaster. The only way was up.

Barry Diller

While we were doing the deal with Ticketmaster, major changes were taking place in their boardroom. Microsoft co-founder Paul Allen purchased 80% of the company from the Pritzkers for $240m. He could see the future revolved around the Internet, and figured his technology team could build a world class platform which would make Ticketmaster a leading light on the web. Fred was more cautious, as the Internet was very new and he wanted to avoid any problems or issues. He had a dominant position in the market, and, aware of how Ticketron blew their business because of technology issues, he didn't wish to upset his clients.

Fred also cut a fine deal for himself with Allen, a five-year contract worth $20m plus stock. But it didn't take long before Paul and Fred locked horns. Fred ran the company as he had done under the Pritzkers, practically ignoring Paul. It was a recipe for disaster. Paul had bigger fish to fry, and sold 47% of his stock in the now publically-traded company to Barry Diller. Fred mistakenly thought he could do the same with Diller.

Diller had dropped out of UCLA and started working at the William Morris Agency, sorting and delivering mail to the executives. He quickly moved through the entertainment industry and became Chairman and Chief Executive of Paramount Studios at the age of 32, the youngest ever CEO of a major Hollywood studio. Under his stewardship came some of the biggest blockbuster movies of the 1970s and 1980s, including *Saturday Night Fever, Grease, Beverly Hills Cop, Raiders of the Lost Ark* and numerous others. He became Chairman and CEO of Fox News, and was responsible for launching *The Simpsons*. He left Fox News in 1992 in search of his next venture.

Friendly with fashion designer Diane von Furstenburg (later to become his wife), one day he accompanied her to QVC, the home shopping TV studio, where she sold almost 30,000 dresses to the public in two hours, netting $1.2m. Diller was fascinated by the scale of the operation and became involved in QVC, but departed after two years and formed his own company Home Shopping Network. It's still a very successful company.

Diller was a visionary and could see where the Internet was heading. Citysearch was one of the first online companies dedicated to city listings, replacing the years-old paper model of listing events, restaurants, hotels etc. in various markets. Diller invested in Citysearch, and further invested in technology and manpower. In 1998 he'd bought additional shares in Ticketmaster and now had control of the company. But there was no way that the giant egos of Fred and Barry could fit in the same room, and Fred soon left. That was a pity, but I'm not sure if he ever grasped the enormous potential of the Internet for the ticketing business.

There was a dot com bubble at the end of the 1990s with everybody was piling in. Diller fused the online portion of Ticketmaster with Citysearch, forming Ticketmaster Online-Citysearch. He launched it on the stock market, leaving the old Ticketmaster, minus outlets plus phone centres, as was. This was somewhat confusing, but it didn't affect Ticketmaster Ireland. While Fred hadn't invested enough in the online business, Barry changed all that. Over the next few years he put hundreds of millions of dollars into the Ticketmaster infrastructure which was to reap tremendous rewards in the coming years. Ticketmaster Online-Citysearch didn't really gel. It made no sense to have two Ticketmasters. Shortly afterwards, Barry brought back the online part to the existing Ticketmaster family so there was now just one Ticketmaster, while Citysearch remained as a stand-alone company.

Denver 2001

Eamonn and I attended the Ticketmaster annual conference in Denver in 2001. I'd been highly impressed with the 1999 conference, but this was on an even higher level. The company had grown enormously in two years and Diller had hired the best new technology talent in the US. The opening evening was held in the Denver Aquarium with hundreds of new staff in attendance, all technology talent.

I was introduced to the new CEO John Pleasants and his Executive Vice President of Technology Operations, Sean Moriarty. Genius that I am, I figured Moriarty had to have

Irish connections ..... and he did. In fact Eamonn's and Sean's great-grandfathers were buried in the same cemetery in Kerry! Sean's grandfather had emigrated to the US and settled in Springfield, Massachusetts. Needless to say, we all bonded, and that meeting began a fantastic friendship that continues to this day.

Diller flew in next morning, gave a bland 15-minute speech, and flew out again. Most of the day was taken up with technology teams outlining their plans for the future. These guys were the best brains in their field. Sean and John had re-built the technology platform so we had one of the best Internet operations in the world. Eamonn and I were drooling, imagining how we could grow our Irish operation with such fabulous technology and back-up from the whole Ticketmaster family.

9/11

I was back in Los Angeles for a budget meeting in September, 2001. It was meant to be a quick trip, out Monday and back Wednesday night. It was a running joke with Ticketmaster executives that Ticketshop never prepared a budget. I joked with them that we did our budget at the end of each year, and wherever we ended up with revenue and expenses was the budget!! So I was regularly teased come budget time, and we had to change many habits as part of a major multinational company. Ticketmaster Ireland was doing terrific business, and we always exceeded our targets. The Odyssey Arena in Belfast was opening shortly and I knew it would grow the business in Northern Ireland, so achieving our 2002 targets would be a doddle.

I arrived on September 10. Travelling westward is a killer for me with the eight-hour time difference, and I was awake around 4am on the 11th. I made some phone calls and worked on my computer. I was watching the news on NBC, when a newsflash popped up saying a plane had crashed into the Twin Towers in New York. It was after 6am in Los Angeles, 9am in New York. The next few hours were extraordinary.

I watched riveted as the second plane crashed, then another hit the Pentagon and then came the crash into the field in Pennsylvania.

Eileen and the girls called to check if I was ok. The scary thing was that nobody really knew what was happening. Is this the start of an all-out attack, maybe a nuclear attack? As word came through that all aircraft were grounded, I realised I'd be stranded 6,000 miles from home for a while. We were now in unchartered territory, and the uncertainty was disturbing. Our daughter Melanie was due to get married in November, and I wondered if I'd make it.

I was staying at a hotel on Wilshire Boulevard just a short walk from one of the Ticketmaster offices in an insalubrious part of Los Angeles. Nigel Grant, Ticketmaster's UK CFO, and his assistant Valerie were staying in the same hotel. We went to the nearby office around mid-day, but hardly anybody turned up until later in the afternoon. The nation was in shock. As people had been required to travel from all over the US and beyond, it was pointless expecting the budget meetings to happen. Jules Boardman and others were in the air from London, but we'd had reports that transatlantic flights had been ordered to land at St John, Newfoundland, and Bangor, Maine. So John Pleasants postponed everything until the position became clearer, and I had a sombre dinner with him and Sean Moriarty.

Soon, all flights were cancelled until further notice. Jules Boardman called. His flight was about three hours out when it turned back to London. They weren't told why, and he only found out back in London. He was lucky, in that thousands were stranded and sleeping in aircraft hangers in Canada.

I told Nigel and Valerie that it looked like we'd be stranded for some time and should make ourselves comfortable, and I suggested we head to the beach in Santa Monica and bunker down somewhere pleasant. Because of the travel disruption, there were numerous cancellations, so I booked three rooms in Le Meridien Hotel on Pico Boulevard, a few blocks from the Ocean. I love Santa Monica's unique vibe, and considering the overall situation, we were ok in a fine hotel, lovely neighbourhood and beautiful sunshine, and had cash and credit cards.

As this had originally been intended as a short trip, I had few clothes with me, so off I went for some retail therapy. We also hired bikes, and cycled down to Venice Beach and, on the following day, rode north on the bicycle path up to Malibu. The airways were still closed, and it was impossible to get through to Virgin Atlantic whose website had the same message for day, i.e. keep logging in for information.

After a few days, I suggested we head to LAX airport. It was like the apocalypse there, thousands of travellers milling around or sleeping outside on the pavement. It was obvious they'd been there for days. It was particularly tough for families travelling with children, and for airport staff, under severe pressure from travellers seeking information that nobody could give with certainty. It was hopeless, so we returned to our hotel to continue the 'holiday'.

By the weekend, flights were thankfully moving again, so we went back to LAX. It was still chaotic, with a queue for Virgin stretching for hundreds of yards. However, Virgin had two desks allocated for business class customers so we were dealt with in less than 30 minutes. We got tickets for the following Tuesday, so our extended stay lasted only six additional days.

It was good to get home.

SFX

From the mid to late 1990s another major play was taking place in the music industry. Bob Sillerman, a New York-based media entrepreneur, started buying up major entertainment companies, promoter companies and venues. Bob had a track record of accumulating businesses and selling them on. In 1996, his company SFX Broadcasting owned 71 radio stations, the 7th largest chain in the US. In 1998, he sold the business for $2.1b, reportedly netting $250m personally.

Bob then turned his attention to the wider entertainment industry, founded SFX Entertainment and started buying up businesses at a furious rate. Promoters could not believe their luck. Bob wasn't interested in diligence or serious attention to detail. He had a huge war chest, and simply wanted to acquire major entertainment businesses fast. He mostly succeeded in buying up the No 1 promoter in every major market in the US, Canada and Europe. Some who'd previously thought their company had little value, soon had Bob waving huge cheques, some in excess of $100m.

Promoting is a very precarious business. Promoters operate on low margins and must make risky calls when booking acts. A top artist can demand a very high guarantee against 90% or 95% of the gross receipts, whichever is higher. If a promoter gets it wrong, he/she can lose a lot of money. For one well-known tour the artist demanded 105% of the ticket price. So the promoter had to add in car parking fees, ticket rebates, food and beverage receipts, and live off the scraps. If one promoter doesn't take the act, another one will. Almost every promoter wants his/her name on the poster... *XYZ Promotions presents U2 at........* and there's little that irritates a promoter more than seeing his competitor's name on that poster.

So, when Bob waved his cheque book, there was a stampede to sign up, and many sold their companies for unheard of amounts of cash. They remained in charge of their businesses, but with very little risk, as the parent company SFX was now guaranteeing artists' fees.

Sillerman reckoned he could change the model by buying up all the promoters, venues and entertainment companies. He reckoned he'd have enormous buying power, which would drive down the artist prices with greater profits for SFX. But there was a major flaw. In order to keep his venues full and his promoters working, he needed content. Artists reckoned that Bob's model would fall apart if he didn't achieve the numbers and the profits he promised his investors. So instead of them squeezing the artists, they put the squeeze on SFX, and Bob had to overpay for artists in order to populate his venues and keep his promoters happy. The result was that ticket prices jumped 80% between 1996 and 2003.

Bob created a monster. Historically, promoters had to invest their own money and so were more cautious. Now they were playing with SFX money, so didn't care what they paid acts. In order to succeed with his model, promoters had to go for market share...i.e. pay enough to secure the act. Bob argued that the industry was undervalued and the artists didn't disagree.

Between 1996 and 1999, SFX spent over $2b buying entertainment assets. It was now time to sell, so Bob had to create a story to attract a buyer, and went back to his old stomping ground, the radio business. He entered into negotiations with Clear Channel Communications, a leading communications company based in San Antonio, Texas. In 2000, they owned 1,000 radio stations, 500,000 outdoor advertising hoardings and 20 TV stations. The company was majority-owned by the Mays family headed by its patriarch Lowry Mays. I'm assuming Bob went to Lowry saying, "*Our artists and venues, and your radio stations and advertising hoardings, make a perfect match*". Lowry took the bait, and paid $4.4B for SFX Entertainment.

It was rumoured that Clear Channel was so hot on the deal they didn't do any proper due diligence and just wrote the cheque. Five years later, SFX was valued at a little over $800m. What I've learned through the years is that the economics don't need to stack up....it's far more important to have a story for Wall Street. There are always suckers ready to write a cheque if the story is sexy enough. In the end, Sillerman had a great story to tell and rode off into the sunset with a big bag of cash. This deal would re-appear on my radar 10 years later.

Melanie's Wedding

Melanie was married in November, 2001. She met her future husband Sean O'Reilly when they worked in the same company in Ireland. Sean was from New York, his father Tony having emigrated from Cavan in the early 1970s. When they became engaged, I placed a notice in the Personal section of the *Irish Times*. I couldn't help smiling as the *Irish Times* lady counted the words and told me the cost. It was more than the entire cost of my own wedding almost 30 years earlier!

When discussions about the wedding were mooted at home, my first reaction was to employ a wedding planner. But after talking it over with Eileen, we decided to do it ourselves. I'd probably lose patience with a wedding planner anyway, and as Eileen is a brilliant organiser, we figured we could do a proper job ourselves. The ceremony was to take place in Sligo Cathedral, and the reception in Harvey's Point, Co Donegal, 40 miles away.

What made a wonderful day even more special was that it was the first time in four years our entire family would be together. Clodagh had moved to Australia, and apart from home visits, Melanie lived Stateside. In fact, it was probably the only time both our extended families were together. In a break from tradition, both Eileen and I walked Melanie up the aisle, and Clodagh was one of five bridesmaids.

We were especially delighted when our next door neighbour Emma Gilligan accepted the invitation to become a bridesmaid. Emma was born a month before Melanie, and they grew up together. Emma had Cystic Fibrosis but had had a successful liver transplant some years earlier. She still has a special place in our family.

There was a large contingent of guests from the United States, despite some nervousness about flying so soon after the Twin Towers atrocities. However, everybody who came enjoyed an extended holiday based around the wedding. Sean and Melanie opened a restaurant in Stroudsburg, Pennsylvania soon after. Clodagh went back to Sydney, and Eileen and I became empty nesters again.

New House
Although we bought the site in 1999, we didn't begin building our new house until May, 2002. There was no rush, and I wanted to give sufficient time to researching and planning. Some people

don't like this stuff, but I loved every minute of it. Despite being very busy with Ticketmaster, I still found time to work on the plans. Eileen and I designed the floor plans to suit our needs, and had an architect design the elevation and do the paperwork. We decided to build a large house with a high specification, as I figured it better to build something decent rather waste the money on some stupid idea. If we were lucky enough to live a reasonably long life, we'd downsize to a smaller house when we get older, so the new build would be a good investment.

The builders came on site mid-May, 2002 and the plan was to move in by Christmas, 2002. The site preparation was very difficult, as hundreds of mostly rotten trees had to be removed. It's a fatal mistake to constantly change plans during a build, because builders use this as an excuse to delay the build and charge for extras. But we'd spent over a year planning every detail to avoid changes and delays. I was away working, but Eileen visited the site practically every day as the builders' tormentor-in-chief. She reminded them we were moving in on December 16, prompting the running joke ... *"that's fine but December 16th of what year? 2003 or 2004?*

But we were relentless, and actually moved in on December 16, 2002. About 95% of the internal work was completed, and we decided to wait for the Spring weather to complete the landscaping. We sold our house on the Green Road where we'd had 27 very happy years.

Deals and Donuts

By 2003, Ticketmaster Ireland was enjoying a great run. The economy was taking off and promoters were on a roll. When we joined the Ticketmaster family in 1997, we were selling almost 700,000 tickets a year, a respectable number. By 2003, we were nudging 3 million, an impressive figure from a population of 5 million. The internet contributed greatly to our success, especially with major events.

There's always tremendous excitement in the week leading up to a big show going on sale. The promoter is anxious, our ticket outlets want extra tickets, phones go bananas, the media demand information, and 'friends' come out of the woodwork looking for tickets. For example, I got a call to my mobile 15 minutes before a major on-sale for U2 in 2001. *"Tommy, you probably don't remember me, but I met you in Seapoint, Galway with Martin Johnson in 1969"*. F.F.S! Never heard of the guy, don't know how he got my number. My second word was *"off"*.

The deals with promoters and venues got tougher. We'd multi-year contracts with our clients, so we'd be back to square one when re-negotiating. It's the law of the jungle. Artists squeeze agents, agents squeeze promoters who in turn have to squeeze the next in line. We all understood the game.

All our big deals with Denis Desmond's MCD and Aiken Promotions were concluded over sticky buns and donuts. So it's no wonder Eamonn and I both gained weight over the years. We'd meet Denis in his office in Dun Laoghaire and would always stop at a bakery on the way to pick up a box of pastries for the meetings. Over mouthfuls of goo, we did multi-million euro deals. At one meeting Denis jokingly said he wasn't impressed with the quality of the sticky buns, so maybe don't bother bringing any next time. Of course when we arrived empty-handed it was, *"Hey man....what's the story, no box"*?

On our way to the next meeting we stopped at Manning's home bakery at the top of George's St. in Dun Laoghaire and bought the largest, messiest box of sweet pastries imaginable. Denis called to his secretary.....*"forks are no good.... bring up some straws"*. It was hilarious, three big kids slobbering over mouthfuls of cream pastries between arguments over ticket volume discounts. Many major deals are done over dinner and fine wines, but I'd wager we did the best deals on the highest amount of calories and sticky buns.

Jim Aiken had a different routine. He always dropped into our office and would phone when en route from Belfast. We'd then head off to Bewleys, the Westbury Hotel, or across the road to our 'local', Bruxelles. We talked about everything from politics to football in a mixture of debate, lecture and advice, depending on the mood on the day. Jim was always on a diet, but, like myself, had no resistance. *"I definitely won't have anything sweet today.....maybe just a spoonful....ah might as well"*, he'd tell us. Eamonn would scout the landscape in advance, sussing what promoters were expecting in a new deal. Then the cat and mouse game would start until eventually we'd settle on a contract. Jim would sometimes say *"There's no fun in this. I can't get a row going with you, Higgins"*. Have another donut and apple pie, Jim!

5

GOING GLOBAL

UK and Ireland

In June, 2003, I travelled to the Ticketmaster Conference in Phoenix, Arizona. With no direct flights from Dublin I had to change in Chicago. I'd just boarded when I heard a large round of applause coming from behind. It was for Muhammad Ali, and he sat next to me for the entire eight-hour trip. His voice had gone, but I could understand his whisper. As a teenager I'd set my alarm for 3.30 am so I could listen with my father to his epic fights with Sonny Liston and others on the radio.

Ali is arguably the most loved sportsperson ever, a truly iconic figure. He'd been to Dublin the previous day for the Special Olympics and spent most of the flight doodling with a felt pen. He asked if I'd like a drawing. Would I what? He did a fabulous drawing of the famous 'Rumble in the Jungle' with Joe Frazier on the back of an Aer Lingus menu card. When finished, he relayed the story and showed me Frazer on the canvas and pointed to himself, Ali, the winner. That treasured drawing is framed and hanging in our home. That it's on an Aer Lingus menu card makes it more quirky.

Terry Barnes was now Chairman of Ticketmaster, John Pleasants, Chief Executive Officer, and Sean Moriarty, Chief Operations Officer. Terry, John and I were sitting outside the hotel on the opening evening of the Phoenix Conference, casually chatting. I asked Terry why Phoenix was chosen, because the heat in June was almost unbearable. Terry said *"In Summer, the room rate in Phoenix is lower than the temperature"*. Message understood!

Jules Boardman had left Ticketmaster UK to set up his own mentoring business. Peter Jackson had relocated from Vancouver to become UK and Ireland Managing Director but was now returning to Vancouver. Ticketmaster was in the process of buying out the remaining 50% of our shares. John asked me what would I do next, perhaps assuming I'd leave the company after the buyout. I told him I really liked the business and intended staying around in some capacity.

He then asked me if I'd take over the running of the business for the UK and Ireland. He explained that Diller wanted to expand the business in Europe, and the company was gearing up for this task. I told John I would accept his offer, but expressed the view that bringing US executives to manage the UK business was not the best way forward. I suggested we hire a British-born Managing Director for the UK alone, and he gave me the green light to proceed with filling the post. Following a conversation lasting five minutes, Eamonn would take over as Managing Director of Ireland. There was no need for much discussion, as I knew he'd take the business to the next level.

Picking the right new Managing Director for the UK was a crucial call. If I got it wrong, the consequences would be horrendous. The UK was a potentially enormous market, but I believed it was underperforming. A headhunter put forward six candidates. I suggested that Chris Edmonds, Ticketmaster's General Manager for the South East, should throw his hat in the ring as he had a very good reputation. He'd previously been box office manager of Tottenham Hotspur Football Club. He was the only in-house candidate.

Jim Warner, our in-house lawyer, helped me with the process. Most of the interviewees were very good and had excellent experience running large companies. John Pleasants sat in on one of the interview sessions but said *"you have to work with the guy....it's your call"*. Ticketing is a peculiar business. You either get it or you don't. For me, the choice boiled down to who would command the room at our Tuesday morning management meetings. I really didn't fancy trying to educate somebody in the peculiarities of the ticketing business no matter how good they might have run a business in another sector or sectors. I had faith in Chris, and proposed him to the Executive in LA. I believed he had all the essential skills and sense of authority, and I was given the green light instantly.

Chris hit the ground running and within months had his own team in place. This was the start of a remarkable run as we struck up an excellent working relationship. I always believe you must have trust with colleagues, and we were very straight with one another. If you surround yourself with people who are better than you, and develop a strong sense of community and trust within the team, success will surely follow. If there's bad news, I always want to hear about it and sort it out. The same principle applied to my relationship with the guys in LA. I always gave them unwelcome news early because, given time, we could deal with any problem. But it was Chris's management skills that made Ticketmaster UK so successful.

China

In October, 2003, *Riverdance* was due to embark on a short tour in China, including Beijing and Shanghai. It was too good to miss. On behalf of the Irish Government, our President, Mary McAleese led a trade mission of Irish business leaders. They were all to attend the opening night of *Riverdance*, as was the Chinese Premier, in the Great Hall Of The People in Tiananmen Square, Beijing. I was really looking forward to this historic occasion. I'd seen the Great Hall on TV when Mao Tse Tung ruled the country, and wondered what it would be like inside.

Maurice was the co-promoter and had travelled out earlier. On the evening before the opening performance, he and I went to the venue to check things over. It took an age to get inside as, apparently, there'd been a crisis earlier. The Irish technicians had built the set over a few days, but some flunky insisted it must come down as a meeting was scheduled to take place. This was a serious problem, as there wouldn't be enough time to take the set and sound system down and rebuild it in time for the performance the following night.

Then came a Chinese solution to an Irish problem. Within 45 minutes, two trucks pulled up with 50 men who hauled out the equipment and obediently sat in the trucks while the meeting took place. They then hauled the gear back in. We learned later that a phone call to the local prison had sourced the 50 men in the trucks. No negotiations necessary!

The opening night was such a memorable occasion. I attended with Irish journalist Sam Smyth and Australian promoter Gary van Egmond. Gary had previously co-promoted, with Maurice, a tremendously successful *Riverdance* tour in Australia. He also enjoyed a long-term relationship with Australian supergroup AC/DC and promoted their shows all over Asia for over 30 years.

While waiting in the lobby, we noticed a line of men marching directly into the auditorium. There must have been 100 of them, dressed identically in grey suits, white shirts, and red ties. Weirdly, they were exactly the same height and had the same features, the nearest thing to cloning I've ever seen. It turned out they were Secret Service guys, and, like human shields, they occupied the outside seats on either end of the rows where the dignitaries were seated.

I was amused at other aspects of the set-up. The Great Hall was designed for Government business and has about 10,000 seats. Although built in 1959, the décor seemed like something from the early Roman era, with large marble columns and colourful carpets adorning the vast spaces. There was a small writing shelf and an ink-well in front of each seat, not unlike a college lecture auditorium.

It was a privilege to see this great Irish show totally enchant a Chinese audience in such a prestigious venue. Indeed, rapturous applause resounded all through the show. Afterwards, we attended a reception in the inner sanctum upstairs. At the back of the reception room was a large marble throne, with two others each side, presumably designed for Mao and his senior people. Unfortunately, no cameras were allowed, so I couldn't take any photographs.

Over the next few days, I hit the tourist trail, including the Forbidden City, Silk Market and the Great Wall. I wasn't aware that the cast of *Riverdance* were due at the Great Wall to dance there, but as they didn't have the required permits, the plan was abandoned. However, you can't underestimate the Irish. The cast arrived with their costumes under their coats, and before anyone could shout the Chinese equivalent of "stop", fiddles and concertinas were produced. And that's how a *Riverdance* flashmob performed on the Great Wall of China and I was lucky enough to witness the wonderful occasion.

Shanghai

The show then moved to Shanghai. Maurice, Sam, Gary and I reckoned a flight would be boring, and went by train. Whereas to-day's high-speed bullet trains have reduced the trip to less than five hours, in 2003 it was a 14-hour overnight journey. We decided to take no chances and bring our own food. We were staying at The Ritz Carlton in Beijing, and they prepared food for our evening dinner and breakfast the following morning. Indeed they prepared enough to feed the whole train. As I was leaving, the concierge gave me some plastic cable ties. Puzzled, I asked about them. *"In addition to locking your door while you sleep, you must secure the handles with these cable ties."* Useful, but not exactly comforting news.

Beijing Central Station is massive. The crowd was like one coming out of a football stadium, tens of thousands of commuters hustling and bustling about. The trip was comparatively uneventful, and we had our own sleeping compartments. Sometime around 4am the train stopped at a grim place in the middle of nowhere, while vendors stood outside in freezing cold trying to sell food and trinkets. An extremely hard life.

Shanghai was amazing. As Gary knew the ropes, we had dinner on the first night at M on the Bund Restaurant. The food was average, but the view from the balcony was just marvellous. The following day, Sam and I took a trip down the river. The level of river traffic was extraordinary, with every conceivable vessel, from huge tankers to small junks, churning up and down 24 hours a day. I've never seen so many skyscrapers in a city. Indeed, the scale of everything was mind-blowing.

I have one unusual memory from that trip. While breakfasting at the hotel, my attention was drawn to an elderly gentleman working on his laptop at a table opposite me. In the same moment, through the window I spotted a guy on a bicycle. He must have been carrying the entire contents of his house on the back of the bicycle. I'd caught the old and the new China in one memorable scene.

If the Beijing audience for *Riverdance* was enthusiastic, it was nothing compared to the Shanghai reaction. This was pure rock 'n roll. Every piece received thunderous applause, and there were loud shouts of encouragement for the cast throughout the show. The director, John McColgan, had placed screens on either side of the stage showing the storyline in Cantonese so everybody could follow the story.

This was a tremendous trip, one of the best.

EVP Europe

Within a year of assuming responsibility for UK and Ireland, I was asked to run Ticketmaster's European business. I was in Barcelona for a break with Eileen and sitting on a bench in Las Ramblas when John Pleasants called me. We concluded the very generous arrangements in less than 10 minutes. I'd be Executive Vice-President of Europe and also included in the Global Executive Management Team based on Sunset Boulevard, West Hollywood.

Ticketmaster had been acquiring ticketing companies in other European markets, and it was becoming difficult to manage from Los Angeles, especially with the time differences, 8 hours in UK/Ireland, 9/10 hours elsewhere in Europe. Business was over for the day in Europe but just starting in Los Angeles, and we couldn't really grow the business without dealing with that issue.

Some of the European team were already in place. Jim Warner was our corporate lawyer. Our other lawyer, Bruce Geyer looked after contracts. Paul la Fontaine was responsible for Business Development with Steve Machin. Joe Carino had just arrived from the US, to take responsibility for finance. Tim Chambers was running Ticketweb, a UK Internet company we'd bought. He had a long history in the entertainment business, from running venues to tour managing artists. Like myself, he'd been down some dark alleys late at night.

COO Sean Moriarty called me one evening and said that we were completely under-resourced in the technology department, but that the company was making a major investment in this area. He was on the look-out for a top-class Chief Technology Officer (CTO) to help me build the business. This was welcome news.

At the 2004 Ticketmaster conference in Las Vegas, Sean introduced me to Selina Tobaccowala who would lead the new technology team in London. We hit it off straight away. Selina had graduated from Stanford University and been one of the founders of the company Evite. Diller's IAC purchased Evite, and Selina became part of Sean's technology team. I was delighted to have her on the European team, and she re-located to London shortly afterwards.

During the closing night party at The Palms Hotel, I watched from the balcony as flights descended into McCarron Airport. It was some sight, with a plane arriving every 60 seconds. But I couldn't help thinking that every minute at least 150 visitors came to the casinos to be dispatched (mostly) empty-handed four days later.

The London office on Leicester Square was bursting at the seams, but, luckily, we acquired another floor in the same building. The UK team remained on the second floor, and we created space for the European team on the fourth floor. Selina was aggressively hiring staff, and the technology team also moved her team to the fourth floor. Some of our US colleagues re-located to London too, including Scott Boecker, Briget Krull, Lauren Mugglebee, and Kevin Schmidt, all dedicated and focused for the cause.

Ticketweb enjoyed a fantastic growth rate. Clients loved Ticketweb because it was NOT Ticketmaster. Instead, it was mainly a self-service model, ideal for small venues and clubs. We also owned the software company Synchro Systems, with over 80 staff based in Stoke-on-Trent. Synchro specialised in sports technology, and was used by the majority of top clubs, including Manchester United, Arsenal and Glasgow Celtic. Manchester United always sold out their games, so hardly any tickets went on sale to the public, but we managed their season ticket clients via Synchro. In addition to the season ticket fans at Arsenal, we managed the allocations for their 200,000 members. A certain allocation was put aside so these members could purchase maybe 2-3 games throughout the season.

We opened an extensive call centre in Manchester. Although the Internet was growing rapidly, many customers, especially theatregoers, still preferred to book by phone. The call centre was also a support resource for those buying on the Internet. In the early days of the Internet, customers were unsure if they'd followed instructions properly, and would call to check if everything had gone through. We had a management team looking after promoters and venues in the north-west, another huge market for us. In the late 1990s we acquired the ticketing platform Microflex, whose development team was based in Quebec City, Canada, and this system was used mostly on mainland Europe. Selina also had the responsibility of looking after all technology platforms, including Microflex in Quebec.

Each ticket bought from Ticketmaster anywhere in Europe generates a considerable amount of work behind the scenes, almost like a massive plumbing network. Somebody in London, Manchester, Copenhagen, Gothenburg, and Quebec City plays a part in producing each ticket, and there are warehouses full of servers in East London and Amsterdam.

Printing a ticket is one thing, but managing the money is a different matter. When an event organiser puts an event on sale, each ticket has to be reconciled with cash, and this has to be managed over different platforms and maybe in many currencies at the same time. Joe Carino managed all cash traffic with his own finance team. Selina oversaw hundreds of staff managing all aspects of these transactions in multiple currencies, with varying local VAT rates and languages. It was a huge responsibility.

The next few years were simply wonderful. The team was united, and the office atmosphere was terrific. Paul and Steve would acquire ticketing companies across Europe, and my team would take over the running of these companies. We had a fantastic run (with one failure, which I'll come to later) and the team delivered in spades. Some business leaders and football coaches stifle talent by ruling with fear and paranoia, but I believe it's much better to allow people to express themselves without having to worry about making mistakes or wrong decisions. Of course we had some disagreements, and some lively discussions in our boardroom on what direction to take, but they were always constructive.

Tim Chambers was particularly vocal at times, but I recognised his vast knowledge of the European ticketing business, and very much valued his contribution. As in soccer, I believe every team needs a 'redhead', somebody with attitude in the middle of the park disrupting the flow and providing the platform to move forward. I'd hate to work in an environment where everybody nodded at the leader. Tim was our redhead, and despite some disagreements we never fell out, and he's still a good friend today.

I figured that it would be best for each market to retain its 'local' dimension. As with our business in Ireland, each market usually moulded it business to the requirements of local clients. We acknowledged that promoters in one country did things completely differently to those in another.

These different approaches proved a huge challenge for the product and development people. It was not very cost effective, but it had to be done. The Danish Opera might request a special software programme that would not suit the Finlandia Opera House in Helsinki. It was different in the US, where we could roll out a new piece of software right across the entire market, as what worked in Boston generally worked in Seattle. But not having this luxury in Europe simply made the challenge all the more enjoyable.

IAC Conference

Inter Active Corporation (IAC) owned Ticketmaster, and I attended my first IAC conference in 2004 in Laguna Beach, California. Diller always held his retreats in luxurious resorts, and the Montage Hotel was no exception. It stood on the cliffs overlooking the Pacific, a stunning location. By now, Diller had acquired or founded a stack of companies, and I think almost 24 of them attended the conference, including Ticketmaster, Ask.com, Match.com, (the successful on-line dating company), Lending Tree, Vimeo, Evite.com, Citysearch.com, Real Estate. com among many others. About 400 delegates attended, including about 30 from Ticketmaster. I found the experience most valuable, as the leaders of these companies made presentations from which I picked up valuable information. Diller coldly questioned each leader about success/failures. Nobody was spared, but that was ok too.

Diller's next two "retreats" were held in Miami and Santa Barbara. The IAC Board was a who's who of highly successful US companies, and one year most of the Board attended. Don Graham, owner of The Washington Post, Michael Eisner, former CEO if Disney Corporation, Jack Welsh, former CEO of General Electric, Don Keough, former COO of Coca Cola, all participated. The legendary Welsh had lead General Electric for decades, his brutal regime producing stunning results. He believed you should fire the lowest performing 10% of the workforce every year. As you can imagine, nobody wanted to be in his lowest 10%.

I particularly remember the speech given by Don Keough. He explained that to demonstrate specific points to university students, he'd bring them to a nearby river. He'd throw a stick in the water and they'd observe it flow immediately downstream. He'd then throw a stick way upstream and watch it meander from upstream. The point he was making to the students (and to the room) was, you can't do anything about the past or what's gone downstream. Forget about mistakes and bad decisions, but learn from them. Concentrate on what is coming into view, and avail of the opportunities coming from upstream. This reminded me of my refereeing career. No point dwelling on a mistake, it can't be undone, get on with the game.

During another fascinating section of the Miami conference, Diller arranged for five students aged between 14 and 19 to come on stage. A moderator posed a number of questions to them about trends and how they managed their time. It turned out they all multi-tasked, texting, e-mailing, talking to friends on the phone, watching TV, studying, many at the same time. Regrettably, perhaps, I've become like this myself, apart from the studying!

The moderator then asked them *"what was the last CD you bought?"* Most looked at one another and shrugged their shoulders. Only one, the oldest, had bought a CD in the previous six months, as kids were now mostly downloading music and listening to live streaming. I knew then that traditional record industry was doomed.

Problem in Finland

Eileen and I travelled to Australia in late 2005 to visit Clodagh, stopping off in Shanghai for four days. We'd not been with our daughter for a few years, and were looking forward to seeing how she was enjoying life in Sydney. We loved Sydney, a vibrant city in which nearly everybody has access to water. I spent a day in Melbourne, as Maria O'Connor had invited me to the Ireland v Australia Rules game in the Telstra Stadium. I also visited the Ticketmaster office. I found a distinct difference in culture between Melbourne and Sydney. Melbourne is much more formal and more business-orientated. While staff in Sydney wear flip-flops and t-shirts, it's mostly shirts and ties in Melbourne. I even had to borrow a tie to gain admission to the hospitality section of the Melbourne stadium.

Eileen and I returned to Melbourne a few days later as guests of Maria at the Melbourne Cup, one of the great days in the global horse racing calendar. Over 100,000 people attend the Flemington Racecourse on the first Tuesday of November each year, and all dressed up to the nines.

When I got back to our hotel after the races, I noticed an e-mail from Los Angeles asking me to participate in an urgent telephone conference call at 9am PST (4am in Melbourne). This must be serious, I thought. It was. Jim Warner and Joe Carino were on the London call with a roomful of people in LA. Joe had discovered discrepancies during a routine inspection of the books, and it seemed the MD of our business in Finland had committed a number of serious breaches. We had to take action. This was a very disappointing development, as we'd bought the Finland business less than a year earlier. Eileen and I had been planning to leave for home the following evening, stopping off for a few days shopping in Dubai. I agreed with the Executive in LA that waiting an extra few days would not make much difference, and I'd visit Helsinki five days later.

Eileen and I parted ways at Heathrow, she continuing on to Dublin and I to Helsinki. I hooked up with Jim Warner, and had a meeting with the MD. It was not a pleasant encounter. After a number of meetings with our local lawyers in Helsinki, we removed him. Mats Brandt, our MD in Sweden, was a tremendous help and found a short-term replacement until we could recruit a new permanent MD.

Although we owned the company, called Lippupalvelu, we hadn't rebranded as Ticketmaster. Lippu is Finnish for ticket, and the brand was renowned all over Finland, so why change it? Jim, myself and the replacement, Seppo (I can't remember his surname) arrived at the office early the following morning to inform the staff of developments. They were shocked, and some traumatised. This was understandable, as the departing MD was a dominant type who had done well building up the company which had been formed in 1946.

This was bound to be a very difficult period for the staff, and I could understand what was going through their minds. Is my job safe? What'll happen next? What will clients say? Although most of the staff spoke English, Seppo translated my speech into Finnish. I gave a clear undertaking that I'd visit them every week for as long as it took to stabilise the difficult situation we were in. I also emphasised that our head office in Los Angeles was fully supportive of our actions, and there was absolutely no threat to job security. There was no way we would let the business suffer.

I believed it was important to follow through on the promises I'd made, so for 11 successive weeks I worked out of the Helsinki office. Every week I'd leave home in Rosses Point around 5am on Monday morning and work from the Dublin office during the day dealing with routine European business. I'd fly out on the 6.30pm flight to Copenhagen, and after a 90-minute layover take a 90-minute flight to Helsinki, arriving in my hotel around 2.30am local time. Boy was it cold in Helsinki that winter. It was not unusual for the temperature to hit 20 degrees or more below, with a further wind chill blowing from the Russian tundra, so the hot reindeer soup was very welcome!

Joe Carino was a terrific help, spending a lot of time in the Helsinki office working on a new financial plan. Some of our clients suspected we were a major global corporation bullying our way around Europe and firing local employees. I visited them and re-assured them that I was a small player in Ireland, that Ticketmaster treated me extremely well and there was nothing to fear. Time, and face-to-face conversations, can be great healers, and we lost no clients during this period. The local staff were brilliant too, and the unpleasant episode was soon behind us.

We hired Kimmo Rannisto as Managing Director, a wise appointment. Kimmo took control immediately, and within a few weeks I was able to hand over completely to him and reduce my visits to once a month. Kimmo had a great personality, and impressively took our business to the next level. He left after four years to become Managing Director of Heineken Finland, and later landed his dream job as CEO of the Finnish Ice Hockey Association. Ice Hockey is the national sport, and Kimmo was an ex-player. I continue to stay in touch with this great guy.

Despite much reflection, I've never understood why the previous MD had acted so disappointingly. He was a very good operator, street wise, smart, ideal for the ticketing industry. He had a promising future with Ticketmaster and we'd discussed expanding into Estonia and other Baltic countries that were only a few hours away by ferry or 20 minutes by helicopter One summer we'd sold over 25,000 tickets in Finland for a Metallica concert in Tallinn, Estonia's capital. My own theory as to why he fell off the wagon is that he simply became star-struck. Within a few weeks of our purchase of Lippupalvelu, we'd had our conference in Las Vegas, and he'd seen the huge numbers and caught the excitement of a big corporation. Still, no excuses.

Governments come gunning

And there was more trouble up ahead, as within six months we were hit with three "competition" investigations. One morning Peter van Ruivjen, Managing Director of our business in Holland, called me. Investigators from the NL Competition Authority had made a dawn raid on our offices in The Hague. I told him not to leave the premises, sit tight, say nothing, and call our lawyers in Holland and Jim Warner in our London office. *"I've already done so"*, Peter told me. The investigators also raided Mojo, Holland's Number I promoter company.

I knew this would be painful. Ticket Service, a Ticketmaster company, was by far the market leader in Holland, and Mojo the largest promoting company. I guessed what the authorities were looking for, assuming collusion between the market leaders in each genre. So the investigators sought every letter, e-mail, memo between the two companies over the previous years, an enormous disruption for our staff and our business on top of our normal day-to-day activities.

I happened to be there when, within a month, they hit our office in Dublin. The Irish Competition Authority was going down the same path. I'd read various articles in the newspapers where uninformed reporters talked about 'cosy cartels' and collusion between promoters and Ticketmaster. There's no question we dominated the market, and two promoters, MCD and Aiken Promotions, had the lion's share of the promoting business. So the Competition Authority must have been reading the newspaper articles, and assumed it was all true.

The lead investigator made it clear they were running a full investigation. He was a smug type, and from the smirk on his face I could see he was salivating at the prospects of a prosecution. I discussed the problem with Jim Warner. I was absolutely sure we'd done nothing untoward and had nothing to worry about. But, again, it'd be a huge distraction to our business. Governments have all the time in the world to send out reams of paper, and they really excelled themselves in our case. We hired a blue chip firm of lawyers with offices in Dublin and Brussels, as well as forensic accountants, to assist with our case.

Just as in Holland, they wanted every e-mail, letter, memo and contract between Ticketmaster Ireland and MCD and Aikens. It was exhausting. If the Competition Authority sent 100 pages of questions, we sent 200 pages of answers, on and on for over 12 months. Convinced we were involved in price fixing, they wouldn't give up.

Separately, Eamonn and I were summoned to the Competition Authority for question-and-answer sessions over two days. They wouldn't allow our in-house lawyer Jim Warner to attend. This was a bizarre decision, as they would allow the outside lawyer to monitor proceedings. I was up first. Four members of the Competition Authority, including the Deputy Chairman, sat at the top of the table, our lawyer and I at the other end. It was clear from the start that they'd been completely on the wrong track for 12 months, and their assumption that Ticketmaster controlled everything was nonsense. The sessions became tetchy at times, but, to the credit of the Deputy Chairman, he was prepared to listen to our points.

I drew a chart of the procedure from the point when an artist decides to go on tour to the day tickets go on sale. In reality, the ticketing company is on the bottom of the food chain. The artist's agent contacts the promoters and invites bids for the concert, so a promoter in Norway or Germany competes with a promoter in Ireland, where MCD and Aiken Promotions are fierce rivals. The promoter has to assess what he can bid for an artist, and the agent can accept or refuse. It's only after the promoter's bid is accepted that the ticketing comes in. We never have anything to do with fixing the prices, and the same with promoters. As I outlined the scenario, the blood was draining from their faces.

Eamonn was in for questioning the following day. I recently read the transcript of his testimony, and it's one of the funniest pieces I've read for years. He had them tied in knots, and it was clear they'd no idea what he was talking about. I guess they knew the game was up, and they were simply trying to see if there were any major differences in our testimonies.

We underwent the same type of investigation in Sweden at the same time. However it didn't last as long before the case folded. We had to make some concessions to the Competition authority in Holland, but nothing serious, and business continued as normal. Jim Warner was planning to return to the US to work with Diller's Home Shopping Network when he was told we were in the clear in Ireland and there would be no further proceedings. Before he left for Florida he sent me a plaque containing excerpts from the Competition Authority closing letter.

"The Competition Authority has concluded that the market for outsourced ticketing services results in certain benefits to end consumers"
Lower prices for ticketing services
Greater choice and variety of events
Easier and faster access to tickets.

It was a very sweet victory, but just as one Irish Government investigation closed, we had to take on the Revenue. It started in 1998, when the Revenue said we weren't accounting correctly for Value Added Tax. VAT is a minefield, and it can be interpreted in a variety of ways. We were absolutely sure our books were correct, but Revenue thought otherwise, and we were hit with a monster tax bill. We appealed the assessment, but it took seven years before it came before the Appeals Commissioner. Again, we hired the best barrister in the country, one who'd never lost a tax case either in Ireland or in Europe.

I faced a tough questioning session lasting over five hours. I thought the Revenue legal team had been very poorly briefed, despite having seven years to prepare, and we won the case hands down. This episode was entirely avoidable. Ireland was the only country in Europe that didn't apply VAT on certain events, but that was the way the VAT law was written. The promoters had no problem applying VAT to tickets, and within three months of the verdict the Revenue called all the stakeholders for a meeting and a new VAT arrangement was agreed. Rather than pursuing us for seven years Revenue should have focused on their own flaws. Instead, they followed a stupid strategy, and cost the Exchequer a fortune.

The Competition Authority investigation and the VAT debacle cost Ticketmaster Ireland over €500,000 in fees. Even though we won both cases, we had to pay our own costs. We were fortunate, in that we had the resources, but what happens the small guy who doesn't? Governments can be very nasty when they're gunning for you.

Germany

We'd been looking for an opportunity to enter the German market for some time. It's an enormous market, 80m people and a thriving economy. Our preference was to acquire the market leader in the ticketing sector, or a strong Number 2. But CTS Eventim, the market leader, wasn't available. Klaus Peter Schulenberg was their Chairman and CEO in the mid-1990s, and he brought the company to the stock market in 2000. He'd acquired a controlling interest in some of the top promoter companies, so by the time Ticketmaster started looking at Germany, he'd a tight grip on the market.

But Ticket Online was a strong Number 2, and up for sale, so Paul and Steve started negotiating, and we very nearly crossed the line. From my memory, we were at €14m and the vendors wanted another €1m. Diller and his deal guy Victor Kaufman balked at the extra million, and we walked away. It proved a very expensive €1m. Ticket Online was sold to Stage Entertainment, who rebranded the company as See Tickets, Germany. See Tickets sold the company to CTS for a whopping €140m in 2010.

We then turned our attention to another ticketing company called Kartenhaus in Hamburg. This was a small operation owned by Gudrun 'Goodie' Barthel Chumee, and run by Goodie, her boyfriend Nils and an Italian IT guy called Luca.

We purchased Kartenhaus, and also did a deal with DEAG, a promoting company in Berlin whereby DEAG would take a small stake in Ticketmaster Germany in return for providing tickets from the DEAG stable of promoters. On paper, the model made sense, but it never worked.

I mentioned earlier that we had one failure and this was it. Our plan was to install the Ticketmaster system and attack the market. Hindsight is wonderful, but we should never have bought Kartenhaus because it was too small for our needs. I also have to take responsibility for not researching the market enough, and we installed the wrong ticketing system. The Microflex system we used in Holland and the Nordic countries would have been much more suitable for the German market. CTS and Ticket Online had a terrific system in place for Germany, and everybody liked the way those models worked. We tried to introduce a different model, and it was doomed to fail.

The Kartenhaus office was a madhouse. I liked Goodie, but she was very highly strung, and a bunch of our team descending on the office didn't help. She had a very nice, simple business until we arrived, and caused her a lot of stress. It didn't help that the office was unsuitable, a small space, three rooms crammed with staff. So to grow the business, we'd have to move, and found very nice offices just across the road.

It would take a year to install a new ticketing system, a very stressful time for everybody. The German staff really didn't buy into the plan. They had a point, as we didn't have the right system for the market, yet they couldn't articulate what was required. Meanwhile, Selina's technical staff in London were driven to distraction. Despite operating well with the local staff in each market in 10 countries, we could see Germany was going to be a challenge.

Peter Schwenkow, the CEO of DEAG, was expecting instant success from his deal with Ticketmaster. He was a colourful but likeable character in a strange sort of way. DEAG at one time was the largest promoter in Germany, but had hit a few rocks, and it didn't help when CTS Eventim became market leader. I understood Peter's frustration. He was expecting the big Ticketmaster machine to steamroll into Germany and take on CTS Eventim, but it wasn't going to happen.

While we were endeavouring to sort out the technology, I tried to land a few big clients so that we could at least be seen to be making headway in the market. The contract for the Bundesliga soccer team Hertha Berlin was up for renewal, and we tried hard to get it. Hertha played at the Olympic Stadium, the iconic venue built for the 1936 Olympic Games. Tim Chambers, Selina, Goodie and I made the presentation to Hertha's executive team. We played a blinder, and walked out with the deal. But now we had to deliver.

The German Bundesliga is probably the best run sports league in the world, with a strict set of regulations for each team, including electronic entry to venues. We had to build the Olympic Stadium seating plan, sell the tickets, and ensure the bar codes on the tickets were compatible with the venue's turnstiles. Everything was progressing fine, until three weeks before the opening day of the season, when we found that the engineer for the turnstile software system had gone on holidays, and wouldn't return until a few days before the game. This had the potential to be an utter disaster, so Selina and her team decamped to Berlin for the final week. Fifteen minutes before the gates were due to open, we got the turnstiles working. It was close, far too close for comfort.

Over 53,000 turned up, Hertha's highest opening day attendance for 10 years, and they beat Stuttgart 3-0. After the game I was introduced to the Chairman of Stuttgart Football Club who said he visited Ireland quite a lot. I asked him what part of Ireland. *"You probably don't know where it is, it's called Ransboro in Sligo. My sister lives in an old church there"*. It's a small world. I can see Ransboro old church from our kitchen, just across the bay.

We were requested to make a presentation for 1899 Hoffenheim, another soccer club in Bad Wurttemberg. It looked very promising. 1899 Hoffenheim had formed as a village team, and was owned by Dietmar Hopp, the billionaire owner of the global software giant SAP. Dietmar had played for the team, and his ambition now was to get them into the Bundesliga. When we arrived at SAP for the presentation, the team was fourth in the Division 2, and confident they'd win promotion.

SAP headquarters was a luxurious campus built around about 10 stunning buildings. We enjoyed a fabulous lunch in the executive boardroom, and proceeded to the presentation for which they wheeled out all the top executives of the club, including the General Manager, Coach and Sponsorship person. There was a sting at the end. Hoffenheim was prepared to award the ticketing contract to us, but they also wanted Ticketmaster to take up the naming rights of their almost-completed new stadium. They put a slide on the screen super-imposing our logo on the stadium plan. It looked fabulous, but they were looking for €5m per season for four years for the naming rights. We had to walk away. We were bleeding enough in Germany, and this deal was too expensive. Hoffenheim did gain promotion at the end of the season, and they still do very well in the Bundesliga.

Goodie was drowning and needed help. I tried to hire Klaus Zemke, who'd recently finished with Ticket Online, but he had a strict non-compete agreement and was off limits. We hired a number of people who didn't work out. Everywhere we turned in Germany we got killed by CTS Eventim and Ticket Online. It's the way the game is played. I'd have done the same myself, never giving the opposition a chance.

After our lawyer Jim Warner moved to Florida, Tom McLean from Lending Tree replaced him and fitted into the European team seamlessly. We had a further crisis in Germany when the old Kartenhaus system was hacked and customer data was stolen. It was a major embarrassment. We decided to deal with it full on and I spent the best part of a week being interviewed by the German media. We must have dealt with it correctly, as the story went away very quickly. No doubt the opposition were delighted with our embarrassment.

We eventually got Klaus Zempke on board after his non-compete expired. Goodie decided to move on, and relocated to a home she had in Thailand. Klaus completely revamped the company and moved the headquarters to Berlin. The last I heard was that Ticketmaster Germany had turned the corner, with, I hope, better times ahead, although it'll still be a huge challenge to make headway against CTS Eventim.

One day I noticed a new German name over the door of Walmart's big store near our office. Relatively few know that the largest retailer in the world couldn't make their model work in Germany, and pulled out of the market. Later, the CEO of Kellogg's Europe told me that Kellogg's also pulled out of Germany for the same reasons. It still doesn't make me feel any better! *Lesson: Never enter a market while small and try to take on Goliath....it cannot work.*

On a footnote, I recently met Klaus Peter Schulenberg, the CEO of CTS Eventim, in London. He'd entered the UK market and paid a high price for the Manchester, Newcastle and Leeds arena contracts. He'd also invested in a joint venture with AEG, acquiring the Hammersmith Apollo, now called Eventim Apollo. But I believe he made the exact same mistake in the UK we'd made in Germany. The CTS Eventim brand meant nothing in the UK. It's too small, and they have difficulty selling tickets. Klaus Peter thought they'd make it work, and conceded he'd have a tough challenge in the UK, unless he acquires a major company.

The Passing of Jim Aiken

As a great horse racing fan, Jim Aiken had for years suggested I get involved in a horse syndicate. He said we'd have great fun and enjoy visits to the racetracks. It was not a top priority with me, but I knew Eileen would like the adventure as she loved horses. Jim and Maurice were acquainted with horse breeder Mike Watt who had a horse in France called Albanov that he was bringing back to Ireland. We did a deal with Mike, who also became part of the syndicate of five that included Pearse Farrell, and Albanov was placed with well-known trainer Jessica Harrington.

Jim, Eileen and I attended a race meeting in Naas on January 20, 2007. We'd had a few seconds and thirds in previous meetings, but that day Albanov produced the syndicate's first win. We normally would've gone for a meal afterwards, but Jim said he had 'flu symptoms and returned to Belfast.

Unfortunately, it was more than a 'flu. Within a few weeks he was diagnosed with a terminal illness and given only weeks to live. It was hard to get my head around this terrible news. I was truly dreading the trip to Belfast to say goodbye. It was a very difficult conversation, but it couldn't last too long as hundreds of people were calling to see him. Jim passed away on February 28, 2007, only about five weeks after our great day at Naas. He was just 74.

Jim's buried in the family plot in Jonesboro, Co Armagh, and anytime I drive to Belfast I visit the graveyard to pay my respects. In addition to being one of the great promoters in the business, he was a wonderful man in all respects, and I reflected on his kindness in guiding my band out of Belfast back in 1969. Nor could I ever forget his generosity in providing funds for Ticketshop in a time of crisis. I'll always treasure his advice. He'd say that a jar of honey is much sweeter than a jar of vinegar. He reasoned that you can achieve much more by being strong, reasonable and pragmatic, than being bitter and argumentative. It doesn't mean that you have to be weak in business, but you don't have to be a jerk either. Wise words indeed.

Simone

There was great joy in the Higgins and O'Reilly families when Melanie and Sean announced they were expecting a baby. Eileen travelled to Stroudsburg for the birth, with me to follow. I was alone in my office in London when Eileen called on September 3, 2008 around 8.20pm to say that baby Simone had arrived, and both mother and daughter were fine. Within a few minutes, Sean e-mailed a photograph. It was a very emotional experience, as everybody had gone home and I'd nobody with whom to share the good news. But, thanks to technology, I circulated the photograph to family and friends around the world. It was mid-morning in Sydney when a thrilled Clodagh knew she'd become a new auntie.

It would be fair to say our lives have changed completely since Simone arrived. Over the next few years, Eileen spent two weeks in the US every 6-8 weeks. It was a gruelling schedule, but she loved every minute of the experience, apart from saying tearful goodbyes at Newark Airport. I was over and back to Los Angeles quite often, and stopped in Stroudsburg on the way home.

As I write this, Simone is now almost 7 and living in Sligo, as Sean and Melanie returned to live here some years ago. Being a grandparent is wonderful, and Simone has brought so much happiness to all our families.

Irving Azoff

Sometime around 2007, Irving Azoff arrived on the Ticketmaster scene. The legendary Irving is one of the most powerful people in the music business. He began, like many music industry people did, by booking bands in college. He had attended the University of Illinois before moving to Los Angeles in 1970 where he managed singer/songwriter Dan Fogelberg out of David Geffen's management office. Los Angeles was then a hotbed for artists. The Eagles had recently formed, with Glen Frey and Don Henley from Linda Ronstadt's backing band. The Eagles were managed by Geffen who also founded Asylum Records which released Eagles' records.

However, the band felt that Geffen would have a conflict of interest, and Geffen suggested Irving as manager. That was in 1972, and Irving is still their manager. The Eagles enjoyed a remarkable decade between 1972–1982, a period the record business was at its height, and the band sold over 100 million albums, including *Hotel California, The Long Run,* and *Eagles Greatest Hits.*

The band broke up around 1981, burned out through the excesses of touring and creating music. Irving went on to run MCA Records for 10 years and later moved to Warner Brothers where he set up Giant Records. But The Eagles' band members were constantly being asked when they'd reform, to which their answer was usually either *"when hell freezes over"*, or *"ask*

Irving". So, that explains why, when the band reformed in 1994, their new album was titled *When Hell Freezes Over*. If anything, their success over the two decades from 1994 onwards even surpassed the 1970s. In between, ticket prices had shot through the roof and Irving squeezed every last dollar on behalf of the band. Today, The Eagles rarely go out on the road for less than $1m per show. Great money if you can get it. Irving also managed such other world-class artists as Van Halen, Christina Aguilera, Jimmy Buffet, Steely Dan, Neil Diamond and more. He and his partner Howard Kauffman set up Frontline Management as an umbrella operation for some of the top artist managers in the world. By the time Irving showed up on the Ticketmaster radar, Frontline was an extremely successful company with 70 managers representing over 200 artists.

Artist management is a strange business. People will find it hard to comprehend that many of the top artists have no written contracts with their managers. It's a trust arrangement that either works or doesn't, and some artists have worked with the same manager for over 40 years without a contract. Although not an artist/management deal as such, one of most enduring 'contracts' I've heard of is between singer Frankie Valli and his bandmate, songwriter Bob Gaudio. As teenagers in the late 1950s they 'signed' what's often called a New Jersey contract, basically a handshake, and it's still in place. There are endless other similar arrangements between artists and managers.

Around 2006, Irving had a chat with Ticketmaster Chairman, Terry Barnes, and mentioned he was selling a piece of Frontline to the promoter group Live Nation. The paperwork, though not signed, was in place. It made a lot of sense. Irving had over 200 artists, so a deal with the largest promoters in the world was mutually beneficial. In an audacious move, Terry contacted Barry Diller and argued that if the deal was mutually beneficial to Live Nation/Frontline, it could be equally good, or even better, with Ticketmaster. Over a weekend Diller and the Ticketmaster team negotiated a deal with Irving who basically left Live Nation CEO Michael Rapino at the altar, and sold

30% of Frontline to Diller. We didn't know that that was the start of the most cunning plan of all cunning plans. Irving the fox, was now in the Ticketmaster chicken coop. When I opened Star Records in 1974, my first sale was *Desperado*, The Eagles LP. Now, almost 35 years later, The Eagles' manager had the destiny of Ticketmaster in his hands.

Wonderful years

The European business was growing at an impressive rate year on year, despite us operating at a loss in Germany. Our footprint across Europe was extensive, with clients from eastern Turkey to the Arctic Circle and down to southern Spain. Most members of the public associate Ticketmaster with musical concerts, but we sold a diverse range of events. We handled ferry tickets in Sweden, helicopter trips between Helsinki and Tallinn, a sheepshead festival in Norway's Arctic Circle, a wrestling festival in Turkey that has taken place continuously for over 500 years, and entry to the Alhambra in Granada. The list is enormous.

We also sold tickets for most of the major soccer clubs in Turkey, including Galatasaray, Fenerbache and Besiktas. Their fans are passionate but extremely troublesome, and we faced major challenges selling tickets for local derbies, at which there would invariably be riots and the police would come down heavy. Hardly a season went by without some clubs being fined and being forced to play games in empty stadiums. So we lost considerable income from the fans' transgressions.

The Nou Camp in Barcelona is one of the most iconic stadiums in the world. Season tickets are sold out every season and often handed down in families to the next generation. However, not everybody attends games against weaker teams, so we negotiated to resell the tickets on behalf of the seat-holder who would split the proceeds with the club.

The box office manager told us about a scam involving club staff. When the club refurbished the stadium some years previously and were replacing the seats, they discovered an additional 300 seats in the stadium that were not on the ticket computer system. As the stadium capacity was over 90,000,

300 seats were not going to be noticed too easily if at all. The scam worked like this: A special gate allowed fans to pay cash to the turnstile operator and a colleague would direct the 'customer' to these 'special' seats. Taking a low rate of €20 a ticket, it must have been a nice little earner for years even if they only filled half the 'special' seats. Nobody knew how long the scam had lasted, probably for at least five years, and might never have been discovered if the club hadn't decided to replace the seats.

Clouds on the horizon

Our global business was doing wonderfully until mid-2007. Our global contract with Live Nation was due to expire in 2008, and, as per normal, re-negotiations started 12 months earlier. Diller wanted to play hardball, probably not the smartest tactic. Live Nation was our largest client with 15%-20% of our business worldwide, but was in very poor shape. From the time in the late 1990s when Sillerman put SFX together (renamed Live Nation), they'd never made money.

The promoter arm of the business was loss making, with the venues barely profitable. For one of the largest entertainment companies in the world, their performance was abysmal. They survived by selling assets, and it was only a matter of time before they ran out of cash. We suspected something was seriously wrong when they offered all their 24 theatres in the UK for sale. The theatres were actually very profitable, and Live Nation management in London were totally against this. But the theatres were bought by the Ambassador Theatre Group for close to £100m. Live Nation also sold some assets in the US. The promoting arm of Live Nation had to be funded from somewhere.

Around the same time Live Nation entered into new 360 deals with Madonna, U2, Jay-Z and other top acts. Such 360 deals involved Live Nation looking after publishing, record deals and touring, like a one-stop shop for the artists. They were enormous deals lasting maybe 10 years, and requiring substantial upfront payments to the artists. But it was noticeable that after the initial flurry of 360 deals, they soon stopped. They are highly speculative ventures, and only time will tell if they've paid off.

So in 2007 Live Nation CEO Michael Rapino had to make some crucial calls. He decided not to renew the Ticketmaster contract, and later announced he was entering into a new long-term deal with German company CTS Eventim to commence early in 2009. It was an unusual deal. Live Nation would license the CTS Eventim system for the US and run it themselves as Live Nation tickets. In Europe, they would sign an exclusive service contract with CTS Eventim, just as Ticketmaster did for the previous eight years. This would be a major loss to Ticketmaster, both in the US and Europe. In the Netherlands, Live Nation would have supplied 50% of our inventory and be impossible to replace. It was a lesser problem in some markets, but we had only a year to find a strategy for replacing the Live Nation tickets.

It was clear from the outset that the CTS Eventim license deal would never work in the US, and the system duly collapsed on its first major outing for a Phish concert on-sale. Everybody thinks ticketing is merely a question of pulling out a plug and putting it into another socket. As CTS Eventim developed its system to suit the German market, and it works extremely well there, Ticketmaster had developed our system to suit US clients. Over 30 years, layers of development went into the system to satisfy thousands of clients, including the major sports teams and arenas. It was naïve to think this infrastructure could be replaced overnight.

The Ticketmaster Annual conference took place in Pasadena, California in February, 2008. Although losing the Live Nation ticketing contract was a downer, the mood was generally buoyant, the company having enjoyed two knockout years in 2006 and 2007. So our team produced a three-year plan to aggressively grow our business. Using a large white board on the fourth floor office in Leicester Square, we'd spent months on the strategy in advance of the conference.

Without question, Tim Chambers knows most about every market in the ticketing industry in Europe and beyond, so he laid the groundwork for our plan. I loved those sessions, with various opinions offered and debated, maps drawn and redrawn, as we pushed each other for new ideas. Our lawyers Tom McLean and Bruce Geyer advised us on the dangers of anti-trust legislation in each market, as what's legal in Denmark might not be allowed in Sweden or Norway. Joe Carino and his finance team provided all the financial spread sheets, and Selina Tobaccowala gave her opinion on what technology and timeframe would be required for each market.

Tim and I presented our plan to the delegates in Pasadena, proposing that the company expand from 10 to between 16 and 20 countries in Europe over the next 3-5 years. In addition, there would be opportunities for consolidation in existing markets. The UK was our flagship in Europe, and Chris Edmonds had a blueprint for expansion there. Of course this would require a lot of capital, and we accepted that sometimes capital might not be available due to priorities elsewhere. Our job was to produce the plan, and then apply for the capital if and when the opportunity arose.

We were introduced to Irving who outlined how the artists in his Frontline Company would be a great asset to Ticketmaster, and as the most powerful person in the music business his words had a very positive impact. The company had recently purchased two secondary ticketing companies, Tickets Now in the US and Get Me In in the UK, so with all the stars aligned, the company was in great shape.

Brian Regan had joined from Expedia as Chief Financial Officer. His ancestors came from Cork and, in a unique twist, his father owned a New Jersey construction company called Sligo Construction. Sean Moriarty joked that an Irish Mafia ran Ticketmaster, with himself CEO, Brian CFO, Maria O'Connor CEO of Australia/New Zealand, and I managing Europe. We were confident we'd overcome the loss of the Live Nation tickets. Unfortunately, our optimism was misplaced.

Ticket Online

A few weeks before the Pasadena conference, I attended the Noorderslag Music Conference in Groningen, Holland where Sean was a guest speaker. A message from Bart von Shreik, CEO of Ticket Online enquired if we could meet for dinner that evening. This was strange. Was something up? We drove to Amsterdam and met Bart at the Intercontinental Hotel. I'd met him before and he was a decent guy.

Ticket Online was owned by Stage Entertainment, one of the largest producers of theatre shows in Europe with over 70 shows in production globally. It emerged from another TV production company Endemol, founded by Joop van den Ende and John de Moll. Endemol was massively successful, responsible for major global TV blockbusters such as *Big Brother* and *Deal Or No Deal*.

Bart was forthright. He said Stage Entertainment was concentrating on theatre productions and would be divesting Ticket Online in Germany and Holland. They were acquiring See Tickets in the UK, and would be co-operating closer with Andrew Lloyd Webber's Really Useful Company. This was totally unexpected, but logical. Bart said they'd sell the ticket company and then enter into a long-term ticketing contract for Stage content. It was basically a sale and lease back arrangement, perfect for Ticketmaster.

My brain was spinning, but I tried to appear calm. By acquiring Ticket Online, in a swoop we'd be a strong Number 2 in Germany, and replace the Live Nation content in Holland. Overnight it would solve the loss-making German operation problem as well as a problem in Holland. It was a clever play, and the sale would finance the purchase of See Tickets in the UK. We couldn't buy See Tickets as the Competition Authority would forbid the merger. Van den Ende and Lloyd Webber were cut from the same cloth, brilliant, eccentric, and hugely successful. Bart said he'd appoint a major bank to handle the process, and we'd be informed in due course.

Sean and I took a long walk along the canal to digest this. If ever a deal was perfect for Ticketmaster, this was it. Yes, we'd lost out to Ticket Online previously in Germany, and it would cost much more this time. But that didn't matter as I knew the numbers would stack up. As we walked, Sean took a call from Roger McNamee, CEO of the private equity company Elevation Partners, with whom Ticketmaster was in advanced discussions about investing in Ticketmaster. Elevation Partners had a track record in technology investments and had been early investors in Facebook. Bono of U2 was on the Board and on the advisory team. This would be a terrific fit for Ticketmaster. Unfortunately, Diller wouldn't do the deal because Elevation's terms were not acceptable, although I suspect it was more about ego.

Over the next few months we had various meetings with Stage. Sean and Terry Barnes attended one meeting which I remember most because of a 6am flight and two women talking all the way from Dublin to Amsterdam, head-wrecking stuff. Another meeting in Amsterdam was attended by Tim Chambers and Eric Korman from our Los Angeles office. At this meeting the body language from the Stage team was strange and Chairman Henk Kivits seemed rather nervous. Every 10 minutes he asked if we wanted tea or coffee and he drifted in and out of the room repeatedly. After the meeting, he gave us a tour of the spectacular Stage offices, adorned with beautiful pieces of art and situated on the Museumplein opposite the Van Gogh Museum.

With negotiations coming to a head the next meeting was in the JP Morgan bank building in New York. Our team included myself and Eric Korman, while Henk and Bart, plus their Chief Financial Officer, represented Stage Entertainment. Including bankers, lawyers and advisors, there must have been over 20 in the room. The fees must have been astronomical! Stage made it clear that we were not the only bidders, which was understandable. We'd long suspected that CTS Eventim would be somewhere in the mix.

We were advised to have our bid in place by August 1, but in September Eric told me we'd been unsuccessful. Parcom Capital, a subsidiary of ING, a major bank in Holland, had purchased a majority shareholding in Stage. This was very disappointing, but I'm sure Parcom paid a big price as our bid was very strong.

Good luck to Stage, who might have been able to persuade Parcom who knew little about the entertainment business.

The collapse of Lehman Brothers bank in September 2008 triggered a catastrophic set of events in the financial world everywhere. It created no immediate problem in the entertainment world, although some shows were taking longer to sell out. But while we ended 2008 in good shape, all was not well in Los Angeles, and, not unexpectedly, we were hearing mixed signals. Personally, I couldn't see how Diller and Irving could get along. No room could hold such big egos.

It's getting messy

Despite the uncertainty in the aftermath of the financial crisis, it was generally business as usual for Ticketmaster. We were going head to head with Billetlugen in Denmark, and then received word that Billetlugen was for sale. It was owned by an Icelandic bank, and Iceland was in meltdown. They wanted a quick sale, so this was a golden opportunity. We were profitable in Denmark, but nothing to boast about, but our competitors were in the same position. Basically we were head-butting each other for modest profits. By merging the two companies, economies of scale would really improve. Tom McLean said there would be no legal issues in merging the two companies. It'd take only about $3m-$4m to acquire Billetlugan as the guys from Iceland were desperate. But our request for approval from Los Angeles was turned down. This was crazy. The price was chump change to Ticketmaster. Something must be up. Billetlugen was then acquired by a Danish media company and is still going head to head with Ticketmaster, a lost opportunity.

Irving and Sean arranged a Ticketmaster executive meeting in Santa Barbara in October, 2008, an intensive two-day affair to work out a future strategy. In addition to the Ticketmaster executive team, Irving brought along his long-time finance guy Colin Hodgson, and his publicist Larry Solters. It was a little frustrating that nothing had really happened since the conference in Pasadena nine months earlier. I presented the earlier European plan, but said we needed capital to move forward. Irving promised that this would be taken care of. During one meeting, Irving, who was managing rocker Axl Rose at the time, was using his Blackberry. *"I've just been fired"*, he told us. Minutes later it was *"I've been hired again"*. Axl must have hired and fired Irving six times that day. I suppose that's rock'n'roll!

Eric Korman told us he'd had a conversation with the guys in Parcom who said that if the Lehman's collapse had happened a week earlier, they wouldn't have done the deal with Stage. Timing is everything, and we lost out.

It was announced at the end of October that Irving would be CEO of Ticketmaster Entertainment with Sean still CEO of Ticketmaster. I wondered how could this work? Irving was up to something. He rarely worked from Ticketmaster's office in Sunset Boulevard, preferring the Frontline office nearby. I reckon he's one of the best artist managers in the world, but he just didn't fit in with ticketing. The situation was getting very messy.

Merger announcement

We heard rumours that discussions were taking place between Live Nation and Ticketmaster. The relationship between Live Nation and CTS Eventim wasn't working, and could never work in the US. So on February 10, 2009, Live Nation and Ticketmaster announced a merger of equals. It was a seismic announcement, and the industry went nuts, claiming that two of the largest players in the industry would destroy the business. Individual promoters screamed the loudest, claiming they'd be squeezed out of the market. Immediately, politicians jumped on the bandwagon, denouncing the merger because it'd drive up ticket prices. Furthermore, the merger could take at least a year to go through the anti-trust mechanism.

Initially we were delighted, but as the dust settled we realised it wouldn't be easy. Who'd run the company? What would be the new structure? Putting together two major entertainment companies would be a huge task, especially as this is not a normal business where people obey the rules.

Sean resigned in March 2009. Los Angeles was now very untidy with a lot of uncertainty about. I was very sorry, as we'd a fabulous relationship, but we all figured that the team would be breaking up. It became clear that Irving was behind the manoeuvres. It was extremely well thought through and began to make sense. Live Nation had ongoing difficulties as CEO Michael Rapino stated in the subsequent Senate hearings. Ticketmaster was very profitable. Irving had to keep Live Nation alive so they could continue paying top dollar for his acts. As soon as the merger received Government approval, Live Nation would have access to the Ticketmaster cash cow, and continue to pay a premium for talent. I believe Irving was working on this merger since the day he arrived at Ticketmaster, or maybe even before he arrived.

Michael Jackson

The announcement that Michael Jackson was doing 10 comeback shows in the O2 in London was a huge story worldwide. We'd had no idea this was coming when Michael appeared at a bizarre press conference in London at which he hardly said anything. There was even speculation that it wasn't Michael on the podium but a look-a-like.

Not surprisingly, the shows sold out in record time, and 10 more were added. Like a fever, the run of concerts was hastily increased to 50. This was unprecedented. Upwards of a million people wanted to see Michael performing in London. We were delighted with this unexpected windfall.

I was having dinner in a hotel at Copenhagen airport on June 25, 2009 when Chris Edmonds called me saying that Irving had been asking who was holding the money from the Michael Jackson tickets sales. Apparently, Jackson had been rushed to hospital in Los Angeles suffering from cardiac arrest. I did a quick trawl through the Internet, but couldn't find anything relating to this story. 30 minutes later, the Internet exploded with the news that Michael had passed away. Irving must have had good contacts in UCLA Medical Center, and I smiled ironically at the thought of him focusing on the money aspect. He was right, but....typical!

We now had to focus on the nightmare of refunding all tickets. We'd already transferred the ticket receipts to the promoter AEG, also owner of the O2 venue. Transferring cash before a show takes place can be risky. If something goes wrong, the problem reverts back to Ticketmaster because we are the first point of contact with the public. Total ticket sales came to almost stg£50m (around $80m), of which we were responsible for £35m, and AEG returned the money to be distributed to our customers. Refunding money for cancelled shows is a horrible process, because in addition to losing the income, you incur additional costs. Purchasers change addresses, credit cards, names, get divorced, separate, all sorts of issues arise and we've to deal with them. Yes, we'd had to do refunds before, but never on this scale.

It was sad that such a magnificent performer had died. But many people have since asked one crucial question, would Michael have been able to perform the 50 shows anyway? It's hard to know, but in the documentary *This Is It* he looked in fine shape. In some of the footage taken just a few days before he died he seemed on top of his game. I believe he would have delivered a spectacular series of shows.

Merger goes through

At the end of June I lunched with Irving who was in Dublin with The Eagles for a show at the RDS. He told me that he'd a guy, Roger Ames, who would help raise finance for the European expansion and he'd introduce Roger to me in a few days. I was pleased with this development, as, frustratingly, nothing much had happened since the Pasadena conference. Roger Ames was a serious player in the golden age of the record business. He started in EMI in 1975, and later founded London Records which he sold for a huge sum to Warner Brothers. He later ran Warner's US division, before returning to EMI and leaving again in 2008.

A few weeks after the Dublin meeting, Irving and Roger arrived at our Leicester Square office in London to meet the European team. Out of the blue, Irving announced that I would report to Roger instead of Los Angeles. Thank you, Irving! He could have told me that in Dublin or called me in advance. Roger was going on holiday, not returning until September. The meeting maybe lasted 30 minutes. It reminded me the words of the great American writer, Hunter S. Thompson: *"The music business is a cruel and shallow money trench, a long plastic hallway where thieves and pimps run free, and good men die like dogs. But there's also a negative side"!* Indeed there is, but we all know the score.

After the two guys departed, Tim, Tom, Joe and I went into the boardroom to discuss what was coming down the line. We saw that Ticketmaster in Europe would face serious challenges, especially in the UK. There was no way that Live Nation's competitor, AEG, would continue with our contract, and we'd lose the O2 contract in London, among others. The future didn't look encouraging. More competitors would come into the market and margins would drop. We drew a chart on the whitewall and speculated on what was to follow.

It wasn't really a 'merger of equals' but a full blown take-over of Ticketmaster, a coup. Irving was now installing Roger as an enforcer to ensure Ticketmaster's European team would toe the line. We couldn't understand how the Ticketmaster Board could go along with it. Ticketmaster, a company that always made money, and always knew how to make money, was handed over to Live Nation, a company that had difficulties since the SFX roll up. Irving was a genius to orchestrate such an audacious move.

Roger returned in September but never really fitted in. Everybody knew he was on a mission for Irving, but I found him very likeable, with a quirky sense of humour and he was obviously very talented in his field. But he was just in the wrong place and I don't think he had his heart in the gig.

We were tendering to supply ticketing services for the 2012 Olympic Games in London, a serious commitment, but well within the UK team's capabilities. Ticketmaster had lost money with the Beijing Olympics which turned out to be a nightmare, but London would be different. In Beijing, we had to install a complete infrastructure and partner with a Chinese company (basically the Government). But we had a superb infrastructure already in place in the UK and merely needed to beef up the existing team for 2012.

We were awarded the contract, but nobody in Los Angeles would sign off on the budget. Roger questioned the viability of taking it on at all, which was crazy. I'd a major difference of opinion with him and said it was inconceivable that Ticketmaster UK, the largest ticketing company by far in the market, would turn down the opportunity of ticketing the Olympic Games in London. After many exhaustive sessions we eventually signed off the budget. The 2012 Organisers had budgeted for 7.2 million admissions for the Olympic Games and Special Olympics, but over 11 million tickets were sold. It was one of the most profitable events in the history of Ticketmaster.

The US Department of Justice hearings into the merger with Live Nation were acrimonious and did indeed last almost a year. Irving and Michael Rapino testified at length. I'm not telling tales, because it's all on public record, but all the dirty laundry from the entertainment industry was aired in public. The industry feared the merger would create a gigantic monopoly, but what came out was that the only true monopoly was the artist.

Finally, the Department approved the merger. Ticketmaster was required to divest a number of companies within the group, and to license a copy of its software to its client AEG. Irving and Michael had pulled off one of the most daring coups in the history of the entertainment industry, and Live Nation, a company in serious difficulties, now had access to the Ticketmaster cash.

There are nearly always casualties when two major companies merge, and in this case the casualties fell on the Ticketmaster side. It wasn't pretty, it never is, but it was understandable that Live Nation would put its own people in place. Ticketmaster would have done the same if the positions were reversed.

Of course it was disappointing to see good colleagues move on. Selina was head-hunted by Survey Monkey and moved to San Francisco. Joe moved to Dublin to work alongside Eamonn as Chief Operating Officer. Tom went back to the US, and is now with Bob Sillerman in New York. Tim was offered a new position in Live Nation, and continued to work on mergers and acquisitions for a year before moving on. Roger moved to Frontline where he should have gone originally. For the previous six months, he'd let us get on with running the business and never really got to grips with ticketing, like a square peg in a round hole. I was treated very well in the process. I had two years left on my contract, and it was extended by a year.

Irving resigned as Chairman of Live Nation in 2013. It was inevitable. I met him in Dublin in June, 2014, and he admitted he didn't like the mechanisms of running a public company and was more at home in the artist community. He sold his company (again!) and teamed up with the Madison Square Garden group where he is now Chairman and CEO. I don't doubt he's plotting his next move.

Live Nation today (2015) looks on the surface to be ok. According to the last published accounts, the promoting arm continues to be challenged, but sponsorship and ticketing are doing very well. The share price is strong which I suppose is what counts. Can they continue with this model? Time will tell.

Band reunion

Many times over the years I always thought about getting our old band together for a few dates just for fun and tell stories. The problem was that the guys were scattered all over the world and I had lost touch with George Kaye. Anyway, it would have been pointless without George. As the years went by it looked less likely as four of the original band, Lenny, Dave, Bernie & Martin had sadly passed away prematurely. I learned later that our road manager, Fergus had also passed away in Vietnam.

Early in 2012, I was browsing through Facebook and spotted a cartoon drawing. I was very curious.....I know that....its George Kaye's work. George had this magnificent mural covering most of his living room depicting battle scenes from WW2. The drawing on Facebook came from one of the battle scenes. I had not been in touch with George for over 30 years although I had heard he was living somewhere in Germany. It turned out that George was a Facebook friend of Fabian Murphy, son of another former road manager Frank Murphy.

I got in touch and arranged a call. He was living in Germany, was a partner in a wellness hotel and played some tunes there at weekends. It was the same old George cracking silly jokes. I asked him if he was up to coming to Ireland to play a few tunes.....was he what? I had wondered what shape was he in after 35 years...was his voice ok ? Could he still play the fiddle? I need not have worried...he started singing some tunes down the phone and the voice was as strong as ever.

Over the next few months we put a plan in place. Francie Lenihan was always very enthusiastic and came on board on lead guitar and mandolin. Francie recruited the rest of the band. Liam Gilmartin on rhythm guitar, Gerry Gallagher on bass. Gene Berrill was on drums but he had an illness and had to drop put, Tom Jamieson replaced him. Our original lead singer Pat Ely was always up for it.

Mattie Fox put some dates together and after 2 weeks of rehearsals we headed out for 3 weekends all around the country. It was never meant to be a commercial venture, it was always about the friendship and a bunch of old guys shooting the breeze for a few weeks. It was also an opportunity to reminisce about our departed colleagues and regale about the madness of the early years. The experience was very enjoyable and great fun......another one off the bucket list.

August 2013

My contract with Ticketmaster finished in July, 2013. I'd had a fabulous run and enjoyed the overall experience. I realised I hadn't had a summer free since I'd left school at 16, and looked forward to some time off.

It didn't last long. Within a week Steve Machin asked me to become Chairman of his company, Accent Media. I'd worked with Steve in Ticketmaster where he was part of the acquisitions team with Paul La Fontaine. He and his business partner Gary Fisher had been working on a business plan for some time with the aim acquiring the Internet domain name *.tickets* (dot tickets). I knew there were major changes coming via the Internet, and I really liked what the guys were doing with this initiative. I could see great potential, and accepted his offer. I would later invest in the company.

In August, Steve asked me to go to the US West Coast for a road show to raise funding for the project. I dined with my friend, former Ticketmaster CEO Sean Moriarty in San Francisco, and on the following night, Steve, Gary and I went down to Palo Alto for dinner with another former Ticketmaster CEO, John Pleasants, now with the Disney Corporation. Another former colleague from the early Ticketmaster days, Tom Stockham, happened to drop by. He was living in Utah but was in the San Francisco area researching a new venture, having previously set up the very successful Heritage.com. We'd a wonderful evening of storytelling and reminiscing, and John and his wife Jen were perfect hosts. The following morning we breakfasted with my former London colleague Selina Tobaccowala. Later we had a succession of meetings with financiers and other industry people.

I had meetings scheduled in San Francisco for the following week so I had five days to spare, perfect for a road trip. There's something about a road trip in the US that lifts the spirits. No matter where you travel, there's always something interesting to see. One of my favourite bands, Asleep at the Wheel, were playing that weekend in Telluride and Durango, both in Colorado, so I flew to Grand Junction via Phoenix, and drove to Telluride. But when I checked in at San Francisco airport I was told the flight was overbooked. The check-in clerk wanted six people to surrender their seats and re-book on a flight two hours later.

This didn't suit me or anyone else, and there was little or no response. *"I'm offering $400 for anybody to give up their seat"*, said the clerk. Now there was a stampede to the counter where a commotion developed. Some Bubba with a mullet haircut and no teeth was having words with a big Mamma. *"I wuz first in line"*. *"No, ah was first in line"*. It was terrific entertainment. Then security arrived, two big burly guys with guns and batons. I thought I'd better get out of there before the shooting started. Only in America!

Telluride is a beautiful place, a ski resort in Winter and outdoor activities in Summer. The town has been restored exactly as it was back in the late 19th century, and old wooden shop-fronts line both sides of a long main street populated with fabulous art galleries and restaurants. Asleep at the Wheel played in the saloon of the Sheridan Hotel, again with everything as was back in the 1880s, and they were simply brilliant. On checking out the following day, the owner, while processing my bill, sang verse and chorus of the Chuck Berry hit 'Route 66'.

The wonderful drive to Durango had sweeping views of the Rockies, but the show in Durango was not as good as the previous night. It took place in the University concert hall which was sterile, although there was a very large crowd. I'd planned to drive the following morning to Santa Fe, New Mexico as I'd never been to Santa Fe before, and *Riverdance* maestro Bill Whelan said it was one of the nicest cites he'd visited. The drive was terrific, right through Colorado National Park. There was hardly any traffic and no cell-phone coverage. It was not a place I'd want to suffer a break-down. But a breakdown would have been more welcome than what was to come.

6

LOSING A FRIEND

An Unwelcome Call From Eamonn

I was lunching at Taos, New Mexico when I took a call from
Eamonn. *"I'm in hospital"*. I was not particularly surprised.
Although I'd talked to him on the phone several times, I'd
last met him at the Bruce Springsteen concert in Kilkenny two
weeks earlier and he didn't look too good. He'd lost weight,
which I put it down to a very busy Summer. I knew he had
diabetes, and would not be the best at taking care of himself,
so I assumed he was in hospital for a check-up. *"They think it's
cancer"*. I still wasn't overly concerned, as cancer is common
and, if detected in time, the cure rate is very high. Eamonn was
having more tests that evening, and said he'd keep me posted.
I drove on to beautiful Santa Fe, an old Mission town with no
high rise buildings. The following day, Eamonn called again.
*'"TH......I'm fucked...doctor gave me three weeks to live...it's
pancreatic cancer"*. I couldn't believe it. I was so shocked. I
don't know which of us hung up first, but I knew pancreatic
cancer was fatal. Most of us accept that when parents get older
time eventually runs out. But Eamonn was only 51. I called
Eileen to tell her the horrible news, but I couldn't talk and cried
throughout the brief call, and cried for hours. Eamonn was one
of my closest friends, and we'd been in the trenches for 27 years.
Memories came flooding back, the days on the road hustling,
ducking and diving, and early morning breakfasts in 'greasy
spoons', and through it all uproarious laughter and non-stop
fun. We'd built a great business which I couldn't have done
alone. Even in the early days when we were hanging by a thread,
and problems mounting, Eamonn would come up with a funny
line to lift the gloom. I've said on numerous occasions that his
loyalty was unprecedented. We talked on the phone ten times or
more a day when either of us was out of the office. Even when

I was doing the European job, we talked practically every day by phone.

We'd even adapted the 'good cop, bad cop' routine when negotiating with clients. It was hilarious. I was the 'bad cop'. When a client sought difficult terms or changes to the contract, Eamonn would say "*Oh, I don't think we can do that. Tommy will never get it through the Executive in Los Angeles*". It was a tactic. Sometimes you can squeeze a bit more through smart negotiations, and we did. Those and other memories flashed before me.

Eamonn attended every show. I knew his routine. He left the office around 6pm and went to the venue to chat with the promoters and bring the paperwork for the tour accountant. The promoters loved to see him arrive. Tour accountants can be particularly nasty. I suppose they need to justify their existence, but they unnecessarily throw their weight around during the show settlement, always trying to find holes in the numbers. But Eamonn deflected the attention away from promoters, and always had an answer. I often wondered if they could understand half of what he said, because he spoke very quickly and with great authority. I reckon the accountants presumed he was right. I remember being at a settlement when one nasty piece started questioning our fees. Eamonn was in like a shot. "*Have you looked at the map of Ireland? It's all islands. We have to get tickets to the islands at a huge cost*". End of debate.

Often I'd get a call around 9.30 or 10pm. "*TH, guess what I heard tonight?* I'd get to catch up on all the gossip as he drove home. I could visualise his journey, up the north quays, over the bridge and on to the south quays. The phone went dead when he passed the American Ambassador's residence in the Phoenix Park where they zapped the phone signal. 10 minutes later, when he was home, the call would resume for another 30 minutes or more. We were always planning, plotting, constantly trying to stay ahead of the game.

Now I couldn't bear to think of what was ahead. The next few weeks would be horrible. I called his wife Breda, but his son

David answered. The conversation was short but the crying started again. I tried calling everybody I knew, but it was so difficult. The news spread like wildfire and with disbelief. I called Sean Moriarty in Los Angeles but he'd already heard and said he'd contact the US crew.

Eamonn called me the next morning. *"I'm going to fight this, TH, I'm going to America"*. I encouraged him, although I had doubts. If he got a few additional months it would be worth it, so he had to go for it. What happened next was magnificent. Sean, John Pleasants and another ex-Ticketmaster colleague David Goldberg got to work and within 24 hours paved the way for Eamonn to receive treatment with world-renowned oncologists in three of the top cancer hospitals in the US. I guess a lot of favours were called in by such wonderful people.

The next few days were hectic. Eamonn called regularly, feeling upbeat about the treatment. After initially breaking the horrendous news, he reverted to his upbeat self, and an army of family and friends supported him at home. I was now back in San Francisco, where Selina drove me to a meeting in Menlo Park. We reminisced, and she was clearly very upset. It was very hard to concentrate. The first person I met said, *"How's Eamonn? I plan to come to Dublin soon"*. He was shocked when I told him. He'd never met Eamonn, but his reputation for hospitality had preceded him.

Eamonn was due to go the Sloan Kettering hospital in Baltimore on the following Monday. I considered going to Baltimore, but after talking to Eamonn I said I'd go home. Peter Aiken (Jim's son) and Mick Devine were making Eamonn's travel arrangements. Mick, a close friend of Eamonn's, provides transportation logistics to the entertainment business. We agreed to put a roster together to support Eamonn while he was having his treatment in Baltimore, provisionally estimated to last 4-6 weeks. There was no shortage of friends offering to travel and stay as long as needed. I flew back via London, and Eileen took me from the airport to Eamonn's house. The place was full of people, so many friends wanting to help in any way. He was in fine form and it was difficult to comprehend that he was seriously ill. I stayed a few hours, and told him I'd see him in Baltimore in a few weeks.

Eamonn flew to Washington two days later, accompanied by his wife Breda, son David, Peter Aiken and Mick Devine. Sean Moriarty travelled from California. John Pleasants was launching a major video game with Disney in New York that morning and had an interview on CNBC, yet found the time to be in Washington when the flight arrived. To save time, Sean and John had a helicopter bring Eamonn to Baltimore to waiting consultants.

In the coming days, Sean kept me informed of progress. With a second consultation arranged in the Lahey Clinic in Boston, the crew flew there on Wednesday. Within four days, Eamonn's condition had deteriorated rapidly, and he returned home on Thursday's night flight out of Boston. Arriving on Friday morning, he was taken directly to the Mater Hospital in Dublin. I went to see him a few days later, but although he was very weak he was still joking. *"I'm still here TH, still here"*, delivered with a big grin. It was very sad. We both knew there was no way back, but we said nothing.

Over the next few days a constant stream of visitors said their goodbyes. Breda was exceptionally strong. She was a nurse, and I presume she could read the situation. I visited the hospital almost daily, but mostly stayed outside with Eamonn's friends to allow his family some precious time with him. Mick Devine kept all informed via texts.

Eamonn died the following Tuesday morning, September 3. Although I knew the end was very near, the text from Mick was still heart-breaking. I never thought I'd receive this news. His wish was to be buried in Kilbaha, Co Clare where he had a beautiful holiday home, beside Loop Head lighthouse. He visited the place as often as possible, and was as popular there as in Los Angeles. He'd purchased a plot at the local cemetery a year earlier, although I wasn't aware of it at the time.

Sean arrived from Los Angeles. I collected him from the airport and we went to Eamonn's house in Castleknock for the Dublin wake. There would be another wake in Kilbaha the following night. The Mass in Dublin took place on the Navan Road, with a massive attendance. Over the previous 27 years with Ticketshop and Ticketmaster Eamonn had interacted with countless people, and it seemed they'd all attended, including colleagues and ex-colleagues from Ticketmaster around Europe. People I'd not seen for years came to pay their respects, and were genuinely shocked and upset. Eamonn's brother Shay delivered a perfect eulogy. The stories were humorous, just like him.

Sean, Eileen and I travelled to Co Clare, stopping at Shannon to collect John Pleasants and our former Chairman Terry Barnes coming from Los Angeles. I don't think the US guys were prepared for an Irish country wake with so many people in attendance. Terry lived in Beverly Hills, and I jokingly told him this was the complete opposite of Beverly Hills. John said maybe 20 people were at the last funeral he attended.

Following Mass the next day in Kilbaha Church, we carried Eamonn the mile or so to the cemetery. It was a beautiful sunny day in West Clare, and the scenery was stunning. Breda and David requested that all who touched Eamonn's life would carry the coffin for a while. There was a lovely moment when children from the local school stood outside holding flowers as we passed by.

But amid the sorrow there had to be a typical "Eamonn O'Connor" moment. A local guy appointed himself the unofficial "director of operations", and was guiding us along the way from the church. Carrying the coffin, David was in the middle between Peter Aiken and me. Dave Egan from Bruxelles bar in Dublin, Mick Devine and Eamon's cousin Paud were on the other side. Peter and I were slightly taller than David, so the "director" told Peter, *"bend yer knees so David can feel his father's weight on his shoulder"*. Peter bent his knees. The "director" said, *"bend them more"*. As Peter was already struggling he came out with the classic line *"If I bend my knees any further I'll be able to join Cirque du Soleil"*. We all laughed, knowing Eamonn would have enjoyed the moment so much. At the graveside Eamonn's sister-in-law Joan sang a beautiful version of 'Danny Boy'. It was just perfect.

Following the funeral, John, Terry, Sean and I retired to Doonbeg Lodge where over a three-hour dinner we discussed the past few years. I love these guys, and we'd gelled as a team. Working with them was the most exciting and rewarding part of my career. There's still a bond between us, and even though we've moved on to other things, we're in touch regularly.

Writing this nearly two years later upsets me. So it must be so much more difficult for Breda, David and the rest of his family. Life can be very unfair. Eamonn had worked extremely hard for 30 years, and brought the company to a new level after taking over from me. He had done all the heavy lifting, and was at the peak of his profession. I know I'm speaking for a multitude of people when I say we'll never see the like of him again. Our colleague Vicky Ni Dhomhnaill appropriately mentioned the Pink Floyd song 'Shine On You Crazy Diamond'. How appropriate.

Now the company is in good hands. Keith English, who joined in 1997, is Managing Director and nearly all of the former staff are still in place.

7

STILL ON THE ROLLERCOASTER

Big win for Accent Media

When Steve Machin asked me to become chairman of Accent Media, I'd a limited knowledge of what he was about. But I learned quickly. Steve had been on our European acquisitions team before Tim Chambers took over. The Internet was expanding in a new direction. In addition to the familiar domain addresses, .com, .net and .org and country addresses such as .i.e., .co.uk, .de etc., ICANN, the governing body of the Internet, was issuing a range of new domains and inviting entities to apply for the new addresses. Steve and his business partner Gary Fisher had set up Accent Media and began the process of applying for the name .tickets in April, 2012.

The global ticketing industry is a very broad canvas, covering entertainment, travel and sports. It was obvious from early on that there would be considerable interest in acquiring the rights for *.tickets*. The winner would have the rights to sell the name with *.tickets* and have the whole world to play with. I could see that *Broadway.tickets, Football.tickets, Travel.tickets, Las Vegas.tickets* plus thousands of other names would be very valuable Internet real estate.

Steve and Gary attracted some initial investors, including family and friends, and they'd provide the seed money to prepare for the application. It was a very difficult procedure, involving endless meetings with lawyers, accountants and various other advisors, over the next year. I came on board as chairman in August 2013, immediately after I'd finished my stint at Ticketmaster.

Over 2000 entities applied for the rights, but only five companies fulfilled the criteria to take part, including Accent Media Limited. The five would take part in an auction, with the winner acquiring the global rights for the domain name *.tickets*.

Originally the auction was due to take place at the end of 2013, but was postponed a few times. But we eventually received a firm date, September 18, 2014.

Our challenge was to estimate how much to pay for the name. There was no guide price, and all we had to go on was what had happened at previous auctions. Google had paid over $18m for a basket of names, Amazon had paid $4.3m for *.buy* and a tech company had paid $6.7m for *.tech*. Google later paid $25m for *.app*. It was difficult to call, but we produced a business plan with the figure we thought we'd need to acquire *.tickets*.

We spent a year fundraising. Some original investors subscribed to the next round, and we secured some new investment. Then we hit a major roadblock. A few weeks before the auction, a major investor had to pull out. We knew our existing level of committed funding would not secure the rights, so we frantically tried to secure new investment. Four days before the auction an Australian investor came on board, yet we were still short.

We knew our competitors. 1) Ticket Network, a large ticket brokerage company based in Connecticut, 2) The Shubert Organisation, major theatre owners in New York, 3) Famous Four Media, a private equity company in Gibraltar, and 4) Donuts, a highly capitalized domain business based in Seattle. All had considerable financial firepower.

The auction was to be conducted on-line from an auction house in Hong Kong, and each company would place an initial deposits of multi million dollars just to "sit down" at the table. Bidding would then commence with additional substantial increased bids every 30 minutes. Each bidder would have 20 minutes to place a bid before the next bid. Although we knew the identity of our competitors, the bidding was blind, and nobody could see if a rival was bidding or not. At the end of 30 minutes, we'd only know how many were going through to the next round.

We assembled at Gary's house in West London on September 18. In attendance were Gary, Steve, Ivan, Marc, and myself. We'd be joined later in the evening by our lawyer Daniel. The mood was not great. We'd cobbled together some more investment, including some I'd put in, but we expected to be well short of a winning bid. But it was still worth coming to the auction to play out our available funds, as we'd nothing to lose.

We logged on to the auction web site on a number of devices, laptop, iPad, iPhone. We decided to place all our available money down as a precaution in case there was an Internet connection issue or a power blackout. The auction started late in the afternoon, and we estimated we'd enough funds to last until later in the evening. Early on, one of our competitors dropped out, so only 4 remained. This was encouraging. Maybe it'll go for a lower price than we expected? However, this was a false assumption. For the next number of rounds nobody dropped out, and eventually our funds had run dry. We'd placed our last bid. Two more competitors had dropped out. So only ourselves and one other remained.

The next hour was the hairiest, scariest, and most exhilarating emotional rollercoaster I ever encountered. We had 20 minutes to decide what to do before the next round closed. After over two years of dedication and hard work, it would be negligent for the people in the room not to try to find a way to get us to the next round. But we had to raise upwards of $1m in 20 minutes. By this stage, our lawyer Daniel had arrived.

Ivan led the charge, and said he'd find money somewhere. Steve, Gary and I said we'd punt again, but this was our last chance. We then called the other investors and explained the situation. One came through immediately. Another was in favour of stepping up, but had to contact his two partners to get permission. By this stage, the clock on the screen was showing we were running out of time. Then the phone rang and the last investor came through. There were only 55 seconds remaining on the clock when we hit the keyboard on the laptop to place our bid. We then waited an agonising 10 minutes for the result. Daniel was frantically writing down notes, basically IOUs of who owed what, as somebody had to keep track.

The screen went blank for about 30 seconds as the results were loaded up. "*You, plus one other*". Shit, the other competitor was still in. There were mixed emotions in the room. Disappointed that we didn't win outright, we were a little hopeful since we were still alive, albeit with no funds, having agreed that the previous bid would be our last. There was no way we could go back to the investors and couldn't see how we could raise around $1m for another bid.

Again, we had 20 minutes to decide. We had to strategically work out the options and allow cool heads to prevail. Did the one competitor remaining want it enough? Do *we* want it enough? Funds from the winning bid had to be with the online auctioneer within 6 working days after the auction. If we gambled and won, we'd six days to raise the money. If we gambled and failed to raise the money, we'd lose the substantial deposit. It was a huge risk.

I could see the look of horror on Daniel's face, as if he thought we were crazy to be even considering another bid without the money. He was looking at me as if to say, *"you are the chairman, stop this"!* We decided to place the bid on the assumption that we would raise the extra money if we had the deal in the bag. Some might say it was completely reckless, others that it was brave, but we believed it was worth the gamble. We all had a lot to lose.

We pressed the button and placed the bid! We then had to wait for the result for what seemed like 10 hours. Again the screen went blank as it loaded......then.....*There are no other bidders.* There was silence in the room. What did this mean? Are we out? No, the auction was over. The other competitor had folded, we'd won. Pandemonium! We lifted the roof with a cheer that must have been heard in Dublin. It was a great moment, with an added bonus. The other competitor's previous bid had not increased and we would have won anyway, but we did not know it at the time...it was basically a poker bluff.

I don't want to appear to glamorise the occasion, and yes, it was dramatic, but it was also very serious and we had to make crucial decisions that would affect many people. We had to find a way to make it happen, but also to take a balanced view against the considerable risk. Time will tell if we did the right thing, but we'll do everything humanly possible to make a success of this exciting project, and we have the whole world to play with.

I've been around so many corners in my time and I know nobody can ever tell what lies ahead. I recently had a rude awakening from a previous disastrous investment, *Batman Live*. I thought the show couldn't fail and guess what? A large investment was lost completely. However, I'm very confident that Accent Media and *.tickets* will succeed.

We launched in July 2015 and in the first 2 weeks, hundreds of major global brands acquired the *.tickets* name including Facebook, Google, Amazon, Real Madrid, Manchester United, Live Nation, Ticketmaster, U2, all Major League Baseball teams among many others. We have also agreed a major partnership with the Shubert Organization which owns seventeen Broadway theatres. Shubert and Accent Media is launching www. broadway.tickets which aims to give theatre-goers a single web platform to purchase tickets.

When consumers see Broadway.tickets, theatre-goers will immediately understand they've discovered the right place to purchase tickets. Early days yet but it is looking very encouraging. For me, one chapter with Ticketmaster has closed, and another opened. One way or another, it's bound to be an exciting journey, and who knows where it might lead?

CONCLUSION

Well, that's about it. As I mentioned in the foreword, I never intended writing a book but it just came out. I never kept a diary so everything has come from memory. I am sure you will excuse some of the rawness in the writing, I was never cut out to be a writer or a journalist so excuse the imperfections.

People talk about the ups and downs of life, but in truth I've had hardly any 'downs'. By some strange twists of fate, I fell into the general entertainment business and have had a fabulous life so far. Nobody could ever call it boring. It's been a life full of fun and laughter, the unexpected and the unreal, the serious and the light. I meet friends in the entertainment business for dinner every few months, and we've all shared similar experiences. Once upon a time each of us set out from small towns around the country with little more than a suitcase, a dream and a work ethic. There were no grand plans, we simply winged it all the way, and somehow made it work. I'm genuinely blessed to have an enviable circle of friends, from Sligo and across the world. I met my close friend Maurice in 1971 and rarely a day goes by without us having a conversation either in person or by telephone. These friendships are invaluable to me.

I am constantly being asked *"when are you going to retire, or have you retired yet?"*....retire to what? I am very fortunate that I have buckets of energy and I am having so much fun. I can understand people wishing to retire from a job that is difficult and soul –destroying, but I never felt I worked a single day in my life.

Finally, I have to thank my loving family who have taken so much care of me. Somebody said that behind every businessman there's a woman rolling her eyes!! I must have given Eileen many eye-rolling opportunities with my hair-brained schemes, but she has been an immense confidante and supporter. She's always supported me unconditionally as have my children, Clodagh and Melanie, as well as my sister Maura.

Here's to the next chapter.....................

My Most Memorable Events

I've been asked many times over the years to name the best shows or events I've ever attended. But having seen thousands of events by top local, Irish and international artists in numerous genres, and in venues all over the world, it's impossible to rate them all. One thing is certain, there's nothing to touch the experience of a live performance, or that feeling of anticipation during those few seconds when the lights go down and the first notes are about to be played and sung. But the shows I've listed below are some I'll always remember for a variety of reasons.

Harry Chapin, National Stadium, Dublin, April 1977
The Stadium, as we called it, was really an old boxing venue, with a capacity of 2,200. Harry was a charismatic American singer and songwriter, and this concert was simply brilliant. It was a marathon, over four hours, so I also remember fans reluctantly leaving early to catch the last buses as the concert didn't finish until 12.15am. Sadly, Harry died in a road crash on the Long Island Expressway four years later. He was only 39.

AC/DC, O2 Dublin, April 2009
What a show for sheer raw power. It was probably the loudest concert I ever attended and the crowd went absolutely crazy. It was wonderful to see Angus and the guys still belting out the rock hits with the same fervour they'd always brought to them.

Luciano Pavarotti, Stormont, Belfast, September 1999
This was an historic evening for a number of reasons. The setting was the lawn of Stormont, the seat of the Northern Ireland Government. It was not long after the IRA ceasefire, and it was quite possible that some in the audience had tried

to blow the place up a few years earlier! It was a chilly night, and for the first six arias, Luciano appeared on stage wearing a big parka coat over his tuxedo, as well as an outsized tweed cap. After he warmed up he discarded the winter gear, and lit up the whole of Belfast with some beautiful singing together with that huge smile.

Dire Straits, The Point, Dublin, August 1991
Dire Straits started their *On Every Street* tour by selling out seven nights in Dublin. We could have sold another seven. It was a brilliant show, exploding out of the blocks with *Calling Elvis*, and I can still hear Mark Knopfler bending those beautiful notes on *Brothers in Arms*.

Bruce Springsteen, Seeger Sessions, The Point, Dublin, May 2006
I'd seen Bruce and the E Street Band many times, but didn't know what to expect from these *Seeger Sessions*. But it was just wonderful, a huge multi-talented band featuring folk, blues, gospel...everything. It was so different and uplifting.

Bob Dylan, Vicar Street, Dublin, September 2000
Bob had sold out The Point, but decided to play a small club gig the previous night. Vicar Street is a warm, intimate venue, holding about 900. As you can imagine, there was an extraordinary demand for tickets. Outside the venue, desperate Dylan fans frantically waved wads of notes trying to buy tickets for this unique gig. Bob didn't disappoint. The first part of the show was completely acoustic with his five-piece band, including an outrageous version of 'Tangled Up In Blue' ...magic. The second part was all electric, but best of all was the encore of six or seven songs, including 'Like a Rolling Stone', 'Blowin' In The Wind', and 'Rainy Day Women'. Uproarious applause and cheering greeted every song, but Bob just stared silently back at the crowd, unmoved. The atmosphere was electric. After two hours he said thank you, smiled, and walked off.

The Highwaymen, The Point, Dublin, April 1992
Four legendary performers, Johnny Cash, Willie Nelson, Waylon Jennings and Kris Kristofferson on the same stage and at the peak of their powers. Wow! The guys were backed by a bunch of red-hot session musicians from Nashville, and it was hit after hit for almost three hours. In addition to the great music, I remember on my way in I noticed a man sitting directly in front of a large pillar. I also noticed a dog beside him, and Eamonn fussing over both. The man was blind and the dog was his guide. He'd bought two tickets, one for himself and one for the dog who was taking up a space. Eamonn explained, *"I badly needed two good tickets and re-seated the man and his dog. It's ok, he can hear everything"!* The man was sitting in front of a large pillar and couldn't see the stage. However, he was directly in line with the PA system and could hear every note perfectly. But it looked terrible if you didn't know he was blind. It was a typical Eamonn O'Connor solution to a problem. I guess the dog was happy too.

Leonard Cohen, Lissadell, Sligo, August 2010
What a setting. The audience could see Benbulben on one side, Knocknarea on the other, and a great poet Leonard Cohen, performing at the location where one of his favourite poets William Butler Yeats wrote so many beautiful works. What a magical setting for a truly magical evening.

Elton John, Fitzgerald Stadium, Killarney, July 2002
This was an outdoor concert and around 6pm the rains came. Elton was due on stage about 9pm, and the concert was in doubt due to the monsoon conditions. He tried to approach the stage from the dressing room on a golf cart, but it stopped backstage in a big puddle of water. I was sure he'd cancel. Not alone did he go on, he played a complete 2.5 hour set full on. Several times the crew had to sweep sheets of water off the stage. We often hear of prima donna behaviour from artists, but I've a lot of respect for Elton since that night. He could have taken the easy way out, e-mailed in the performance and skimped on the stage time, but instead he looked after the fans who came to see him.

Asleep At The Wheel, Austin, Texas, October 1978
During a road trip I arrived in Austin. The concierge at the hotel suggested I go to the Armadillo World Headquarters. I'd been told the 'Dillo was a great venue, but I'd no idea who was playing that night. It only held around 1,500, but there was a great vibe and the place was jumping to local band Asleep At The Wheel. They were fabulous, and this started my love affair with AATW. Every time I'm in the US, I try to take in a show with a band still going strong over 40 years later. The 'Dillo closed its doors on New Year's Eve, 1980, with Asleep At The Wheel and Commander Cody on the bill. I'd have loved to have been there. Sadly, the 'Dillo is now an office block.

Prince, O2 London, August 2007
Everybody though it was crazy when Prince announced seven shows in London's O2. Usually artists initially announce one or two shows, and if demand is strong they add more. But Prince had a thing about the number 7. It was still very ambitious, but not alone did he sell out 7, but eventually did 21 shows to over 400,000 fans, a stunning achievement. The stage was set up in the centre of the venue for what was a spectacular production, and he practically changed the set list every night. After the show ended, he announced he'd play another set at midnight in the 1,700 capacity Indigo Club located within the O2 entertainment complex. He did this for 17 of the 21 nights, sometimes playing until 4am. The overall experience was both unique and artistically brilliant.

Michael Jackson, RDS, Dublin, July 1997
I was working at the gig that evening but decided I'd have a look only for the first few songs. I got into the mosh pit, and stayed for the whole show. Up close this guy was unbelievable. He put on the show of all shows. His singing and dancing were in a different class. It's such a tragedy that such a wonderful talent is no longer with us.

Led Zeppelin, O2, London, December 2007

I didn't see Zeppelin back when they were the biggest stadium rock band on the planet in the 1970s. This reunion was a one-off, and it was estimated that there were over 20 million requests for the 20,000 tickets. People travelled from all over the world for this unique occasion. The sound that John Paul Jones, Jimmy Page, Jason Bonham and singer Robert Plant produced was tremendous, one of the best gigs I ever attended, and heavy rock at its best.

Riverdance, Radio City, New York, March 1996

The opening night of *Riverdance* in Dublin was special, but taking the show to Broadway was on another level. Radio City is an iconic venue, and Broadway is a notoriously challenging market. The opening night was a lavish black-tie affair, followed by a celebratory after-show party in The Plaza Hotel, attended by a who's who from the industry. The show was a smash and swept the US for the next 20 years. But the American invasion began that night.

Carmen, Verona, Italy, August 2014

Arena di Verona is my favourite venue in the world. It was built in AD30 and re-constructed after an earthquake in 1117. I'd seen *Carmen* and other operas there many times, but the 2014 production was my favourite. The night was perfect, no wind, and a balmy 22 degrees. 15,000 listened to a wonderful 80-piece orchestra, with over 150 performers on stage and no amplification. There was a new stage set, and the opera was directed by Franco Zefferelli. This is as good as it gets.

Van Morrison, Culloden, Belfast, June 2012

In 2012, Van Morrison began a series of shows in small venues in Northern Ireland. My friend Brian Kabatznick, a lifelong fan of Van, invited me to this show in the Culloden Hotel. It was an intimate experience for 250 devoted fans, with dinner followed by an electrifying performance from Van. As always, he had a world class band, and the atmosphere in the room was terrific....a magic gig.

Westlife
Westlife had a remarkable career and I lost count of the number of concerts we ticketed. Having started as a boy band they developed into a wonderful pop act. Normally, boy bands lose impact after a few years, but Westlife constantly re-invented themselves. They decided to take a break after 12 years with three sell-out shows in Croke Park, and I've no doubt that any further re-unions will be equally successful. Westlife are a credit to Sligo and their families.

Sporting Days
The Irish Soccer International team had a golden 6-7 years, and Maurice and I attended all the big occasions.

Ireland v England, Stuttgart, Germany, June 1988
We only decided to go to the Ireland v England Euro Championship game in Stuttgart at the last minute. Unable to get direct flights we flew to Zurich the previous day, and travelled by train to Stuttgart on the day of the match. I vividly remember arriving at Stuttgart Banhoff with scores of trains from all over Europe. We were met by a sea of green flags and jerseys as the supporters were out in force, a heart-warming sight. With Ireland winning 1-0 we rid ourselves of 800 years of baggage with one game!

World Cup, Italia, June 1990
The Ireland v Romania game in Genoa was tied 0-0 after 90 minutes, but the penalty shoot-out was so exciting and we went through to the quarter finals. I'll never forget the atmosphere in the Piazza afterwards. Italy had beaten Uruguay, and the Italian fans descended on the city centre along with 20,000 Irish supporters. The noise level was off the scale. A stage had been erected in the Piazza for entertainment, and a guy in a green shirt went up on stage and took the microphone from the singer. In a very strong Cork accent he said, *"I have an announcement. If Ger O'Sullivan is here could he phone home, his mother is worried about him"*.....brilliant! Among the madness, Ger was

probably romancing some Italian damsel at the time, and not too worried about his ma.

We were back in Rome a few days later with re-enforcements for the quarter final game, Ireland v Italy. We lost 1-0, but it was still a very special occasion. I suspect it'll be a long while before Ireland see a quarter final of a World Cup again.

Ireland v Italy, Giants Stadium, New York, June 1994

This was a terrific Italian side and we were very much the underdogs. What was most surprising was the number of Irish supporters in attendance, perhaps 80% of the stadium. I just don't know where they all got tickets. We scored after about 12 minutes, and it was an excruciating wait to the final whistle. Despite the scoreline being a modest 1-0, we dominated the Italians on the day. I've one outstanding recollection of the match, probably my best sporting moment ever. Centre-half Paul McGrath was running towards his goal, his back to play. Looking over his shoulder, he coolly back-heeled the ball away from danger.....genius. Italy went on to the World Cup Final and lost to Brazil on penalties.

World Cup Final, Germany 2006

I suppose it is on everybody's bucket list to attend a World Cup final and I got to see the final in Berlin. Maurice and I also got to see both semi-finals. ....Germany v Italy in Dortmund and France v Portugal in Munich on the following night. The final is a wonderful spectacle and Berlin's Olympic Stadium was a perfect location.